An Introduction to Accounting

James Gachihi MSc. CPA
& David Spurling BSc, D.G.A, F.C.I.T, P.G.C.E, M.Inst.T.A.

Published 2006 by arima publishing

www.arimapublishing.com

ISBN 1-84549-143-2
ISBN 978-1-84549-143-7

© David Spurling 2006

All rights reserved

This book is copyright. Subject to statutory exception and to provisions of relevant collective licensing agreements, no part of this publication may be reproduced, stored in a retrieval system, or transmitted in any form or by any means, without the prior written permission of the author.

Printed and bound in the United Kingdom

Typeset in Palatino Linotype 10/14

This book is sold subject to the conditions that it shall not, by way of trade or otherwise, be lent, re-sold, hired out, or otherwise circulated without the publisher's prior consent in any form of binding or cover other than that which it is published and without a similar condition including this condition being imposed on the subsequent purchaser.

abramis is an imprint of arima Publishing

arima publishing
ASK House, Northgate Avenue
Bury St Edmunds, Suffolk IP32 6BB
t: (+44) 01284 700321

www.arimapublishing.com

Table of Contents

Preface 4

Chapter 1: Introduction to Accounting 5

Chapter 2: Double Entries for Assets, Liabilities and Capital 23

Chapter 3: Double Entry for Incomes, Expenses, Stock and Closing T-accounts 47

Chapter 4: An Overview of Financial Statements 71

Chapter 5: Recording Financial Transactions 109

Chapter 6: Nature of auditing and Fundamental Auditing Principles 129

Chapter 7: Nature and Capital Structure 141

Chapter 8: Company Accounts 151

Chapter 9: Ratio Analysis 183

Chapter 10: Budgetary Planning 203

Glossary of Accounting Terms 216

Subject Index 225

Preface

This book has been written as an introductory companion for students beginning accounting courses at professional and degree levels. It aims to break down the basic concepts of accounting and does so in a way that is practical and easy to follow. The authors have taken particular care to ensure that the most up-to- date information has been included both on academic and professional points of view.

Each chapter has both worked examples and self-test examination questions. It is important to realise that accounting like other practical business courses is best studied through rigorous revision and working through accounting problems. Do not merely read this book, but ensure that you can complete at least 95% of the problems at the end of each chapter. It is also important to discuss these problems with your class tutors as well as other students.

This book is supported by a live feedback facility on the internet. The authors welcome any comments and views.

Chapter 1: Introduction to Accounting

The aim of this topic is to give learners an overview of the accounting function at a professional entry level. The accounting function or equation connects liabilities to assets and capital.
At the end of this topic, the learner should be able to:
- *Explain double entry as the basis of accounting systems*
- *How to generate double-entries in business*
- *Name and explain stakeholders and how they use business accounts*
- *How the accounting equation remains balanced throughout the life of a business*
- *How to record assets, liabilities and capital*

1.1: Introduction

The term accounting derives from the 13th century word 'aconter', to count. Accounting is more informally derived from the expression 'to keep account' which refers to the activity of monitoring through well-kept record, the performance of a business. In today's world, accounting is a key business activity and central to the operation of successful businesses because it enables them to keep track of their money and provides a key source of information about the performance of the business. Consequently, accounting is essential to the running of any business or organisation since it is also an important tool in ensuring that the business not only uses resources as allocated but it does so efficiently and effectively. As we shall see later in this book, businesses require the investment of valuable resources that belong to the owner of the business or other people, who are not owners. These people have sacrificed the immediate 'good' they would derive from using those assets and have deferred that 'good' by investing in a business.

Accounting can therefore be defined as the process of identifying, measuring and communicating economic information to permit informed judgements and decisions by users of the information. (*American accounting association (1996) Statement of Basic Accounting Theory, p.1*)

In the next section of this chapter, you will find out what business is and a more detailed definition of accounting will be explained. This should not confuse you as it still refers to the same concept only in detail.

What is business?
A business, in our context, refers to a commercial entity whose purpose is to generate wealth. A business can be defined as the allocation of productive resources to the creation of wealth. It is the combination of different productive resources to create more value than can be assigned to the productive resources prior to the business activity. This can sound

like a highly technical definition yet it is not. Every one who goes into business aims to produce more than he puts in; in terms of labour, land, capital, technology or even entrepreneurial know how. This applies to businesses all over the world be they successful international car companies or the tiny grocers at the corner of the street. The grocer at the corner of the street uses his or her money to buy groceries, which they then transport to the corner shop. Sometimes the groceries may have to be washed and the bulk purchased broken down to smaller packages that we can buy. This is known as adding value and a key characteristic of a business. The grocer has 'added value' by transporting the groceries and breaking them down into smaller packages. The grocer aims to produce more than he or she spent in getting the groceries. Therefore, if he or she spends £200 on the groceries then they hope that they will make a further £80 after sales. The same principle applies for huge multinational carmakers such as Toyota by using skill, a lot of capital, land, labour and entrepreneurial savvy they are able to produce cars that will make a profit. Profit is the difference between the cost and the revenue gained from sales in a business activity.

This brings us to an important point: that business may be formed for the purposes of making a profit, which profit may be saved for future investment or immediately reinvested to create more wealth. Therefore, one reason for which businesses are formed is to produce wealth. However, defining businesses as simply entities that are aimed at producing wealth would be leaving out a significant amount of human occupation. There are other entities that are not profit oriented in nature yet they use up productive resources. They must therefore serve a business purpose as they take up productive resources and time. Voluntary organisations, charitable organisations, government departments and so on confer a benefit different from profit. Business does not therefore just refer to organisations created for the sole purpose of turning a profit but also to create value and benefit to humanity. A broader, more inclusive definition would therefore be that business refers to all human activity that confers benefits to human beings. We can further define benefit as increased wealth, better living conditions, alleviation of poverty, better medicine, freedom from oppressive rule, lowering of carbon dioxide emissions, maintenance of law and order in a society. All these activities, and others not included on this list, can be referred to as business as their successful completion is dependent on the usage of productive resources.

Another undeniable fact about businesses is the clear organisation and predetermination of activities that use productive resources. The outcome is often anticipated and the benefits of using the resources in that manner are foreseeable. This means that the wastage of productive resources in unclear pursuits is not business. A lot of thought and planning goes into successful businesses, as we shall see later in this course.

We can therefore define business as:
'Any human occupation that uses productive resources in an organised and predetermined manner to confer benefit to humankind'

Activity

Look around your locality; how many local, national and international businesses can you identify? Make a list of these businesses and the benefits they confer to humankind in that area, nationally or internationally.

Business can also be defined as any economic activity. Where economics is further defined as the study of how scarce resources are allocated to unlimited wants. Hence, business is the activity of allocating scarce resources to unlimited wants. Business is characterised by the allocation of resources in the production of goods and services. Every businessperson would like to produce as many goods and services as he or she can using the least possible resources. Success in business could thus depend on how efficiently the scarce resources are allocated to the production of goods and services. Businesses are set up for three basic reasons, these are:

1. Profit making
2. Provision of public services or
3. To offer voluntary, not for profit goods or services

Each business will thus be seen to use resources to meet one or more of these three objectives. Inherently resources are scarce; this means that there are more needs than there are resources to meet those needs. It is important therefore, to allocate resources optimally to ensure that the most important needs are met before other less important needs. To ensure that the optimal allocation has been achieved businesses will keep records. The most important of these records are financial records, which relate to the monetary transactions of a business. These records are used to evaluate what happened to the business in the past in terms of money movements. It helps determine whether these movements were beneficial to the business. Secondly, the records can be used to pass on information about the performance of the business to other interested parties. These parties are known as stakeholders (see Section 1.3). Lastly, these records form the important basis on which future performance of the business can be forecasted.

The Chartered Institute of Management Accountants a UK based professional institute of management accountants has defined this as accounting.

Learning point: *Accounting is defined as the classification and recording of monetary transactions for presentation and interpretation of the results of those transactions in order to assess performance over a period of time and the financial position at a given date of a given business. Accounting is also concerned with the projection of future activities arising from a planned course of action*

Bookkeeping was the former name of accounting since financial records were written in books. Hence, the process of maintaining those books was known as bookkeeping. However, with the increased use of computers less and less accounts are kept in books.

AN INTRODUCTION TO ACCOUNTING

1.2: Cash Activities in Business

Money is a medium of exchange. This means that money helps business transactions flow easily and conveniently for both the buyer and the seller. Money has developed over the centuries as a convenient way of holding value. Before money was invented, trade was done by a direct exchange known as barter trade. Goods and services were exchanged for other goods and services. For example, if a person A, who was a beans farmer, wanted meat he had to look for a person B who had meat but wanted beans. This presented many problems. Firstly, some of the goods for exchange could not be kept for long. Person B had to find a person willing to buy the meat within a day or two or his meat would go bad.

Secondly, it was difficult to measure how many kilograms of beans were equivalent in value to one kilogram of meat. Another problem was that the goods and services had to be delivered individually to the people trading. Worse still people could not buy those amounts they needed, as some of the goods were indivisible.

Money was thus invented to deal with all of these problems. Money is used to hold value as it can be kept in the bank until its owner has some use for it. Money can also be used to measure the value of goods and services and this means that one can buy exactly what he or she needs. Another advantage of using money is that it is easy to carry from place to place and thus transactions can be carried out at any time anywhere:
Today money exists in various forms some of these are:
1. Cash
2. Cheques
3. Credit cards
4. Vouchers

Learning point: *Money is an important medium of exchange. It eases the flow of transactions between the buyer and the seller. As already defined, accounting is the recording of monetary transactions.*

Cash is one of the most common types of money. Due to security reasons and convenience, the other forms of money have become more common.

1.3: Financial recording and reporting:

Information about the flow of money is not only important to any business internally, but also useful to other people who get into transactions with the business. These people are known as **stakeholders**.

They include:
1. The **government** that ensures that the business adheres to its tax and legal obligations
2. The **owners** of business who need to know how successful their business is

3. **Lenders** who need to know whether the business is in a position to meet obligations arising from a credit agreement
4. **Competitors** who need to make comparisons between their performance and that of the business in question
5. **Customers** who need to be reassured that the producer of the good or service which they use is financially capable of carrying on with the production
6. **Employees** who are concerned with the security of their jobs and the business's ability to meet the financial obligation arising from the services that they provide
7. **Suppliers** who need to know that their customers are financially robust and also creditworthy
8. **Management** need the information to determine their effectiveness in using the resources of the business.
9. **Prospective investors** who need to find out if the business they intend to invest in is robust and likely to increase in value.

Financial information for these purposes is made up into Financial Reports. People who do not work in the business use the financial reports as a source of information regarding the business. For this purpose, the accounts must reflect the true state of the business. To ensure that they do third parties (people without any interest in the business and its performance) are contracted to check the accounts reflect the performance of the business. This checking is known as **auditing**, the checkers are known as auditors. Auditors are expected to ensure that the accounts of these businesses are 'a true and fair' reflection of the financial situation of the businesses. There are international regulations that govern the reporting of financial information these standards are known as the '**International Accounting Standards**'.

To adhere to these standards as they are set out it is important to maintain very reliable records. The records must also be in line with the general accounting conventions so that any of the stakeholders and accountants can easily understand them.

The most basic of conventions is the use of **Double Entry**, an older form of accounting known as **Single Entry** can be used for very simple transactions that involve cash only. Single entry is rarely used in the mainstream business place.

Learning point: *Financial Reporting refers to a set of final accounts that is presented to the stakeholders to help them evaluate the performance of a business. Financial reports are created from financial records that have been prepared according to Accounting standards that are followed the world over. These are known as the International Accounting Standards. The basic standard is the use of the double-entry system.*

1.4: Double Entry

All transactions in business have two sides: the **debit side** and the **credit side.** A customer who buys an item for £100 gives up the value of £100 at the same time he gains a good worth £100. The direct opposite is that the seller gains £100 in cash but loses a product

AN INTRODUCTION TO ACCOUNTING

worth £100. This double effect then when recorded on financial books generates what is called in accounting a **double entry.** As we will see later in the course when we come to creating final accounts this double recording of transactions is very useful as a way of ensuring that all the transactions have been recorded correctly. This is known as the **'Check of accuracy'.**

Another practical reason why double entry is important is that apart from cash, other forms of money generate a credit agreement between the buyer and the seller. For example, a cheque issued by the buyer is not cash it is a very short-term credit agreement, which implies that the buyer will pay the seller when the bank of the buyer honours the cheque. This might take two or three days within which the seller has not been paid but has been promised payment. This transaction must be recorded to reflect this important information; you will need to make a double entry in the Cheques ledger book and another entry in the Sales Ledger book. However, cheques are not conventional credit agreements, for the purposes of business they are perceived to be equivalent to cash, and are recorded in a three-column cashbook instead.

Before the advent of computers, financial records were made on financial ledgers. A ledger is a book in which the monetary transactions of a business are posted in the form of debits and credits. The left hand side is known as the debit side. All expenses and assets of value to the business are recorded on the left hand side also known as the debit side, whereas all sources of income or liabilities to pay for expenses in the future are recorded on the right hand side also known as the credit side. For example, cash received goes to the right whereas cash paid out goes to the left of a cashbook

Learning point: *Accounts are conventionally recorded as double entries. This represents the gain and loss of the buyer to the seller and vice-versa. This approach is useful as it provides a check of accuracy when financial statements are prepared. It is also easy to follow the progression of the transactions through the books. A T-account is a ledger used for recording accounting double entries in:*

A T-Account is so called as it looks like the letter T

Debit Side	Credit Side
This side of the T-account records: including *Expenses, Assets both fixed and current, value* *Decrease in liability, Cash received*	*This side records: Liabilities to the business what is owing to the suppliers, Decrease in asset and cash paid out of the business*

1.5: The Accounting Equation

To set up a business we must use resources. Resources are defined as the total means available to the business or its owners and other interested parties that can be used to produce further wealth. These resources must be contributed to the business either by the owners of the business or people who have an interest in the business but do not own the business. These resources are divided into two: Equity and liability. Equity refers to resources contributed by the owners of the business whereas liability refers to resources contributed by the non-owners with an interest. The resources contributed as either equity or liabilities are used to acquire assets.

Those who contribute assets to a business have legal claims on those assets. This legal claim to the assets then extends to a legal claim to the business itself. They are in control of the business through their contribution to the business.

Since the total assets of the business are equal to the sum of the assets contributed by investors and the assets contributed by creditors (non-owners with interest in the business) then the total asset value can be expressed as:

$$Assets = Liabilities + Owners'\ Equity$$

This is known as the Accounting Equation

Once a business starts trading, the total value of the assets is affected by other incomes generated and expenses incurred in the course of business. These in turn affect the value of the total assets. Hence, the simple accounting equation is modified to include income (revenues minus expenses, and gains minus losses) and perhaps additional capital contributions and withdrawals such as dividends. At the end of a reporting period, these items will affect the owners' equity as follows:

$$\begin{aligned} Assets = &\ Liabilities + Owners'\ Equity \\ &+ Revenues \\ &- Expenses \\ &+ Gains \\ &- Losses \\ &+ Contributions \\ &- Withdrawals \end{aligned}$$

These changes particularly affect the owner's equity. This is because usually the owner who approaches the creditors and other interested parties to offer resources to his or her business. The owner is also known as the entrepreneur. He or she bears the risk that arises from committing the resources to his or her business. The upside of this is that any gains made in the business belong to the entrepreneur after he or she has paid the non-owners their contributions and any interests that arise from their contributions.

AN INTRODUCTION TO ACCOUNTING

These additional items under owners' equity are tracked in temporary accounts until the end of the accounting period, at which time they are closed to owners' equity. The accounting equation holds true at all times over the life of the business. When a transaction occurs the total assets of the business may change, but the equation will remain in balance as a corresponding change will occur in either or both the liabilities or the equity of the business. The accounting equation serves as the basis for the balance sheet, as illustrated in the following example.

Learning point: *The accounting equation refers to the balance between the assets of a business and the contribution of lenders and investors. This equation is affected by changes during the course of the business, but throughout the life of the business the equation remains balanced even if the value of the assets changes:*

Example 1.1:
John Roberts opens a recruitment agency business. To get started he rents an office, purchases office furniture, office stationery and makes statutory payments to various government bodies regulating the business.

Following is a list of transactions that occurred during his first month of operation:

May 01:	John deposits £3,000 in his business bank account and purchases office furniture worth £500
May 02:	He pays for a telephone line and a business broadband account £50
May 03:	He orders business marked stationery on account from Staples £360
May 04:	He supplies two temporary members of staff to a client earning £360
May 12:	He supplies three temporary members of staff to a client and is paid £300 after billing the client £540
May 22:	He pays three members of staff £450 for services offered the previous week
May 25:	He pays for the annual data protection fee for handling personal information £35
May 30:	He pays rent in advance for the month of June £493.50

What is the value of his business assets at the end of the month of May?

Solution:
The initial value of assets is given as:

$$\text{Assets} = \text{Investors' money (Equity)} + \text{liabilities}$$
$$= £3,500 + 0$$
$$= £3,500$$

In the course of business for one month the business generates a total income of £900, incurs a liability of £360 from lenders and incurs other expenses that are paid for in cash, these total £1,568.50

CHAPTER 1: INTRODUCTION TO ACCOUNTING

The new accounting equation at the end of the month will thus be:

Assets = Investors' Equity +Liabilities +incomes – expenses
= £3,500 + £360 + £900 –£1,028.50
=£3,731.50

At the end of the month, the business will have cash balance of £2,631.50, furniture worth £500, an account receivable worth £240 and stationery worth £360 for which it has not paid. This is the total asset value of the business. The Accounting equation is hence balanced but at a different value.

What has happened can be illustrated using a table:

Dates	Assets =			Investors' Equity + Liabilities		
	Cash + Assets in general +accounts receivable			Equity + Liabilities + Incomes – Expenses + Accounts Payable		
May 01	3,000	500		3,500		
May 02	(50)				(50)	
May 03		360				360
May 04	360			360		
May 12	300		240	540		
May 22	(450)				(450)	
May 25	(35)				(35)	
May 30	(493.5)				(493.5)	
Totals May 31	2,631.5 + 860 + 240			3,500 + 900 – 1,028.5 + 360		
	= 3,731.50			3,731.50		

The above table represents in simple terms the double entry effect of business transactions. The only difference is that all the transactions are recorded in ledger accounts with debit and credit sides. *A ledger is a book in which the monetary transactions of a business are posted in the form of debits and credits.* Ledger accounts do not have negative figures as the table in the example does. In double entry accounting, rather than using a single column for each account and entering some numbers as positive and others as negative, we use two columns for each account and enter only positive numbers. Whether the entry increases or decreases the account is determined by choice of the column in which it is entered. Entries in the left column are referred to as debits, and entries in the right column are referred to as credits.

1.6: The Balance Sheet

A balance sheet is a statement of a business or institution that lists the assets, debts, and owners' investment at a specified date. It lists the assets, liabilities, and the difference between the two, which is the owner's equity or net worth. The accounting equation (assets = liabilities + investors' equity) is the basis for the balance sheet. All balance sheets refer to the changes in assets and liabilities of a business during a specific period, as quoted at a specific date. Assets and liabilities in a business change continuously and their values

AN INTRODUCTION TO ACCOUNTING

cannot be quoted over a period due to these changes. As a result, it is conventional to quote balance sheets at a specific date.

The balance sheet is a useful tool in analysing the performance of the business. It is used to determine the movement of assets and liabilities in the business. One very important aspect of the balance sheet is determining the stock of cash available for the business. This is known as liquidity. Availability of cash determines the ability of the business to meet maturing financial obligations.

Stakeholders use the balance sheet to evaluate the performance of the business. The balance sheet shows whether the business is a robust, worthy investment. It can be used to discover trends in the business for example the efficiency in the collection of accounts receivable.

Example 1.1 is a very simple balance sheet made up to the 31st of May for John Roberts' business. At the end of this chapter, you will have a chance to review what you have learnt. You will also be called upon to prepare simple balance sheets.

Example 1.2:

Angela started a business on 1st of April with a cash deposit of £10,000 in her savings account at the bank. She then carried out the following transactions:
- 4th Jan: bought goods for resale £3,000
- 11th Jan: purchased more goods for resale on credit £2,500 from Valour Suppliers
- 12th Jan: purchased a second hand van from an auction yard at £2,100
- 21st Jan: a sudden illness made her withdraw £2,000 from the business savings
- 25th Jan: paid Valour Suppliers £2,500
- 28th Jan: Jack a long-time friend of Angela's offers her £2,500 loan to cover for the amount she withdrew and continue running the business.

Prepare a balance sheet for the month of January:
Remember: Assets = Equity + Liabilities

	£s	£s
Total Assets:		
Business Car	2,100	
+Stock (2,500 + 3,000)	5,500	
+Cash (10,000 – 2,500 – 3,000 + 2,500 – 2,000 – 2,100)	2,900	**10,500**
Financed by:		
Initial Capital from Savings	10,000	
-Withdrawal of Capital	(2,000)	
Net Equity:	8,000	
+Loan from Jack	2,500	**10,500**

The balance sheet above traces how money (resources) was used. Notice that the totals of all assets and the finances used to acquire the assets are equal. A balance sheet must 'balance'

CHAPTER 1: INTRODUCTION TO ACCOUNTING

hence the name balance sheet. The net equity refers to the money contributed by Angela in her business whereas the loan lent by Jack is a liability to the business. Note also that the assets at the beginning of the business equal the equity and liabilities of the business and at the end of the one-month transactions the assets still equal the total of the liabilities and the equity.

Note carefully how we treat liability differently. In the above case, two liabilities arise; one is the liability that arises when Angela is offered goods on credit by Valour Suppliers. A second liability arises when Jack lends Angela £2,500. The two amounts are however treated differently as they have different effects on the accounting equation. Whereas the 'trade creditors (those who offer goods or services on credit for a short time and usually without security) are treated as short-term liabilities known as current liabilities. On the other hand, loans and cash offered by outsiders with an agreement for repayment with interest and for a longer period are entered in the balance sheet along with the equity of the business.

The following example illustrates how losses affect the equity of a business and how this is recorded in the balance sheet.

The following information is available from John Simpson's Programmers for the year ending on the 31st December:

	£s
Creditors	4,900
Stock	3,100
Debtors	2,300
Wages due	3,600
Computers and Server system	7,000
John's capital account	15,000
Prepaid rent	2,100
Cash deposit	4,000
Completed software	3,300
Loss for trading period	

Prepare John Simpson's balance sheet for the period to 31st December.

Worked solution:

	£	£
Fixed Assets		
Computers and server system	7,000	
Add: Current Assets		
Stock	3,100	
Debtors	2,300	
Prepaid Rent	2,100	
Cash deposit	4,000	
Completed Software	<u>3,300</u>	21,800

Less: Current liabilities		
Creditors	4,900	
Wages due	3,600	(8,500)
Net Assets		13,300
Financed by:		
Capital account	15,000	
Loss at end of period	(1,700)	13,300

We need to record how the equity of a business has changed over the period ending on the 31st of December. During the period in question, John Simpson's programmers made a loss of £1,700. Just as profits increase the equity levels, losses reduce the equity. Also, note the current liabilities, these are short-term liabilities, which we believe will be paid off in the next trading period. Current assets are resources that are being used in the current productive activity, for example, the debtors are those who owe money to the business for the trading that occurred during the balance sheet period. Rent prepaid is an asset that will be realised, most probably in the next trading period. Fixed assets are longer-term resources for example a computer server may have a life expectancy of about three years during which it will be used as a productive resource.

1.7: Assets, liabilities and capital

A balance sheet is made up from a series of double entry balances. In the example of John Roberts' business (The accounting equation), you may have noticed how the balance sheet changed appearance every time there was a transaction. In the real world, it is simply not practical to re-write the balance sheet every time a transaction occurs; so we keep a separate account (page of detail) for every item you might find on the balance sheet. If we need to draw-up a balance sheet, we simply write - down the latest values (known as '**balances**') on each account and arrange them into balance sheet order.

A balance sheet contains all these balances; it is formally defined as a financial statement recording the *assets* and *liabilities* of a business at the end of an *accounting period*. Assets are the entries on a balance sheet showing all properties, both tangible and intangible, and claims against others that may be applied to cover the liabilities of the business. Assets can include cash, stock, inventories, property rights, and goodwill and so on.

Liabilities are the financial obligations entered in the balance sheet of a business enterprise. Financial obligations are all the debts that are owed to other people and businesses other than those owed to the owners of the business. The accounting period is the time referred to in an accounting statement; usually this is one calendar year of twelve months.

Learning point: *Capital is the initial financial investments that are made in a business. Assets and liabilities make up the capital. A balance sheet will also show what use the capital has been put to.*

CHAPTER 1: INTRODUCTION TO ACCOUNTING

In the introductory chapter, we looked at the key concepts of accounting:
1) Accounting is the discipline that concerns itself with the orderly recording of financial transactions to provide information to stakeholders on the performance of a business. This information is important as stakeholders are always making decisions regarding the business.
2) The Accounting equation which states that:
Assets = Equity + Liabilities relates the assets of the business to the resources contributed to the business by the owners and the non-owners. Every business transaction has a double effect on this equation, which ensures that the equation remains balanced throughout the life of the business.
3) The balance sheet is the statement produced at the end of a financial period (usually a one-year period) that summarises all the transactions that have occurred throughout the year. It shows the new balance of assets, the level of liabilities and changes in the equity of the business.
4) Stakeholders are all those people who are interested in the performance of a business. Stakeholders include the government, management, employees, competitors, society in which the business operates and so on.
5) Accounting conventions ensure that accounts all over the world are prepared to the same standards and in the same formats. In an increasingly globalised world, this is important. Accounts produced in one country may affect decisions made by stakeholders thousands of miles away.
6) Auditing is the process of checking that the accounts produced by a business give a true and fair view of the performance of the business. Stakeholders rely on the opinions of auditors to make decisions regarding the business. An adverse opinion on the performance of the business will result in adverse decisions being made and the vice versa is true. An untrue report would result in adverse opinions being rendered to businesses that are actually performing well, or more commonly, a good opinion where an adverse one is deserved could lead to stakeholders making the **wrong decisions** and putting their investments at increased risk.

Revision Questions:

Understanding:
1. Define accounting and explain at least two uses that accounting information can be put to.
2. Explain what would happen if accounts did not have international conventions
3. Discuss the effects of unscrupulous auditors on a business' operations.
4. When preparing the financial statements why do we add profits to the equity?
5. Businesses are continually making decisions in allocating scarce resources, discuss the following scenarios and state whether they are prudent business decisions, and whether they confer value to the business' future prospects of creating wealth:
    - Purchase of goods for resale worth £3,000

- Training employees on how to use a new computer system £10,000
- Holiday for best and run-up employees of the year £4,000
- Two transport vans on credit for an anticipated rise in sales in the next year
- Paying for 2 years rent in advance even when the landlord demands for only a 6month down payment £36,000
- Buying a prestigious car to impress potential clients £27,000

Revision exercises:

6. Charles started a business on the 1st of August 2xxx Using the information provided below analyse the effect of the transactions listed below on the assets, equity or liability.
   - 1st August: opened a bank account and deposited in it £47,000
   - 3rd August: bought a van for business at £26,000 putting down a cash deposit of £9,000 and getting a credit facility for the remaining amount of £17,000 this amount will be paid over three years without an interest charge.
   - 7th August: purchased goods for resale at £3,200
   - 9th August: received goods from Berry Wholesalers on credit for £4,500
   - 12th August: got a loan from A. Bank business lenders of £13,000
   - 14th August: prepaid 2 month's rent £2,000
   - 17th August: sold goods on credit at £2,500
   - 21st August: withdrew £5,000 from the bank account and used it to book a holiday in the Caribbean
   - 26th August: paid wages to employees £2,800
   - 30th August: part paid for goods purchased on credit £3,000
   - 31st August: received payment for goods sold on credit £2,500

7. Salome opened a bridal shop on the 1st of July 2xxx following is a list of transactions that she carried out in her first month of operation:
   - 1 July: deposited £7,000 in her business bank account
   - 4 July: borrowed £3,000 from one of her friends payable out of any profits she made
   - 5 July: purchased silk fabrics on credit £2,000
   - 7 July: paid for Bridal Society membership £130 for the whole year. Bridal Society is a professional body that brings together bridal designers and wedding planners
   - 10 July: installed telephone and broadband connections £55
   - 11 July: paid for business stationery (business cards, letterheads, compliment notes and engraved pens) £300
   - 16 July: ordered for a van on a business lease basis of £200 per month
   - 19 July: paid for an advertisement on the local radio station £1,100

- 20 July: bought a sewing machine for £2,600: paid in cash
- 24 July: using the silk fabric made a bridal gown which she sold for in cash for £4,500
- 27 July: bought shares in a high-growth internet business £1,500

Using the information provided complete the following questions:
I. Calculate the cash balance at the end of the period in question
II. How do you account for the money spent on shares in a high-growth internet business?
III. Calculate the total expenses of running the business for the one month
IV. Using your answer from (III) above calculate the profits made during the month (Note: Profit = Total Sales – Total Expenses)
V. Prepare a balance sheet for Salome's business

8. Jane has been in business for two years now. At the end of the first year of trading her balance sheet looked like this:

	£	£
Total Assets:		
Fixed Assets:		
Motor Vehicle	23,000	
Computers	2,500	
Business Furniture	1,900	27,400
Current Assets		
Cash balance	11,300	
Debtors	2,300	
Prepaid rent and rates	1,600	15,200
Current liabilities		
Outstanding Telephone bill	300	
Creditors	3,500	(3,800)
Net Assets		38,800
Financed by		
Capital	20,000	
Loan	15,000	
Profits	6,500	
Withdrawals	2,700	38,800
Net Assets		38,800

During her second year of trading, she had the following transactions:
- She exchanged the van she had bought the previous year for another van worth £27,000
- She bought a new laptop so that she could work while travelling this cost her £1,300 cash

- She paid off her creditors and the outstanding phone bills, she has prepaid rent and rates again for next year £1,400
- She repaid £3,000 on the loan that she had outstanding
- Her profits for this period were 7,200.

Using the information provided calculate the cash balance at the end of the year and the new balance sheet.

9. Complete the table below using the assets, liabilities and equity relationship. Show how each of the transactions affects these three items by putting a '+' sign where there is an increase and a '-' sign where there is a decrease.

Transactions	Assets	Liabilities	Equity/Capital
• Bought a vehicle on credit for the business			
• Sold goods on credit			
• Paid wages to employees			
• Got a loan from a business development agency			
• Sold motor vehicle			
• Repaid an outstanding loan			
• Takes out some money for personal use			
• Paid a creditor for goods supplied			
• Bought more goods on credit			
• Prepaid for telephone usage			

10. Spurling set up a sewage clearance business on the 1st of March 2xx1 he transferred £120,000 from his private account to his business account. He also had the following transactions during the period.

- Paid town council fees for the year £3000,
- Took his three employees for training on health and safety £10,000
- Leased a sewage exhauster for £1000 per month for a period of three years
- Furnished the business premises and bought a business computer for £2000
- Paid for business stationery and memorabilia for £500
- Received payment for the town council for extracting sewage from the high street shops £41,000, the council owes him £2,000 at the end of the operating period
- Paid rent for the year for his office premises at £800 per month
- Paid wages to his three employees at £1,200 a month per employee
- Received £13,500 from private customers, is still owed £3,500

- At the end of the trading period he has an outstanding balance for the petrol charges with his supplier of £7,200, total fuel costs for the period were £10,000.
- Bought a second hand sewage exhauster engine for £22,000 in cash

Calculate the loss or profit for the period ending 28th February 2xx2. Then prepare a balance sheet for Spurling for the period.

Chapter 2: Making double entries for assets, liabilities, capital, expenses and stock

At the end of this chapter, the learner should be able to:
- Describe the theoretical background of double entries for capital, assets and liabilities
- Make double entries
- Relate double entries to the accounting equation
- Use the theoretical background to make decisions on how to account for unusual transactions relating to assets, capital and liabilities

2.1: Double Entry

From example 1.1, it is evident that each transaction in a business leads to changes in the accounting equation. Each new transaction changes the values of balances in the balance sheet but does not alter the equality of the sum of liabilities and capital to the total assets.

In a typical business, there are many transactions each day. That implies that each time there is a transaction a new balance sheet must be drawn up. This, however, is not true in practice. Drawing up a balance sheet each time a new transaction occurs would be very inefficient. A more efficient and widely used approach to recording financial transactions is opening separate **accounts** for each item of transaction.

An account is a precise record of all financial transactions that relate to the same financial item. For example, if a company has bought office furniture all the financial transactions that relate to furniture are recorded in the same list. This list is known as an account.

A list of Furniture Transactions

Date:	Particulars	Values
01/04/2005	Bought 3 Leather Swivel office chairs at £95 each	£285
04/04/2005	Bought 3 office executive tables at £120	£360
06/05/2005	Two filing cabinets worth £45	£90
28/04/2005	One swivel chair was returned to the stores with faults	-£95
Total value of furniture at the end of the period:		640

However, the above list does not represent all the financial transactions that have occurred in the purchase of the furniture. Assuming that the chairs were bought for cash, then a different account showing how the transactions affected the money must be prepared.

A list of cash transactions that have occurred because of the furniture transactions in the same month

Date:	Particulars	Values
01/04/2005	Bought 3 Leather Swivel office chairs at £95 each	-£285
04/04/2005	Bought 3 office executive tables at £120	-£360
06/05/2005	Two filing cabinets worth £45	-£90
28/04/2005	One swivel chair was returned to the stores with faults	£95
Cash spent on furniture:		**£640**

The first list shows that the business has acquired furniture worth £640 and the second one show that the business has spent £640 for furniture. These lists thus represent the double effect of each transaction.

2.2: Why double entry?

However, the above lists are not a convenient way of recording transactions for three reasons. Firstly, that it is difficult to compare the two lists in different pages. A cash account for example will contain many transactions that relate to different items and making a different list for each cash item is inefficient. Secondly, each transaction represents the movement of resources and it is not easy to trace these resources over different lists of transactions if there is a separate list for each transaction. Thirdly, recording financial transaction on simple lists like these can only be used for cash-based transaction. In reality, many credit transactions occur in a business.

For these reasons, the double entry convention has been developed where transactions are recorded side by side. An account is prepared where both lists of the transactions are presented side by side. Each side of the account holds a corresponding entry in another account. It is also important to show how much the business is owed or how much it owes other people.

2.3: The T-Account

A basic account is also known as a T-account because it looks like the letter 'T'. A T-account has a debit and credit side. The left hand side of a T-account is known as the Debit side of the account while the right hand side is known as the Credit side. When making entries in a T-account it is important to understand for whom you are making the entry. If you are preparing asset accounts for a business, then your debit side will record all the increases in value of the business assets, whereas all the credit side entries represent a reduction in the assets of the business. This implies that if the accounting equation balancing figure increases because of a transaction then you make a debit entry in the T-accounts of the business dedicated to that asset. You also make a credit entry in the T-account of the source of this increase in value.

This has a very distinct implication when recording transactions of the three main items of the accounting equation:

2.3.1 Capital

Capital is the contribution of the owners of the business. Capital can increase if the owners decide to contribute more cash or items to the business:

If for any reason, the value of **capital increases** we make a **Credit entry** in the capital account. The reason for this is that capital is owed to the owners. Hence, the liability of the business to the owners increases. We make a debit double entry in the account where this increase goes. For example, if the capital increase has been used to buy vehicles we make a debit entry in the Vehicles T-account.

A **decrease in capital** say, due to the withdrawal of one of the owners, would lead to a debit **entry** in the capital T-account. The source of this reduction is then credited with these funds. This source would most likely be the person's account or if the reductions were made in cash then we debit the cash account with the reduction. You should do a lot of practice with T-accounts to understand how they are worked out.

2.3.2: Liabilities

In business, liability refers to the debts owed by the business to third parties. They do not include debts owed to the owners of those businesses. Resources given to the business by its owners are known as capital. The treatment of capital and liabilities is similar. If the value of **liabilities increases,** then the value of the assets of the business increases. A **credit entry** is made in the liabilities T-account and a **debit entry** is made if there in the corresponding asset account for which the liabilities are used.

For example if a business acquires a Computer system on credit from a computer company XYZ. Then in the business accounts, a debit entry is made in the Computer Systems Assets T-account and a credit is made in XYZ Liability Account.

At the same time if the business sells something on credit then a debit entry is made in the account of the person or business to which that item has been sold. A credit entry is made in the Stock account of the item sold on credit. If a business sells motor vehicles and sells a car to Mr ABC on credit, we will debit Mr. ABC's account with the value of the car and credit the Motor Vehicle Stock Account with the value of the vehicle.

2.3.3: Assets

Assets are the resources available to a business to pursue its goals and objectives. Assets are made up of capital and liabilities. This has special implication to the double entry system. When a transaction occurs, two of the three items are affected simultaneously. This generates a double entry.

Examples:
- Money injected into a business by its owners increases the assets and the capital. This is because capital injected into a business is used to acquire assets. Thus, a rise in capital leads to a rise in assets.
- A machine (Asset) bought on credit increases the assets but also increases the liabilities that the business has with the suppliers of the machine
- If an outstanding debt by the business is paid back, then the cash and bank (Assets) balances reduce and so do the Liabilities to the creditor.
- If a business stops operating and repays the creditors from money in the bank, (Assets), supplied by the owners then the capital and the liabilities will be reduced.

All transactions have this double effect to assets and liabilities or, assets and capital or, capital to liabilities. Businesses also incur expenses in order to produce wealth these expenses are treated in the double entry system in the same way as assets. This is because they serve the same purpose as assets: they are used to produce wealth. We shall see how this affects the double entry system later in this chapter.

The table below shows how to treat three financial items in a T-account:

Debit Side	Credit Side
- Increase in assets	- Decrease in Assets
- Decrease in liabilities	- Increase in liabilities
- Decrease in capital	- Increase in capital

Remember that:

> Assets = Liabilities + Capital

Example 2.1:

Janet has saved up £2,000 and has decided to open a Property Consultancy firm. After doing her budget, she realises that she needs a further £1,000 to set up her business. She approaches her bank, which lends her the £1,000 she needs on the 5 April.

She makes the following purchases:
- Office Furniture on the 4 April worth £300
- She pays membership fee of £158 to a property and housing organisation that regulates the property agencies standards and ethics for practice on the same day
- A local stationery store prepared office stationery on 7 April on credit payable at the end of the month, this cost £98

Solution:

To record Janet's transactions the following accounts are drawn up:

1. Capital Account
2. Bank Account
3. A liability account for the Stationery store
4. Assets accounts: Furniture, Stationery and Membership accounts

The entries for the transactions shown above are as follows:

A: Janet's Capital Account

Date	Particulars	£	Date	Particulars	£
			04-Apr	Cash in hand	2,000

B: Bank Account

Date	Particulars	£	Date	Particulars	£
04-Apr	Capital	2,000	04-Apr	Membership Fee	158
05-Apr	Loan		04-Apr	Furniture	300

C: Stationery Account

Date	Particulars	£	Date	Particulars	£
06-Apr	Stationery	98			

D: Furniture Account

Date	Particulars	£			£
04-Apr	Cash	300			

E: Bank Loan

Date	Particulars	£	Date	Particulars	£
			05-Apr	Cash in Bank	1,000

F: Membership Account

Date	Particulars	£	Date	Particulars	£
			04-Apr	Cash	158

G: Stationery Store Account

Date	Particulars	£	Date	Particulars	£
			07-Apr	Stationery Account	98

T-accounts 'A – G' record all the transactions that have occurred for Janet's business between 04/04 and 07/04. It is important that all transactions in T-account have a date of entry. They must also have particulars that describe the transaction. This makes it easier to cross-reference the accounts. In practice however, we enter the name of the account in which the corresponding double entry has been placed rather than all the particulars of the transaction. For example when Janet purchased furniture in cash we enter 'Furniture' and its corresponding value in the cash/bank account while we enter the word Cash/ Bank in the furniture account to show how we purchased the furniture.

In account 'A' above, we enter the capital on the credit side of the account and a corresponding debit entry on the Cash/bank account. This means that capital has been contributed as cash and/or has been deposited in the bank.

Account 'B' is the cash/bank account; it records all cash-based transactions. In this case, money was received as capital from Janet. The business also received a loan from the bank, which is debited into the Cash Account while being credited in the loan account 'E'. The loan account is a liability account. Another Liability account is the Stationery account 'C'; stationery was prepared for the business on credit and is thus recorded on the credit side of the stationery shop's account' G' and debited on the stationery account of the business as an asset.

CHAPTER 2: MAKING DOUBLE ENTRIES

The cash/bank also records the outflow of cash for furniture and membership fee. The corresponding furniture and membership accounts, 'D' and 'F' are debited with the values of these assets.

Learning Point: *All transactions in a business have an effect on the accounting equation Assets = Liabilities + Capital. A change in total asset will occur if the liabilities increase and the liabilities are used to acquire more assets, then the value of assets increase the same is true if more capital is introduced into the business. This effect is recorded as a double entry as it affects both sides of the equation. Once the business starts operating it starts incurring expenses and generating revenues, it will also have to make purchases and sales all these are recorded in the double entry system. The basic balance of the accounting equation is maintained throughout all business transaction. Another way of understanding double entries is that DEBITS record transactions relating to purchases, expenses and an increase in the assets of the company. CREDITS record transactions relating to revenues and an increase in the liabilities of the company.*

So far, we have looked at the different transactions that occur in a business. The important relationship that must be maintained is that of assets, liabilities and capital. In doing so, we must recognise the double effect of each transaction in a business.

Example 2.2:

Peris started her transport business by depositing into her business bank accounts a sum of £180,000 on the 1 January.

Bank

Date	Particulars	£	Date	Particulars	£
01-Jan	Capital	180,000			

Capital Account

Date	Particulars	£	Date	Particulars	£
			01-Jan	Bank	180,000

This one transaction generates an entry on the debit side of the bank account, which is an asset account and a corresponding credit entry on the credit side of the account. The credit entry from the point of view of the business shows that there is a liability owed to the owner of the business of £180,000

On the 9 January, Peris acquired an articulated lorry worth £60,000 from Leading Truck Company. She pays a deposit of £30,000. She is offered credit for the remaining amount (£30,000). The following entries are made in the books:

Bank

Date	Particulars	£	Date	Particulars	£
01-Jan	Capital	180,000	09-Jan	Lorries Asset Acc	30,000

Lorries Asset Account

Date	Particulars	£	Date	Particulars	£
09-Jan	Bank	30,000			
09-Jan	Leading Truck Co.	30,000			

Leading Trucking Company Account

Date	Particulars	£	Date	Particulars	£
			09-Jan	Lorries Assets Acc	30,000

Peris uses £30,000 to pay for the lorry's deposit and takes credit for the rest of the amount due. Credit is very important in start-up businesses as it allows them to operate beyond their finances using this scheme Peris can acquire six lorries, without the credit facility she can only afford three lorries but would have no money to run the rest of the business.

In the case above, Peris has incurred a liability to the Leading Truck Company, which is entered on the credit side of their account. This account is a liability account. However, she now owns a truck worth £60,000; she has acquired it by putting down a deposit of £30,000 from her bank (credit bank account, debit asset account) and a liability of £30,000. Note that the credit owed to Leading Truck Company is not a long-term liability and is known as a current liability.

On the 14 January Peris pays for diesel, £300 stationery £400 and wages for a short-term drive who was supposed to deliver goods between 10 Jan and 13 Jan: £700

CHAPTER 2: MAKING DOUBLE ENTRIES

Bank

Date	Particulars	£	Date	Particulars	£
01-Jan	Capital	180,000	09-Jan	Lorries Asset Acc	30,000
			14-Jan	Stationery	400
			14-Jan	Wages	700
			14-Jan	Diesel	300

Expenses Account

Date	Particulars	£	Date	Particulars	£
14-Jan	Wages	700			
14-Jan	Stationery	400			
14-Jan	Diesel	300		X	

Wages Account

Date	Particulars	£	Date	Particulars	£
14-Jan	Bank	700	End of period	Expenses Account	700

Stationery Account

Date		£	Date	Particulars	£
14-Jan	Bank	400			

Diesel Account

Date	Particulars	£	Date	Particulars	£
14-Jan	Bank	300			

To record these three transactions we open expense accounts. All expenses are entered on the debit side of the account like the other long-term assets. This means that the money spent in paying for these expenses confers value to the operation of the business. Therefore, the expenses are a type of short-term assets; their lifetime is so short that they cannot be entered into the balance sheet, though they are resources that are used to run the business and create wealth.

AN INTRODUCTION TO ACCOUNTING

All the transactions on 14 January were paid for in cash through the bank. The corresponding entry is made in the general expense account. This is created at the end of the trading period. As we shall see later in the book, we have to create business statements; one of these statements is the Profit and Loss Account. All expenses incurred during the period of transaction are posted to the debit side of the Expense Account as shown using arrow X in the wages account. As we have seen before since cash was spent then we have to credit the bank account with these expenses.

On 30 January Peris paid £5,000 for the truck, she also withdrew £3,000 from the business account to cover for a holiday in Spain.

Bank

Date	Particulars	£	Date	Particulars	£
01-Jan	Capital	180,000	09-Jan	Lorries Asset Acc	30,000
			14-Jan	Stationery	400
			14-Jan	Wages	700
			14-Jan	Diesel	300
			30-Jan	Capital	3,000
			30-Jan	Leading Truck Co	5,000

Capital Account

Date	Particulars	£	Date	Particulars	£
30-Jan	Bank	3,000	01-Jan	Bank	180,000

Lorries Asset Account

Date	Particulars	£	Date	Particulars	£
09-Jan	Bank	30,000			
09-Jan	Leading Truck Co.	30,000			

Leading Trucking Company Account

Date	Particulars	£	Date	Particulars	£
30-Jan	Bank	5,000	09-Jan	Lorries Assets Acc	30,000

Peris has paid £5,000 reducing her liability to Leading Truck Company to £25,000. Note that the value of the truck account does not change, the truck is still valued at £60,000. As we shall see later in the book the value of an asset can only change if the asset is disposed of, or if the asset is extensively damaged or through depreciation. Depreciation is the normal wear and tear that occurs as an asset gets used up. For example, the computer screens of most computers become progressively darker as the computer gets older. Another way of looking at it is that if you bought an ipod player today for £700 two years down the line you will have to sell it at a price lower than that say £300. This is because the ipod has been used and its value has reduced or there are better ipods in the market. In this case, we credit the bank account where the £5,000 came from and debit the liability account reducing the liability to £25,000.

If the owner withdraws money from a business as Peris did to visit Spain for a holiday, the capital is reduced. This is recorded as a debit entry in the capital account and a credit entry in the bank account where the money came from. Any money drawn from the business by the owner for any purpose other than meeting the expenses of the business are treated as 'Drawings' and are recorded in the manner recorded above.

2.4: Sale, Purchases and Stock

Purchases in business are defined as all those goods bought to be resold in a business. For example, a shoe retailing company purchases shoes from a shoemaker and resells them on a high street store to individuals. In some cases, there are no alterations made to the purchases whereas in other cases value is added to the purchases to increase their resale value for example, a ring maker may buy raw uncut diamonds. He or she may then polish the diamond, cut it and set it in a ring thereby making it useful to an end user. Therefore, anything bought to be resold, either in its purchased state or after adding value to it through manufacturing or any other process is known as a purchase.

Sales on the other hand are anything that the business normally sells and usually buys to resell either in its original state or after adding some value to it. Therefore a shoe selling business may buy designer shoes and resell them, this is known as sales, however if the same company bought a computer and for some reason it resells it. The computer is not part of the sales rather it is an Asset that has been disposed of and is treated differently in the double entry system.

In recording transactions that arise from purchases and sale of goods and services, the same rationale applies. If we use cash to purchase goods or services we are reducing the asset of cash or bank, we therefore credit the cash or bank account while we debit the purchase account to show how we have used the money that we had in hand or in the bank. On the other hand we debit the bank account with money we receive for selling the goods or services and credit the sales account which shows that we have 'given-up' the value in the goods or services we have sold. The double entry here again traces the flow of resources.

Stock can be defined as goods meant for resale held by the business at any one time. This means that any goods bought and brought into the business that have not been sold are referred to as stock. Stock can therefore increase if more purchases are made, or can reduce if there are sales. If goods sold are returned to the business then the stock increases, conversely if goods purchased are returned to the wholesalers then the stock levels increase. Business owners want to know how much stock they hold at any one time. Too much stock would mean that there is money tied down with stock that is not required and if the levels run very low then the business is risking turning away customers due to the lack of goods for sale. A car reseller for example cannot afford to hold at his or her premises 200 cars

CHAPTER 2: MAKING DOUBLE ENTRIES

because they require a lot of storage space. It also means that if one car costs £30,000 then he would be holding £6m worth of cars that he does not need. Too much stock may lead to cash flow problems. On the other hand, he cannot hold one or two cars in stock because if two customers bought them he would have to reorder more cars while he turns away customers who want to buy cars.

The following relationships therefore arise between stock, purchases, sales, returns outwards and returns inwards:

Simply:
- **Stock = Purchases – Cost of Sales**

The stock retained in business is equal to the stock that has been purchased less the cost of the goods that have been sold. Note it is not purchases less sales, but less cost of sales, this is because sales include a profit margin. For example, a reseller of office furniture may buy a swivel chair for £70 and have a profit margin of 20% of the cost. Calculate the resale price:

$$\frac{20 \times 70}{100} = £14$$

Sale price = cost of sales + profit margin = £70 + £14 = £84

We calculate stock without including the profit margin. This means that stock is valued at cost (as you proceed further in accounting other stock valuation methods will be introduced)

As we have seen, goods returned to the vendors by a business are called 'Returns Outwards' these reduce the stock held by the business. Returns outwards are subtracted from the purchases. On the other hand, goods returned to the business by its customers' increases the stock. The returns inwards increase the stock held within the business.

Therefore:
- **Stock = (Purchases – Returns Outwards) – (Cost of Sales – Returns Inwards)**

The following example looks at the effects of purchases and sales as well as returns inwards or outwards.

Example 2.3:
Merkel has been in business for six months now. Following are some of the transactions affecting stock that occurred during the month of June

- June 1: Stock held £3,000
- June 3: purchased goods for resale £4,500
- June 5: received goods for resale from Oz Suppliers on credit worth £2,700
- June 6: returned goods to Oz Suppliers that did not meet the specifications he had requested worth £2,100

35

AN INTRODUCTION TO ACCOUNTING

- June 7: Sold goods to Merlin Traders at £3,900 making 30% profit on the sale
- June 12: received goods from Oz Suppliers worth £3,000
- June 17: Sold goods to Angel Traders at £4,000 at a profit margin of 25%
- June 21: received goods from Angel Traders since they had a fundamental defect, these goods were worth £1,500
- June 25: Merkel purchased goods worth £1,000

Using the information provided calculate the Stock at the end of the month of June. Enter the information in the Merkel's ledger books. Note that at the beginning of the solution we have stated that the value of the stock 'as at 30 June' this means that we can only calculate the stock at a certain time rather than over a period. This applies to all the assets that end up in the balance sheet. The asset values are constantly changing and therefore what was true two days ago may not be true today. We therefore state that we are reporting the value of assets at a specific time rather than over a period. We will see more of this as we prepare final accounts.

Merkel's Stock as at 30 June

Example 2.3

			£	£	£
	Opening Stock			3,000	
ADD	Purchases	4,500			
		2,700			
		3,000			
		1,000	11,200		
ADD	Return Inwards (1)	1,200	1,200	15,400	
LESS	Cost of goods sold (2)	3,000			
	Angel Traders (3)	3,200	6,200		
LESS	Returns outwards	2,100	2,100	8,300	
		Value of stock as at 30 June		7,100	

Notes:

(1) Goods sold to Angel Traders attracted a profit of 25% therefore £1,500 is actually 125%

Therefore 100% would be $\frac{100}{125} \times £1,500 = £1,200$

(2) Cost of goods sold on June 7: if 130% = £3,900 then 100% is: $\frac{100}{130} \times £3,900 = £3,000$

(3) Cost of goods sold to Angel Traders on June 17: if £4,000 = 125 % then 100% is:

$$\frac{100}{125} \times £4{,}000 = £3{,}200$$

To calculate the value of the stock held at the end of a certain period we need to remove the profit element of the goods sold and the profit margin that is still attached to the goods returned. However, care should be taken when entering the information in the double entry system. In the following solution, you will be introduced to the stock account. The stock account is used to value the stock at the end of a trading period. In the case below, the stock is valued at cost; therefore, the entries in the stock account are similar to the working out of the closing value stock in the section above.

Double entries for the month of June for Merkel's Business:

Stock Account

Date	Particulars	£	Date	Particulars	£
Jun-01	Opening Stock	3,000	Jun-06	Returns outwards	2,100
Jun-21	Returns Inwards	1,200	Jun-30	Cost of sales	6,200
Jun-30	Purchases	11,200			

Sales Account

Date	Particulars	£	Date	Particulars	£
			Jun-07	Bank	3,900
			Jun-17	Bank	4,000

Purchases Account

Date	Particulars	£	Date	Particulars	£
Jun-03	Bank	4,500			
Jun-05	Oz Suppliers	2,700			
Jun-12	Bank	3,000			
Jun-25	Bank	1,000			

Returns Inwards (Sales Returns)

Date	Particulars	£	Date	Particulars	£
Jun-21	Angel Traders	1,500	Jun-21	Stock Account	1,200
			Jun-30	Profit and Loss A/c	300

Returns Outwards (Purchases Returns)

Date	Particulars	£	Date	Particulars	£
Jun-30	Stock Account	2,100	Jun-06	Oz Suppliers	2,100

Bank Account

Date	Particulars	£	Date	Particulars	£
Jun-07	Sales	3,900	03-Jun	Purchases	4,500
Jun-17	Sales	4,000	Jun-12	Purchases	3,000
			Jun-21	Angel Traders	1,500
			Jun-25	Purchases	1,000

Oz Suppliers

Date	Particulars	£	Date	Particulars	£
Jun-06	Returns outwards	2,100	Jun-05	Purchases	2,700

Angel Traders

Date	Particulars	£	Date	Particulars	£
Jun-21	Bank	1,500	Jun-21	Returns inwards	1,500

CHAPTER 2: MAKING DOUBLE ENTRIES

Both the returns inwards and outwards are transferred to the respective sides of the stock account so that we can calculate how much stock we have at the end of each period. Returns inwards have a profit element (as in the case of Angel Traders); this profit element should be removed from the double entry system by crediting the profit and loss account with the amount.

Both sides of certain accounts such as Angel Traders are equal, this means that at the end of the period of trading Merkel does not owe Angel Traders anything nor do they owe Merkel. Such an account is said to have balanced out. Angel Traders returned the goods they did not want, they were then paid off using the money withdrawn from the bank account. On the other hand, Merkel owes Oz Suppliers £600 as can be seen from that account.

Example 2.4:
Mr. Welfare started a retail business on 1 June. The following is a list of transactions that he carried out during the month of June.

- Deposited £10,000 in his bank account on 1 June
- On 3 June, he received a loan of £5,000 from his friend, on condition that he would be paid a fixed amount at the end of each month.
- Bought goods for resale in cash on 4 June these goods cost £2,000
- On 5 Jun, bought a second hand delivery van from Johnston at £2,200
- Sold goods on credit for £700 to June Traders on 7 June
- On 14 June, received more goods for resale on credit from Goods Wholesalers Company worth £3,000
- Withdrew £1,200 to fix his car, he uses this car to take his children to school on 15 June
- Paid his shop front assistant £300 as part of her wages on 18 June
- Bought furniture for the store and increased the shelving space £800 on the 22 June
- On 29 June paid the shop front assistant the remaining £700 wages
- 30 June paid rent for the store £650

Prepare double entries for the transactions above:

Bank Account

Date	Particulars	£	Date	Particulars	£
01-Jun	Capital	10,000	04-Jun	Purchases	2,000
03-Jun	Loan	5,000	05-Jun	Delivery van	2,200
			15-Jun	Capital	1,200
			18-Jun	Wages	300
			22-Jun	Furn & Shelving	800
			29-Jun	Wages	700
			30-Jun	Rent	650

AN INTRODUCTION TO ACCOUNTING

Capital Account

Date	Particulars	£	Date	Particulars	£
15-Jun	Bank	1,200	01-Jun	Bank	10,000
			03-Jun	loan	5,000

Purchases

Date	Particulars	£	Date	Particulars	£
04-Jun	Bank	2,000			
14-Jun	Goods Wholesale Co	3,000			

Delivery Van Account

Date	Particulars	£	Date	Particulars	£
05-Jun	Delivery Van	2,200			

Sales

Date	Particulars	£	Date	Particulars	£
			07-Jun	June Traders	700

June Traders

Date	Particulars	£	Date	Particulars	£
07-Jun	Sales	700			

Goods Wholesalers Company

Date	Particulars	£	Date	Particulars	£
			14-Jun	Purchases	3,000

Wages Expense Account

Date	Particulars	£	Date	Particulars	£
18-Jun	Bank	300			
29-Jun	Bank	700			

Rent Expense Account

Date	Particulars	£	Date	Particulars	£
30-Jun	Bank	650			

Furniture and Shelving Acc

Date	Particulars	£	Date	Particulars	£
22-Jun	Bank	800			

The best way to learn how to complete the double entries is to do as many examples as possible, the more entries you make the more you become familiar with them.

2.5: Check of Accuracy

The system of double entries enables accountants to check whether accounts have been completed accurately. This is known as the check of accuracy. The rationale behind this is that if each transaction has a corresponding debit and credit entry, then it follows that if all the entries are made correctly, all the debit entries should equal all the credit balances. If we list all the double entries in three-column table, we can easily calculate the totals at the bottom of each column and see if they are equal. This however is not a foolproof check of accuracy, as two wrong double entries, which are equal in value, will not affect the total. It is nonetheless an early indicator that there is an error if the two totals are not equal.

Example 2.5

Ariel opened a business on 1 Jan; the following are some of the transactions that occurred during the month of January.

- Jan 1: deposited £25,000 in his bank account
- Jan 3: bought goods for resale £3,000
- Jan 5: sold goods to on credit to Banda Enterprises £2,000
- Jan 6: bought furniture and fixtures £700
- Jan 11: received goods from Big Traders on credit worth £2,500
- Jan 17: paid for broadband and telephone installation £100
- Jan 25: bought a van for the business £8,000
- Jan 30: received a bank loan from his bank £5,000

Date	Particulars	Debit £	Credit £
Jan 1	Bank Account	25,000	
	Capital Account		25,000
Jan 3	Purchases Account	3,000	
	Bank		3,000
Jan 5	Banda Enterprises	2,000	
	Sales Account		2,000
Jan 6	Furniture and Fixtures	700	
	Bank		700
Jan 11	Purchases Account	2,500	
			2,500
Jan 17	Broadband and telephone	100	
	Bank		100
Jan 25	Van Asset Account	8,000	
	Bank		8,000
Jan 30	Bank	5,000	
	Loan Account		5,000
	Totals	34,6000	34,600

AN INTRODUCTION TO ACCOUNTING

In the previous example, all the debit entries equal all the credit entries. For your practice, enter the transaction in T-accounts.

Revision Questions:

1. Discuss the rationale behind the following double entries: Expenses are entered on the debit side of a T-Account just as assets are entered on the debit side. All the liabilities and capital contributions are entered on the credit side.

2. The double entry system is used to record the double effect of transactions. Discuss why this is important in ensuring the accuracy.

3. Explain how profits, losses and withdrawals affect the capital of a business. Why do they affect the capital account the way they do?

4. In what ways can the value of a fixed asset change?

5. The double entry system is an accepted way of recording financial transactions. What are the advantages of using double entries rather than the single entry system?

Revision Exercises:

6. Following are transactions that have occurred during the period ended 30 November 2xx2 for a business that was started on 1 July 2xx2.

    - 1 July: deposited £55,000 in the business bank account
    - 3 July: bought furniture worth £1,800
    - 5 July: ordered for a broadband and telephone installation £60
    - 8 July: bought stationery in cash £400
    - 11 July: bought goods for resale at £3,000
    - 18 July: sold goods on credit to Jonas Retailers £1,200
    - 22 July: received goods on credit for resale £2,000 from Serious Wholesalers
    - 28 July: paid wages to his shop front assistant £800
    - 30 July: paid rent £1000 and £89 telephone bill
    - 31 July: paid £500 for goods received from Serious Wholesalers

August

    - Aug 3: withdrew £3,000 from his bank account to buy shares in a company that was tipped to grow by 20% by the end of the year

- Aug 12: bought a van for £18,000 to ferry goods from the wholesalers to his store
- Aug 15: received goods on credit from Serious Wholesalers worth £3,000
- Aug 16: sold goods in cash for £4,000
- Aug 16: bought two computers, a desk-top computer for £700 and a laptop for £1,100
- Aug 20: paid Serious Wholesalers £3,000 for goods received
- Aug 22: sold goods on credit to Another Retailer Company Limited at £1,200
- Aug 24: received payment from Jonas Retailers for goods sold to them on credit
- Aug 30: paid rent for his premises at £1,000 and £102 for his telephone bill
- Aug 31: received goods sold goods worth £1,800 to Jonas retailers

Using the information provided above:

Calculate the balance of the following items at the end of the two months:

a) Amount of money owed to Serious Wholesalers at the end of July and then amount owed at the end of August
b) Amounts that Jonas retailers owe at the end of August
c) Enter all the information shown in a double entry system

7. Marion started a business on 1 November following are transactions that occurred during the month.

- 1 Nov: deposited £60,000 in his bank account, where the bank had already deposited a business loan of £30,000
- 3 Nov: bought furniture and fixtures £1,500
- 4 Nov: bought goods for resale at £2,000 cash
- 11 Nov: sold goods at £900 cash
- 13 Nov: sold goods on credit to Easy Retailers at £1,400
- 19 Nov: paid miscellaneous (sundry expenses) £300
- 24 Nov: received £1,000 part - payment for goods sold to Easy Retailers
- 30 Nov: paid rent for the month £1,100 and wages for her assistant £1,400

Using the information presented above:

a) Marion bought goods worth £2,000 yet made sales of £2,300 explain the difference
b) Using the table below enter all the transactions in either the debit or credit side. The first transaction has been done for you:

AN INTRODUCTION TO ACCOUNTING

Account Name:	Debit £	Credit £
Bank Account	60,000	
• Capital		60,000
Bank Account	30,000	
• Bank Loan Account		30,000

8. Mr Didcot opened a shoe retailer business on Oxford High street on 1 Jan 2xx5 the following are transactions for the month of Jan:

- 1 Jan: started business with £20,000 in bank account
- 3 Jan: bought office furniture and fixtures £3,000
- 4 Jan: bought a second hand van for £2,300
- 11 Jan: bought shoes for resale, he paid £4,000 and incurred a credit agreement with Shoe Suppliers Company of £3,000
- 14 Jan: sold 10 pairs of shoes for £1,800 cash
- 21 Jan: paid £1,500 to Shoe Suppliers Company

   Using this information complete the double entries for each transaction

9. Piper has been trading for the last three months following are some of the balances at the beginning of the fourth month:
   - 1 April: Stock £2,500
              Bank Balance £4,700
              Debtors: Dwarves Retailers £1,500
              Creditors: Big Wholesalers £3,600

   The following transactions occurred during the month of April:
   - 1 April: received payment from Dwarves retailers £1,500
   - 3 April: sold on credit goods worth £2,100 to Taller Limited
   - 8 April: received goods from Big Wholesalers worth £4,000
   - 9 April: paid Big Wholesalers 4,500
   - 11 April: received goods from Taller Limited worth £500 that had been damaged in transit from Piper's business premises
   - 15 April: stock takers found that part of the goods received from Big Wholesalers were meant for another customer of Big Wholesalers and already had the initials of that customer embossed on them. These goods were returned to Big Wholesalers they were worth £1,500
   - 16 April: sold goods worth £1,800 to Dwarves Retailers in cash
   - 21 April: took £2,000 from the bank account to help her friend set up a business.
   - 25 April: bought additional furniture for an outer office £700
   - 27 April: paid rent for her office building £1,200

   1) Calculate the following balances at the end of the month of April:
      a) Bank Balance

b) Debtors Balance a
c) Creditors balance
d) Stock levels

2) Make the double entries for the transactions for the month of April.

10. You have been provided with the following table, which shows one debit and credit entry for the month of July for Mona Dressmakers. The following is a list of transactions for this period:
    - 1 June: Deposited £10,000 in bank account
    - 3 June: Purchased fabric for £4,000
    - 5 June: received clothes accessories from ACC ltd worth £1,500 on credit
    - 7 June: bought a second hand car to deliver clothes to customers £3,000
    - 11 June: sold a wedding dress and 4 bridesmaids gowns £5,000
    - 14 June: bought furniture and fixtures £700
    - 21 June: received one of the gowns back it was worth £750. A gown cost £600 to make
    - 25 June: received fabrics worth £4,500 from Sundance Fabrics on credit
    - 27 June: returned fabrics to Sundance Fabrics worth £1,800

Date	Particulars	Debit £	Credit £
1 June	Bank	10,000	
	Capital		10,000

Complete the table by correctly filling in the missing transactions. Ensure that the total of the debits equal the total of the credits.

Chapter 3: Double entry for Incomes, Expenses, Stock and Closing T-Accounts

Learning outcomes: The learner should be able to:
- Describe the theoretical reasons for double entry of incomes, revenues, stock
- Successfully make double entries for these items
- Balance off T-accounts and prepare a Trial Balance
- Explain how the trial balance is important in checking for accuracy of entries and its limitations

3.1: Incomes and Expenses

Once a business begins operations it generates an income. As we already saw in chapter 1, businesses are created for three basic reasons; these are profit, provision of public services or charitable reasons. This book looks at businesses formed for a profit. In chapter 2, we looked at how to make double entry records of day-to-day business transactions. This chapter looks at how to make entries for incomes and expenses. We have already seen how to record expenses and stock on a basic level. We will further discuss these concepts in this chapter. The chapter will show how these transactions are connected through closing off accounts and obtaining balances for the T-Accounts.

People who take the risk to start a business and put in resources are known as entrepreneurs. These people start businesses with an aim of generating wealth. They offer goods or services that are sold for an income. Production of these goods or services requires the use of resources. Resources used in the production of wealth are known as expenses. Hence, incomes are generated by a business through the application of resources (capital, labour, entrepreneurial skill, land and technology) to production. Capital is used to acquire assets that are used in production. Capital is also used to pay for operational expenses of the business. The difference between the income generated from the production and expenses incurred in that production is known as profit – if the income exceeds the expenses. A loss is incurred if expenses exceed incomes.

The cumulative effect of profit is an increase of the resources available to the business. These resources are also known as capital. Therefore, profit directly increases capital. This implies that more resources can be employed for the business and more expenses can be paid for as well as more assets being made available for production.

Expenses and assets are therefore the same in a business; they are paid for with the capital or liabilities that the business holds, for this reason **expenses and assets** are **debited**. Another reason that assets and expenses are debited is that they are used for production and creation of wealth. We are familiar with this concept now, as we have seen it earlier in Chapter 2.

Incomes are also known as revenues. Revenues are conventionally credited in the revenues accounts. Revenues are generated from sales. When a business generates revenues, it uses those revenues to pay for expenses as well as for assets that are acquired through debts. If a business generates the exact revenues that equal the expenses the original value of the accounting equation would be maintained. However, if the revenues exceed the expenses then there is a profit, which increases the capital and thus generates a credit entry. If there were no expenses, which is highly unlikely, yet the business-generated revenue then the profits would equal the revenues. This means that the revenues would also generate a credit entry in the revenue T-accounts. During the normal course of recording of financial transactions, the different accounts are recorded individually according to their nature and a double entry is made in the corresponding accounts. **Revenues** like **profit,** hence **capital, are credit entries**.

3.2: Sales, Purchases and Stock

Sales refer to all the goods or services that a business buys produces and sells its customers. **Purchases** refer to all the inputs that go into the direct production of the final product.

Sales do not include the disposal of assets or other items that the business does not ordinarily sell. For example if a supermarket were to sell one of its trucks this is not a sale, rather, it is the disposal of an asset.

On the other hand, purchases only relate to those goods that are used directly in the production of the good or service that the business sells. For example, sacks of wheat bought to produce bread are purchases whereas rent paid for the building in which the product is produced is classified as an expense. Stock refers to the merchandise that is available with the business for resale or for production of the final product. In accounting, we cannot simply record the inflow and outflow of stock because this does not capture the profit element in the sales.

To record the movement of stock, as products bought for resale at a profit or as raw material bought for production of the final product to which a profit margin is added, we use separate purchase and sales accounts. Sales accounts show the sale of goods at a profit on the credit side, since these revenues increase the capital, and a purchase account shows the products bought for production or resale at their cost price. The purchases are recorded on the debit side of the purchases account. The difference of the balances of these two accounts gives a certain type of profit known as **Gross Profit**

Note: Gross Profits = Sales – Purchases

Recording stock movement in the two different accounts allows the easy calculation of the gross profit or loss. Another advantage is that we can make a double entry for business customers who buy our products on credit. We can also make a double entry recognising the purchase of goods and services on credit.

CHAPTER 3: DOUBLE ENTRY

3.3: Points of reference

It is clear that the double-entry system is very diverse in its applications. This book aims to introduce the learner to both the theoretical and practical background of accounting and aid informed managerial decisions.

Below is a simple tabulation of all the double entries that have been considered so far:

DEBIT SIDE		**CREDIT SIDE**	
Date	£	*Date*	£
Purchases		*Revenues (Sales)*	
Expenses		*Profits*	
Assets		*Capital*	
		Liabilities	

The entries in the table above are presented, as they would appear in their individual accounts. This is to say that purchases go on the debit side of the purchase accounts while sales go on the debit side of the sales account.

Example 3.1

Jon has been operating his business for the last six months. His business retails computers from a major computer brand. His initial capital was £10,000 on the 01st of April

The following is a list of transactions:

April 1: he paid rent for his store of £1400
April 2: he receives 15 computer systems worth £ 7,000
April 3: he sells for cash a computer system for £640
April 3: sells two computer systems on credit for £800
April 7: pays for a new business mobile phone £150
April 12: he sells two computer systems cash for £640 each
April 14: customer who bought computer on credit returns it due to a faulty cooling fan
April 17: the major brand company collects the faulty machine
April 21: he receives a broadband connection pack worth £215; this will be included in his three-month bill from his telephone company

Worked solution:
It is important to make entries as we read down the list. This ensures that none of the entries is missed out.

AN INTRODUCTION TO ACCOUNTING

Capital Account

Date	£	Date	£
		01/04 Bank/Cash	10,000

Rent Account (Expense Account)

Date		£	Date	£
01/04	Cash/Bank	1,400		

Bank/ Cash Account

Date:	£	Date	£
01/04: Cash/Bank	10,000	01/04: Rent	1,400
03/04: Computer Sales	640	07/04: Mobile Phone	150
12/04: Computer Systems	1,280		

Purchases Account

Date	£	Date	£
02/04: Big Brand Computers	7,000		

Sales Account (Revenue Account)

Date	£	Date	£
		03/04: Cash	640
		03/04: Customer 1	800
		03/04: Customer 2	800
		12/04: Cash	1,280

Big Brand Computers (Creditors/ liability account)

Date	£	Date	£
Returns outwards	500	02/04: Purchases	7,000

Customer 1: Asset Account (Debtor)

Date:	£	Date	£
03/04: Computer Systems sale	800	14/04: Returns inwards	800

Customer 2: (Asset Account-Debtor)

Date:	£	Date	£
03/04: Computer Systems Sale	800		

Business Mobile Telephone (Asset Account)

Date	£	Date	£
07/04: Cash	150		

Broadband Pack (Asset Account)

Date	£	Date	£
Broadband pack supplier	215		

Broadband Pack Supplier Account (Liability/ Creditor Account)

Date	£	Date	£
		21/04: Broadband pack	215

Returns Inwards (Sales Returns)

Date	£	Date	£
14/04: **Customer 1**	800		

Returns Outwards (Purchases Returns)

Date	£	Date	£
		Big Brand Computers	500

1. *His initial capital was £10,000 on the 01 April:* Jon starts his business by depositing his £ 10,000 in the bank. This is entered as a debit balance in the cash/bank account and as a credit entry in the Capital account
2. *01/04: He paid rent for his store of £1400 and on 07/04/05: Pays for a new business mobile phone £150* These are expenses that have been paid for in cash, debit the individual expense accounts and make a corresponding credit entries in the cash/bank account
3. *02/04: He receives 15 computer systems worth £ 7,000:* This is a purchase on credit; purchases refer to items bought for resale by a business. Debit the purchases account and credit the account of the supplier as they have provided the computers on credit. If the computers were paid for in cash then a corresponding credit entry would have been made in the Cash/Bank account
4. *03/04: He sells for cash a computer system for £640 and on 12/04: he sells two computer systems cash for £640 each:* These three transactions have the same entries; debit the cash account with the cash received and credit the revenues or sales accounts with the values of the sales.

5. *03/04: Sells two computer systems on credit for £800:* In this case, computers are to be paid for in future by customers. These customers become assets, as they will in future generate an income in terms of payment for the customers. We debit each of the customer's accounts with the value of the computers bought and we credit the sales account.
6. *14/04: Customer who bought computer on credit returns it due to a faulty cooling fan:* This transaction is known as Return Inwards or Sales returns- note that the computer was sold at the sale price of £800 as opposed to the cost price of £ 500. This means that it cannot be debited from the sales account directly since it does not represent the payment of the outstanding amount nor can it be credited in the purchase account as it is still with the company and has not been returned to the vendor of the Big Brand Computers. It is debited in a special account known as Sales Returns or Returns Inwards and this is then credited in the customer's account.
7. *17/04: The Big Brand Company collects the faulty machine:* The machine was then returned to the vendor. We credit the returns outwards account (Purchase Returns Accounts). We then debit the Big Brand Company because we have reduced our liability to the Big Brand company.

It is important that all the account entries be entered along with the correct dates. The name of the corresponding account to which the balancing entry is made is entered as the description of either accounts. For example, in the cash account we enter the word rent on the credit side meaning that we spent that amount on rent. In the rent account, we enter cash, meaning that the rent was paid for in cash.

Many other issues arise in reality when it comes to double entries for a large variety of transactions. We will learn about these transactions as we look at various issues in accounting in this book.

3.3: Balancing off the accounts

Periodically, say once a month or two months a business needs to evaluate its position in terms of its performance and prospects. Financial information is very important for these evaluations. Businesses needed to tell at a glance where each of its transactions stands.

To provide this summary information we 'balance-off' the accounts, this means we add up all the values at the end of each account and find the difference between either sides of the account. This process is known as balancing off as we close each account by equating the totals of the credit and debit side. The difference between either sides is then added on the side that is less, to equate the values. This difference is known as the 'balance carried down' abbreviated as **Bal. c /d.**

CHAPTER 3: DOUBLE ENTRY

The balance carried down is then recorded at the beginning of the next period this is known as the opening balance, this balance is also known as balance brought down and abbreviated as **Bal. b/d**

From example 3.1 above we can balance off the Bank/ Cash Account below

Bank/ Cash Account

Date:	£	Date	£
01/04: Cash/Bank	10,000	01/04: Rent	1,400
03/04: Computer Sales	640	07/04: Mobile Phone	150
12/04: Computer Systems	1,280		
		30/04: Balance c/d	10,370
Total:	11,920	Total:	11,920
Date	£	Date	£
01/05 Balance b/d	10,370		

The arrow shows how the balance carried down from the previous period otherwise known as closing balance is transferred to a new account for the new period.

This account shows a balancing off the value of the balance carried down is arrived at by calculating the difference between the Total and the credit side, which is the lower balance of the total.

Cash/Bank	£ 10,000 +
Computer sales	£ 1,920
Total:	£ 11,920
Less: Credit side:	
Rent	£ 1,400+
Mobile Phone:	£ 150
Total:	£ 1,550
Balance Carried down:	£ 10,370

This balancing figure has a special significance in the case of a cash/bank account a debit balance means that the business has £ 10,370 in Cash or in the bank. A credit

AN INTRODUCTION TO ACCOUNTING

balance in the cash account might mean that the business owes money to a third party as it has paid out more money than it has put into the account.

This should not be confused with a bank's credit balance, which means that the customer has some money with the bank. This is true from the point of view of the bank. Customer's money is a credit balance, as the bank owes the customer that money.

Taking another account from example 3.1

Sales Account (Revenue Account)

Date	£	Date	£
		03/04: Cash	640
		03/04: Customer 1	800
		03/04: Customer 2	800
30/04: Balance c/d	3,520	12/04: Cash	1,280
Total	3,520	Total	3,520

Date	£	Date	£
		01/04 Balance b/d	3,520
		This is a credit balance	

In this case, the account is said to have a credit balance. The sales account is in credit. The entries of the sales account correspond with the debit entries of the debtors and the cash or bank account. The credit balances of the sales account in this case finance the debit entries in assets accounts.

At the start of our new period's account there is a starting balance of £3,520, which will be, added onto the new period's sales. This is a credit balance.

Purchase Account Month of April

Date	£	Date	£
Purchases	7,000	30/04 Balance c/d	7,000
Total	7,000	Total	7,000

Purchases Account Month of May

Date	£	Date	£
01/05:Balance b/d	7,000		
This is a debit balance			

Attempt to close off all the accounts in example 3.1 above

3.4: Trial Balance

After all accounts are balanced off then a list of all balances can be made. This list of balances is known as a Trial Balance. This is a two-column statement, which lists all the debit and credit balances of all the T-accounts. The total at the end of the debit entries of each account should equal the credit entries total if all the double entries have been correctly entered in the T-accounts.

The trial balance thus provides a check of accuracy. If there has been an entry that has been made incorrectly the totals would not balance.

Using example 3.1: A trial balance can be created:

Trial Balance	Dr.	Cr
Capital		10,000.00
Rent	1,400.00	
Mobile Phone	150.00	
Bank/Cash Account	10,370.00	
Sales Account		3,520.00
Purchases Account	7,000.00	
Big Brand Liability Account		6,500.00
Broadband Pack Supplier		215.00
Broadband Pack	215.00	
Customer 1	800.00	800.00
Customer 2	800.00	
Returns Inwards	800.00	
Returns outwards		500.00
Total	**21,535**	**21,535**

Notes:
Ordinarily accounts such as Customer 1's account are not included in the trial balance as it has a balancing entry on the other side of the account making the balance carried down nil.

To determine if a balance is a debit balance or a credit balance, the account is balanced off and the balance carried down calculated and then brought down for the next period. A debit balance is one where the balance brought down is on the debit side at the start of the new period whereas a credit balance is one where the balance brought down at the start of the new period is on the credit side of the T-account.

AN INTRODUCTION TO ACCOUNTING

The trial balance is an important tool for determining the accuracy of double entries. Since every debit entry has a corresponding credit entry, it follows that the total value of the debit balances equals the total value of the credit balances.

However while this could be an important check of accuracy, it is not conclusive for the following reasons:
1. Failure to enter a transaction altogether, this means that the total balances will be equal, as the omitted transaction does not appear on the debit or credit side.
2. Compensating errors could also lead to the two totals equalling each other but being wrong. Two transactions of equal value but with no relationship can have only one entry made each but one on the credit side and the other on the debit side. This would lead to the trial balance totals being equal but incorrect.

Note that the trial balance may resemble the debit/credit table that was introduced in Chapter 2. It however is not the same thing; the trial balance is created after all the T-accounts have been balanced off.

Example 3.2:
Kyle has been in business for the last six months. On July 31, the books showed the following balances:

- Bank balance   £4,400
- Van Asset Account   £12,000
- Furniture and fixtures   £1,400
- Debtors (Mug Traders)   £2,400
- Creditors (Hussein W/Salers)`   £3,000
- Capital   £17,200

The following transactions occurred during the month of August:
- 1 Aug: received goods from Hussein Wholesalers worth £2,800 on credit
- 3 Aug: paid Hussein Wholesalers £3,000
- 4 Aug: received payment from Mug Traders of £2,000
- 5 Aug: paid wages to his employee £1,800
- 9 Aug: sold goods on credit to Robertson Retailers £2,500
- 11 Aug: sold goods to Mug Traders worth £4,000, £2,000 was paid in cash and £2,000 was sold on credit.
- 14 Aug: bought goods from Jalal Traders worth £1,600
- 16 Aug: Robertson Traders returned some of the goods they had bought on credit as they were damaged, these goods were sold to Robertson Traders at £1,300
- 17 Aug: paid for sundry (miscellaneous) expenses £900
- 21 Aug: deposited £5,000 a loan he had acquired from a Venture capitalist into his business account
- 24 Aug: returned goods worth £800 to Hussein Wholesalers, these goods had a different specification from the rest of the goods bought

CHAPTER 3: DOUBLE ENTRY

- 25 Aug: bought new swivel chairs worth £400
- 26 Aug: paid rent and rates for the month of August and September £2,000
- 31 Aug: paid for broadband and telephone charges £140

Note that all the goods were sold with a 30% profit margin

        a) Make the double entry for all the transactions above.
        b) Create a trial balance for the period ending 31 August

Bank Balance

Date	Particulars	£	Date	Particulars	£
Aug-01	Bal b/f	4,400	Aug-03	Hussein W/Salers	3,000
Aug-04	Mug Traders	2,000	Aug-05	Wages	1,800
Aug-11	Sales	2,000	Aug-14	Purchases	1,600
Aug-21	Loan	5,000	Aug-17	Sundry Expenses	900
			Aug-25	Furn & Fixtures	400
			Aug-26	Rent and Rates	2,000
			Aug-31	Tel & Broadband	140
			Aug-31	Balance c/d	3,560
		13,400			13,400
Sep-01	Balance b/f	3,560			

Van Asset Account

Date	Particulars	£	Date	Particulars	£
Aug-01	Bal b/f	12,000	Aug-31	Bal c/d	12,000
Sep-01	Bal b/f	12,000			

Furniture and Fixtures

Date	Particulars	£	Date	Particulars	£
Aug-01	Bal b/f	1,400			
Aug-25	Bank	400			
			Aug-31	Bal c/d	1,800
		1,800			1,800
Sep-01	Balance b/f	1,800			

Mug Traders

Date	Particulars	£	Date	Particulars	£
Aug-01	Bal b/f	2,400	Aug-04	Bank	2,000
Aug-11	Sales	2,000	Aug-31	Balance c/d	2,400
		4,400			4,400
Sep-01	Balance b/f	2,400			

Hussein Wholesalers

Date	Particulars	£	Date	Particulars	£
Aug-03	Bank	3,000	Aug-01	Bal b/f	3,000
Aug-24	Returns outwards	800	Aug-01	Purchases	2,800
Aug-31	Balance c/d	2,000			
		5,800			5,800
			Sep-01	Bal b/f	2,000

Capital

Date	Particulars	£	Date	Particulars	£
Aug-31	Bal c/d	17,200	Aug-01	Bal b/f	17,200
			Sep-01	Bal b/f	17,200

Purchases

Date	Particulars	£	Date	Particulars	£
Aug-01	Hussein Wholesalers	2,800			
Aug-14	Bank	1,600	Aug-31	Balance c/d	4,400
		4400			4,400
Sep-01	Balance b/f	4,400			

Robertson Retailers

Date	Particulars	£	Date	Particulars	£
Aug-09	Sales	2,500	Aug-16	Returns inwards	1,300
			Aug-31	Balance c/d	1,200
		2,500			2,500
Sep-01	Balance b/f	1,200			

CHAPTER 3: DOUBLE ENTRY

Sales Account

Date	Particulars	£	Date	Particulars	£
			Aug-09	Robertson Retailers	2,500
			Aug-11	Mug Traders	2,000
Aug-31	Balance c/d	6,500	Aug-11	Bank	2,000
		6,500			6,500
			Sep-01	Balance b/f	6,500

Returns inwards

Date	Particulars	£	Date	Particulars	£
Aug-16	Robertson Retailers	1,300	Aug-31	Balance c/d	1,300
Sep-01	Balance b/f	1,300			

Venture Loan

Date	Particulars	£	Date	Particulars	£
Aug-31	Balance c/d	5,000	Aug-21	Bank	5,000
			Sep-01	Balance b/f	5,000

Returns Outwards

Date	Particulars	£	Date	Particulars	£
Aug-31	Balance c/d	800	Aug-24	Hussein W/Salers	800
			Sep-01	Balance b/f	800

Trial Balance:

Particulars	Debit	Credit
Bank Balance	3,560	
Van Asset Account	12,000	
Furniture and Fixtures	1,800	
Mug Traders	2,400	
Hussein Wholesalers		2,000
Capital		17,200
Purchases	4,400	
Robertson Retailers	1,200	
Sales Account		6,500
Returns Inwards	1,300	
Expenses	4,840	
Venture Loan		5,000
Returns outwards		800
	31,500	31,500

AN INTRODUCTION TO ACCOUNTING

Example 3.2 shows what happened in one month in Kyle's business. We have completed the double entries to show these transactions and prepared a trial balance. A trial balance is more useful than the previous list of debits and credits that you have encountered in chapter 2. This is because it only deals with balances, for a trial balance to be balanced all the transactions of a given transaction must be correctly entered; therefore, the trial balance provides a better check of accuracy. The trial balance is still not foolproof just more sensitive to error.

The following errors could slip through a trial balance check of accuracy:
- Reversal of entries happens when debit balance is entered as a credit balance and vice versa if this is done consistently for all the transactions that relate to a particular item then the trial balance will balance, however there is an error
- Debiting the wrong account with the correct figures also leads to a balanced trial balance. For example if you debit the Van account with amounts used to purchase the furniture, then the trial balance will balance but the value of the van account will be consistently wrong.
- A compensating error is one where two unrelated amounts cancel each other out in the trial balance concealing the error that might have occurred. An erroneous debit entry of £30 will be cancelled by an erroneous £30 credit.
- An omission of a transaction altogether leads to an overall error, on the financial statement but will not be detected on the trial balance.
- Putting in a wrong figure altogether also leads to the trial balance not balancing. For example if you pay £2,000 to your employees and you enter £1,200 in the wages account and the bank account then the trial balance will balance but the overall accounts will be in error.

Note that the balances at the end of July are simple balance sheets:

	£
Assets:	
Bank Balance	4,400
Van Asset Account	12,000
Debtors Account	2,400
Furniture and Fixtures	1,400
Creditors	(3,000)
Net Assets	**17,200**
Financed by:	
Capital	**17,200**

The balance between the assets, liabilities and capital is maintained even after the trading month of August. It is important that the learner understands the connection between the three items as it is the basis of all the accounting concepts.

CHAPTER 3: DOUBLE ENTRY

Example 3.3:

The following transactions occurred during the first month of trading for Betty Travel Accessories business.

Jan 1: deposited £20,000 in her business bank account
Jan 3: bought a stock of travel bags in cash for £3,000
Jan 4: received on credit worth £5,000 from Boots World
Jan 7: received a van on credit from Van Vendors traders £10,000
Jan 10: paid wages for £4,000
Jan 14: bought furniture and fixtures worth £1,000
Jan 17: sold goods worth £3,000 to a camping team
Jan 23: paid £2,000 to Boots World
Jan 25: sold goods worth £2,300
Jan 27: paid rent for the premises £1,100
Jan 28: returned some boots to Boot World, as they were mismatched, these were worth £1,000
Jan 29: sold goods worth £3,200

Make the double entry for these transactions and prepare a trial balance:

Solution

Bank Account

Date	Particulars	£	Date	Particulars	£
Jan-01	Capital Account	20,000	Jan-03	Purchases	3,000
Jan-17	Sales	3,000	Jan-10	Wages	4,000
Jan-25	Sales	2,300	Jan-14	Furniture and Fixtures	1,000
Jan-29	Sales	3,200	Jan-23	Boots World	2,000
			Jan-27	Rent	1,100
			Jan-31	Balance c/d	17,400
		28,500			28,500
Feb-01	Bal b/f	17,400			

Capital Account

Date	Particulars	£	Date	Particulars	£
Jan-31	Balance c/d	20,000	Jan-01	Bank	20,000
			Sep-01	Balance b/f	20,000

Purchases

Date	Particulars	£	Date	Particulars	£
Jan-03	Bank	3,000			
Jan-04	Boots World	5,000	Jan-31	Balance c/d	8,000
		8,000			8,000
Feb-01	Balance b/f	8,000			

Boots World

Date	Particulars	£	Date	Particulars	£
Jan-23	Bank	2,000	Jan-04	Purchases	5,000
Jan-28	Returns outwards	1,000			
Jan-31	Balance c/d	2,000			
		5,000			5,000
			Feb-01	Balance b/f	2,000

Van Vendors

Date	Particulars	£	Date	Particulars	£
Jan-31	Balance c/d	10,000	Jan-07	Van Asset Account	10,000
			Feb-01	Balance b/f	10,000

Van Asset Account

Date	Particulars	£	Date	Particulars	£
Jan-07	Van Vendors	10,000	Jan-31	Balance c/d	10,000

CHAPTER 3: DOUBLE ENTRY

Furniture and Fixtures

Date	Particulars	£	Date	Particulars	£
Jan-14	Bank	1,000	Jan-31	Balance c/d	1,000
Feb-01	Balance b/f	1,000			

Sales

Date	Particulars	£	Date	Particulars	£
			Jan-17	Bank	3,000
			Jan-25	Bank	2,300
Jan-31	Balance c/d	8,500	Jan-29	Bank	3,200
		8,500			8,500
			Feb-01	Balance b/f	8,500

Returns Outwards

Date	Particulars	£	Date	Particulars	£
Jan-31	Balance c/d	1,000	Jan-28	Boots World	1,000
			Feb-01	Balance b/f	1,000

Trial Balance:

	Debit	Credit
Bank	17,400	
Capital Account		20,000
Returns outwards		1,000
Sales		8,500
Furniture and Fixtures	1,000	
Van Asset	10,000	
Van Vendors Account		10,000
Expenses	5,100	
Boots World		2,000
Purchases	8,000	
	41,500	41,500

A trial balance is used as the basis for the preparation of final statements of accounts. A trial balance is the summary of transactions that have occurred during a certain period of trading.

3.4: Accounting Systems: Manual and Computerised

Financial information is important to all the stakeholders of a business. Accounting systems are used to ensure that this information has been correctly collected and recorded.

The following systemic approach was used in the manual systems of accounting. Firstly, books were accounting information that was entered into the **'Books of Prime entry'** this is the conventional accounts journal that you can pick up in any bookshop. This more or less resembles a list of debits and credits that you encountered in chapter two. If a business is carrying out many of the transactions of the same type for example sales then a specific journal called a 'Sales Daybook' may be prepared. In this journal, all sales transactions are recorded. Different daybooks may be used for purchases, wages, and sundry expenses and so on. Today, computers have removed the need for books of prime entry as initial transactions can be recorded automatically at the check out point using cash machines or bar-code reading till machines. Accounting software, which can track stock movement, eliminates the need to take initial records for goods received or sold. However, this software replicates the records that were kept manually and some will even have the same formats of the normal daybooks albeit on-screen.

Once the initial accounting information has been collected, it is then entered in **ledgers**. Ledger is the other name of T-accounts, which you are familiar with now. Ledger accounts make it possible to record non-cash transaction such as credit transactions. It is also easier to record transactions such as return inwards, discounts and even provisions, as we shall see later in this book.

After balancing off the ledger accounts, a **trial balance** can be created. This is a list of all the balances of the ledger accounts. The trial balance provides information on the performance of the business. Looking at a debtors account for example, a manager can tell that some debtors are taking too long to pay off their debts, or that the stock levels are unsuitably high or low. A trial balance also forms a basis for the creation of the financial statements.

Financial statements are the final statements of the accounting system. This is the information that is required by stakeholders who need to know how the business is performing. Financial statements are prepared according to certain international standards. These standards make it possible for stakeholders the world over to understand what is meant by the statements.

The computerisation of accounting system has however made some of the systemic recording of transactions redundant. Software such as 'Sage' or 'Quick-books' can track stock as it comes into the store, record its movement, sale, damage, returns inwards and outwards even discounts. Such software can produce statements at various points in time on request or trial balances or any other pertinent information as it is required.

There are significant advantages of computerising the accounting system. Some of the advantages include; the records are often accurate, unless the data fed into the system is incorrect. All machines share this weakness; they are unable to discern abnormal entries. For example, if a car dealership that usually sells a cars for £10,000 reports selling a car for £100,000 because someone entering the information made a mistake of typing too many zeros the computer system may not pick this up and may use it for future computations and report abnormal profits. A human being dealing with the same entry can pick up that there is a problem. However, as computers and software become more advanced the system may pick up the error when it tries to complete a trial balance or even the financial statements. If all the information entered into the computer system is correct then the accuracy is likely to be maintained throughout the computations that the computer system performs.

The speed of computation is also very high and therefore convenient. A business requires information that is accurate and up to date. Without computer systems, it took a very long time to record financial information and produce final balances that could be used to evaluate the performance of the business. Using computer systems, we can easily produce the balances and the information we need when we need it. For example if we need to know how much a frequent buyer owes us using the manual system we would take at least a week to collate all the transactions that appertain to that buyer. If we wanted to use this information to offer credit immediately, then it would not be available.

Another advantage of computers is retrieval and referencing, this means that it is easy to find the information that you need by simply using the 'search' facility in the computer system. This makes it easy to compare data from different periods and even create trend information. Finding the same information in a manual paper system would take a long time, there is also the possibility of the information being misplaced.

Computers have been changing rapidly becoming more powerful and faster. This is an advantage in disguise because a business can buy the latest system as soon as they appear and this is at relatively low prices of between £400 and £1000. Compared to retraining staff members to deal with changes in the accounting systems and conventions is far cheaper. Training staff does not automatically mean that they will learn and be proficient in applying the training to their work. Computers generally prevent excessive training and retraining costs.

Connectivity is another advantage that arises from computers. The internet has made automation with stakeholders easier. Computers can monitor the stock levels and reorder when there is need for more stock. Computers can also be used to send tax returns to the UK government. This is very important, as tax computations tend to be complex for the average businessperson. It is also time wasting if done by the businessperson or costly if passed on to an accountant. Software that communicates with the tax department, orders stock, and sends an item out to the customers is also cost effective and efficient.

Consistency arises from the fact that a computer programme is created to perform the same action in the same way at all times. As a result, one of the conventions of accounting is fulfilled by a computer system. For example, a computer programmed to treat furniture as assets always does this unlike two accountants who may disagree on whether or not the value of furniture is high enough to be treated as an asset or a mere expense.

Manual records have always had the disadvantage of storage space. Computers can store massive amounts of information and physically occupy a very small space.

There are disadvantages of using computers, firstly, viruses are known to wipe out computer memories and make all the information stored there inaccessible. Secondly, computers cannot assess situations and make appropriate decisions, as the situation requires. For example, a stock reorder system may reorder stock at the end of a shopping season, like at the end of the Christmas season, leaving the store with too much stock. Thirdly, computers depend on power supply in times of power outages and other power related problems the computer system becomes inaccessible. This is especially a problem in countries where power supply is not reliable. A fourth problem for computers that are connected to the internet is vulnerability to privacy breaches. This means that computers can be accessed remotely by a third party over the internet and the information stored in them stolen or corrupted. This is known as hacking. Though hacking is a crime, the speed and ingenuity of hackers makes it a difficult, expensive and often impossible crime to police.

Human error may also compromise the effectiveness of computers. The most common error is that of data input where the wrong data is entered into the computer. Secondly, the handling of computer access could also compromise the information stored in it, this is especially important where there are specific people who are assigned to access the computers. Computer access is usually restricted to certain individuals; these people are assigned passwords and levels of access. If one of these people were to reveal their passwords inadvertently then the whole system may be compromised. Failure to back-up information in a computer because of over-reliance on the computer could be a precursor to disaster in case the system fails. Some business over rely on computers oblivious of the fact that these systems could fail, they do not set up a parallel system that can act as a fall-back in case the first system fails.

In all the use of computers is advantageous as compared to the manual systems. The implementation of computer system should be carefully thought out. Anti-virus, anti-hacking, anti-spam software should be included in the system set-up. Access to the system should be restricted to very few people. Physical security is also important for the server (a central computer that is usually very powerful and that controls all the information that is required for running the business- it is the brains of the system).

CHAPTER 3: DOUBLE ENTRY

Revision Questions

1. The trial balance can be used to check the accuracy of the entries made in the books of accounts. What errors are likely to be missed out in by this check of accuracy?
2. The balancing-off of accounts is important as it gives the state and the performance of businesses at a certain point. Why is this difficult for a business today and what are the likely solutions?
3. Using computers is a popular business trend, what are the advantages of using computers in business today?
4. What are the problems associated with using computers?
5. State the erroneous entries in the following trial balance:

Item	Debit	Credit
Sales	10,300	
Purchases		7,900
Capital	9,300	5,700
Bank	5,000	
Car Asset		10,000
Furniture and Fixtures	3,000	
Debtors		6,700
Creditors		4,000
Returns inwards	1,000	
Returns outwards		1,900
Loan account	5,000	
Stock		3,000
Expenses	5,600	
Total	39,200	39,200

Correct the mistakes in the trial balance and calculate the balancing figure.

Revision Exercises:

6. The following transactions occurred in the first month of Naima's Fashion Design Business.
   - June 1: Deposited £13,000 into her business account
   - June 2: Bought stock in cash worth £3,100
   - June 4: Bought furniture and fittings £1,800
   - June 7: Received goods from Jared Designers £4,000
   - June 8: Sold goods in cash worth £1,500
   - June 15: withdrew £2,200 to pay for her son's trip to Spain
   - June 17: received goods worth £500 as Sales returns for the goods she had sold on June 8
   - June 21: sold goods on credit to Keenyah Traders worth £3,500

AN INTRODUCTION TO ACCOUNTING

- June 25: paid wages to her employees £2,000
- June 28: Paid for broadband access and telephone bills £300
- June 29: Prepaid rent and rates £1000 and rent for the month at £1000.

Enter the information in the double entry system and derive a trial balance.

7. Robert has been in business for the last six months. Following are the balances at the end of the sixth month:

Stock	4,800
Bank Balance	5,000
Debtors (Eagle Eye Traders)	2,700
Creditors (London Wholesalers)	3,000
Prepaid rent and rates	800
Motor Vehicles	11,000
Computer systems	2,500
Capital	23,800

During the seventh month the following transactions occurred:
01/07: purchased goods worth £3,400
03/07: received goods on credit £4,000 from London Wholesalers
06/07: sold goods worth £4,600 to District Traders on credit
08/07: returned goods worth £2,000 as they were defective
11/07: sold goods in cash £1,500
15/07: Received damaged goods from District traders worth £1,800
21/07: Paid for sundry expenses £2,200
25/07: returned goods received from District Traders to London Wholesalers
26/07: Received £2,700 from Eagle Eye Traders
28/07: paid London Wholesalers £3,500
29/07: on the due date for rent did not pay anything and used the prepaid funds to settle the account.

    a) Calculate the value of the stock at the end of the trading period assuming that Robert made 20% profit for each sale.
    b) Enter the transactions into the double entry system, balance off the T-accounts and create a trial balance

8. Mathers started a business on 1 Jan and made the following entries in his diary. He has hired you to enter this information correctly in a double entry system as well as generate a trial balance:

- 2 Jan deposited £20,000 in my business bank account
- 3 Jan received goods from David, a long-time friend; worth £2,000, he owed me £1,000 for an old car I sold him for his son's 17th birthday. I now owe him £1,000 only

- 5 Jan took out some money from the bank account to buy a vintage Golf Set that was being sold on Drop down TV for £2,500
- 6 Jan sold the goods I received from David to Jonathan for £2,500 in credit
- 7 Jan bought goods in cash worth £4,500
- 8 Jan Jonathan returns some goods worth £500 because they were defective. I reduced the money he owed me by £100 for all the trouble.
- 11 Jan sold one my cars for £3,000 and deposited this amount in the business account
- 12 Jun received payment from Jonathan of £1,500, but did not deposit the money in the bank account; I used the money to refit the Kitchen in my house.
- 17 Jan sold goods worth £2,000 in cash and goods worth £1,500 on credit to Pharell Traders
- 20 Jan paid for my private house broadband and telephone connections £40, also paid for my business telephone connection £30
- 21 Jan withdrew £1,500 from the business account and lent it to my sister in law on condition that she would repay me exactly one month from today.
- 22 Jan paid a parking ticket for the van which had been parked outside my store without the parking permission required £30
- 23 Jan received goods on credit from Parabolic Traders worth £2,700
- 27 Jan paid rent for the store at £900 and other sundry expenses for £300

Using the information in Mather's diary:
    a) make double entries for the business
    b) Prepare a trial balance
    c) What would you advise Mathers to do about how he does business his accounting procedures?

9. The following transactions occurred in John's business for the month of June, his first trading month:

June 1: deposited £3,000 in his bank account

June 4: bought goods worth £300 from Alan, then received on credit goods worth £500 and £800 from Jeremy and Anita respectively

June 10: sold goods to Robertson on credit at £600 also sold more goods in cash at £400

June 12: Robertson returned goods worth £200, which were defective. Later the same day all the goods that were sold in cash were returned, as they were also defective

June 14:	returned all the goods that were defective to Anita who had sold them to him in the first place
June 16:	received goods from Anita worth £1,000 in credit
June 18:	paid for goods received from Jeremy
June 21:	paid wages and sundry expenses £1,800
June 25:	deposited a further £2,000 in bank account
June 27:	received a grant from Local Business Support group a government organisation that finances small businesses £3,000
June 28:	sold goods in cash £900, and in credit to Robertson for £700 received payment from Robertson of £500

Prepare the double entries for the transactions and a trial balance.

10. Why is it important to have an accounting system with a clear sequence of events from the books of original entry to the final statements? Illustrate your answer using the Mathers' business in question 8.

Chapter 4: An Overview of Financial Statements

Learning outcomes: At the end of this chapter, the learner should have a basic understanding of the main financial statements in a simple sole trader business. The learner should be able to describe key financial statements and highlight the list of items for each of the statements:

1. *Cash flow Statement*
2. *Trading, Profit and Loss Accounts*
3. *Balance Sheet*
4. *Other Reports and statements*

4.1 Introduction to Financial Statements

Financial statements are reports that summarise a business' accounting data and indicate its financial state and performance. These statements provide specific information about a business' financial position. They include the Profit & Loss Statement, also known as the Income Statement, the Balance Sheet, and the Statement of Cash Flows

These statements are important to a business for the following reasons:

1. They are used to communicate financial information to third parties interested in the operations of the business.
2. They are used to plan for future operations of the business; they provide information on what operations were successful and which were not successful and highlight changes that can be implemented to rectify this situation.

A **Trading, Profit and Loss Account** is a statement of a business' profits over a given period. It shows how the profits or losses have been computed. Profits or losses are an important measure of a business' performance as they show whether such a business is generating an income from which further investments can be made. This statement is also known as an Income Statement as it shows the net income of business's operations. The term Income Statement is used where the business exists for non-profit purposes or where goods are provided at cost for example in the public sector.

The **balance sheet** is defined as a statement of a business's financial position at a particular point in time. It is for this reason that balance sheets are stated as at a particular date. This is indicated by the title of the balance sheet such as:

'XYZ Business Ltd Balance Sheet as at 31 Dec 2005

The **Cash flow statement** is a record of the pattern of the inflow and outflow of cash in a business over a specific period. The statement can be used to evaluate the business's ability to manage its cash resources. It can also be used to forecast future cash flow in the business.

4.2 Trading, Profit and Loss Account

At the end of every trading year, a business prepares final accounts. These provide a financial summary of all their trading activity during the year.

The trading account shows the gross profit (or loss) that the business has made. Profit is the money made by the business and equals income minus expenses.

The profit and loss account shows the net profit (or loss) made. The Trading account and profit and loss account are often combined as one trading, profit and loss account so that both the gross and net profit can be displayed in the same set of accounts

The difference between total revenues and the total expenses is the income of the business. If the total revenues exceed the total expenses then the difference is known as profit. When the opposite is true then there is a loss.

The trading account constitutes the sales revenues less the cost of sales. The sales revenues are derived from the main business activity and the cost of sales relate directly to those sales. The cost of sales is the total expenditure on the goods or services that have then been resold or that have been directly used in the production of the goods or services that are then resold.

Cost of sales is the total purchases for the period in question less the closing stock. In case this is not the first trading period then it is possible that there was an opening stock at the beginning of the period. In that case, the cost of goods sold (cost of sales) can be calculated as follows:

Opening Stock + Purchases – Closing Stock = Cost of Sales.

Cost of sales shows how much they have spent on buying the goods at cost price before the firm adds its own profit margin. It is divided into three sections:

1. **Opening stock** is the value of stock remaining unsold from the previous year.
2. **Purchases** are the amount spent on new stock during the current year.
3. **Closing stock** is the value of stock left unsold in the current year that is then carried forward to the next trading period.

The difference between sales revenues and cost of sales is known as Gross Profit or Gross Loss where the cost of sales exceeds the sales revenue. The profit and loss account on the other hand includes Gross profits and all the other revenues that the business generates other than through its main business activity. It also shows all the other expenses that the business has incurred in a trading period. The difference between total revenues and total expenses is known as the Net Profit if the revenues exceed the expenses or Net Losses if the expenses exceed the revenues.

The trial balance contains most of the entries that are used in determining both the total revenues and the total expenses. Below is an example of the layout of a trading, profit and loss account (TP&L).

XYZ Distributors

Trading Profit and Loss Account for the period ending 30th June 2xx8

Trading Account
Items:	£	£
Total Sales (Revenues)		xxxx
LESS:		
Cost of Sales	xxxx	(xxxx)
Gross Profits or Losses		xxxx

Revenue Expenses

Provision for Depreciation of Assets	xxxx	
Provision for bad debts	xxxx	
Rent	xxxx	
Telephone charges	xxxx	
Rates, heat, lighting	xxxx	
Bank Charges	xxxx	
Motor expenses	xxxx	
Other expenses	xxxx	(xxxx)
Net Profit or Loss		xxxx

There are different formats of the TP&L account depending on the type of business. These different formats however contain the same information. For example, a manufacturing business will have a Manufacturing Account and A Profit and Loss Account. A retail business will have a Trading Account followed by a Profit and Loss Account, whereas a business that offers professional services will have an Income and Expenses Account. The Income and Profit & Loss Account serves the same purpose and may contain the same entries as a Profit and Loss Account, a professional practice such as a Surgery may not want to reflect its income as a profit due to the nature of services it offers. A doctor might find it hard to recognise someone's illness as a source of profit. Hence, the use of Income and Expenditure account.

4.3.: Items of a Trading Profits and Loss Account:

4.3.1: Stock:

As we have briefly mentioned above stakeholders are interested in the performance of a business for different reasons. This is the purpose of final accounts, prepared at the end of each trading period. The trading period is usually one calendar year. This can be considered a reasonable time within which the performance of a business can be determined or compared to a previous or future period. For the benefit of the stakeholders, all final accounts are prepared according to certain specific conventions, which are agreed on worldwide.

Stock can be defined as the total merchandise held by a trader at his or her premises intended for either resale or direct production of goods or services for sale. In the previous section, we introduced the simple way of calculating the cost of the goods sold. This simple approach assumes a number of things, firstly that the cost of the goods sold remains the same. That is to say, goods bought last year and that remain in stock cost the same as goods bought in the current year. This is not true in practice. In some cases where the goods bought have very volatile prices then the differences in the costs may be so significant as too change the profits or losses made. For example, petroleum prices have changed significantly between 2003 and 2006. In 2004, the average price of crude oil was $45 to a barrel this has increased to an average of $65 in early 2006. A business that resells either petroleum products or use petroleum products as an integral part of its production would have to include these changes in the production. The cost of sales must therefore be adjusted to reflect these changes. This is often difficult if we are dealing with a number of commodities that are not homogenous. A business would try to, as much as possible; use a method of valuation that best represents the actual cost of the goods included in the sale. This has led to various methods of valuing stock.

The challenge is to value the stock as close as possible to its actual cost. There are many methods used to value stock, some of them are discussed in the following section.

The First In First Out (FIFO) Approach:
The FIFO approach refers to the valuation method where we assume that the cost of the goods included in a sale is the cost of the goods that we bought earliest prior to the sale in question. This means that we assume that the goods that came in first are sold (or used up) earlier than the goods that were bought later. Simply, this arrangement is a first in, first out. Using the example that we had already referred to of petroleum, a retail vendor of petroleum on a busy motorway is continually refilling his storage tanks. On 30 December 2xx2, he bought 300 barrels of petroleum products at £50 per barrel. On the 2 of January 2xx3, he had 20 barrels remaining to which he added 400 barrels at £60 per barrel.

From this example, we can see that the value of the stock he holds presently is 20 barrels at £50 whose total value is £1,000 to which he added 400 barrels at £60 whose total value was £24,000. Therefore, his total stock is £25,000. If he assumed a FIFO approach to costing his stock then he would assume that the first 20 barrels of petroleum products he sold cost £50 and then £60 for subsequent barrels. This is in practice not true because he has actually sold a mixture of petroleum products some that had cost £50, and some £60.

FIFO approach to stock valuation is useful in cases where the price of the goods bought for resale or to produce the resale product is constant. Where there are wild fluctuations then it would not be a fair method for valuation. FIFO tends to yield high profits where the prices of the purchases are rising, this is because the sales are assumed to be from the oldest products that business has which could have significantly lower price than newer goods. Since the closing stock is valued at a very high price then it seems that the balance sheet has a higher asset value. Later in the book you will learn about the accounting convention known as consistency, a firm must adapt a single stock valuation approach to ensure that the reports they produce are true and fair. A firm cannot use FIFO and in time of price deflation use another method.

Example 4.1:
Following are sales and purchase transactions that occurred in Attila's store during the year ended 30 Nov. 2xx1:

Month	Purchases	Sales
Dec		
Jan	4000 units @ £7 per unit	2,500 units
Feb	5,000 units @ £6 per unit	
March	2,300 units @ £10 per unit	6,000 units
April	1,800 units @ £11 per unit	
May		
June	1,000@£13 per unit	
July		3,000 units
August	2,400units @ £9 per unit	
September	3,000 units @ £10 per unit	
October		
November		4,000 units

Using the information provided to calculate the value of the stock at the end of the trading period.
Attila's Business

Stock at the end of:

		Units	£	
Jan	Opening Stock		0	
	Purchases	4,000	28,000	4,000units @7 per unit
	Less Cost of Sales	2,500	17,500	2,500units @£7 per unit
	Closing Stock	1,500	10,500	1,500units@7 per unit

Feb:

Opening Stock	1,500	10,500	1,500 units @ £7 per unit
Purchases	5,000	30,000	5,000 units @ £6 per unit
Less Cost of goods sold		0	0
Closing Stock	6,500	40,500	

March

Opening Stock		6,500	40,500	
Purchases		2,300	23,000	2,300 units @ £10 per unit
Less: Cost of sales	1,500 @ £7 per unit	-1,500	-10,500	
	4,500 @ £6 per unit	-4,500	-27,000	
		2,800	26,000	

April

Opening Stock	2,800	26,000	
Purchases	1,800	19,800	1,800 units @ £11 per unit
Less: Cost of Sales	0	0	
	4,600	45,800	

June

Opening Stock	4,600	45,800	
Purchases	1,000	13,000	1000 units @ £13 per unit
Cost of Sales	0	0	
	5,600	58,800	

July

Opening Stock		5,600	58,800
Purchases		0	0
Less: Cost of Sales	500 @ £6 per unit	500	-3,000
	2,300 @ £10 per unit	2,300	-23,000
	200 @ £11 per unit	200	-2,200
		2,600	30,600

August

Opening Stock	2,600	30,600	
Purchases	2,400	21,600	2,400 units @ £9 per unit
Less: Cost of Sales	0	0	
	5,000	52,200	

September

Opening Stock	5,000	52,200	
Purchases	3,000	30,000	3,000 units @ £10 per unit
Cost of Sales	0	0	
Closing stock	8,000	82,200	

November

Opening Stock		8,000	82,200
Purchases		0	0
Less Cost of Sales	1600 @ £11 per unit	-1600	-17,600
	1300 @ £10 per unit	-1300	-13,000
	1100 @ £9 per unit	-1,100	-9,900
Closing Stock as at 30 November 2xx1		4,000	41,700

At the end of trading period, using the first in first out approach the stock held by the business is valued at £41,700 made up of the different prices that make up the 4,000 units.

Last In First Out (LIFO)

This approach is not used in the United Kingdom, in fact very few countries allow this form of valuation as it understates the profit significantly at times of rising prices. Though using LIFO relates sales more closely to sales it is often a fallacious assumption, as businesses tend to use up old stock first to avoid obsolescence and destruction due to long storage. Since the method is neither practical nor recommended by the tax departments of most countries then it is rarely used. The computation of LIFO is the same as that of FIFO discussed above, only in reverse with the newest goods assumed to be sold first.

Average Cost (AVCO)

This approach is not only easier to compute and keep in books of accounts, but it also avoids the extreme distorting effects of either LIFO or FIFO on the profits and loss statement as well as the balance sheet. Every time a new batch is received, the value of the stock held is recalculated and the new average cost is applied to stock until the next batch is received. This is a more representative method where the stock consists of liquids, which are topped up, or other uncountable substances. It is also very good for countable stock whose individual value is minute, such that a stock of nails measured in kilograms and where the kilogram of nails is the same the average price is the most logical method of stock valuation.

AVCO is also advantageous if excess stock is to be resold, by continually updating the price with the latest purchase the valuation of the stock is closer to the market value. Using the example of Attila's business in example 4.1, the following would be the valuations at the end of each month.

AVCO for Attila's Business for Period ending Nov 2xx1

	Units	Total Cost £	AVCO Unit price £
Jan			
Opening Stock	0	0	
Purchases	4,000	28,000	7
Cost of Sales	-2,500	17,500	7
	1,500	10,500	7
Feb			
Opening Stock	1,500	10,500	7
Purchases	5,000	30,000	6
	6,500	40,500	6.23
March			
Opening Stock	6,500	40,500	6.23
Purchases	2,300	23,000	10
Total Stock	8,800	63,500	7.22
Cost of Sales	-6,000	-43,295	7.22
Closing stock	2,800	20,216	7.22
April			
Opening Stock	2,800	20,216	7.22
Purchases	1,800	19,800	11
Closing Stock	4,600	40,016	8.68
June			
Opening Stock	4,600	40,016	8.68
Purchases	1,000	13,000	13
Closing Stock	5,600	53,016	9.47
July			
Opening Stock	5,600	53,016	9.47
Cost of Sales	-3,000	-28,410	9.47
	2,600	24,606	9.47
August			
Opening Stock	2,600	24,606	9.47
Purchases	2,400	21,600	9
Closing Stock	5,000	46,206	9.24
September			
Opening Stock	5,000	46,206	9.24
Purchases	3,000	30,000	10
Closing Stock	8,000	76,206	9.52
November			
Opening Stock	8,000	76,206	9.52
Cost of Sales	-4,000	-38,080	9.52
	4,000	38,216	9.52

Whereas the final figures of the FIFO approach are £13 and £10 for the stock they hold, we get a single valuation figure of £9.52 per unit for stock held using AVCO.

Replacement Value Approach

The replacement value approach looks at how much it would cost the firm to replace stock that has been lost or destroyed. This value is then imputed into the stock value held by the business. This is often the net realisable value of the stock if the stock was resold into the market it had been purchased from.

Taking Attila's example above, the replacement value of the stock at the end of June would be £13 pounds for all the stock held. Therefore the value of the stock value £72,800 (5,600 units at £13 per unit) assuming that there are no costs of selling the product back into the market. This type of valuation while reflecting market conditions, understates the profits that the business has made as it overstates the cost of goods sold where prices are rising rapidly.

Where prices are falling, which rarely happens, then this approach overstates the profit and this may mislead the stakeholders that the firm is doing better than it actually is.

Choosing an appropriate valuation method:

In the discussions of the different valuation methods, we have discovered that a decision on the method of valuation is very important in ensuring that profit is reported as correctly as possible. Stock valuation can be misused to report higher profits for those who earn bonuses tied to the profits made in the period. Methods that reduce profits may be used when people want to evade taxes (as opposed to avoidance). However, using stock to understate the profits will reduce the opening stock value for the next period, therefore the value of the cost of sales is understated, and therefore the profits made are overstated.

The factors to consider when deciding on the valuation of stock:

1. Actual and anticipated changes in the price levels are an important consideration. In periods of rapid price changes, the profits earned can be seriously distorted by the method of valuation.
2. Type of stock is also important, in some instances stock bought and sold cannot be distinguished according to the time that it was bought and therefore prices cannot be allocated using either the FIFO or LIFO. For such stock, the AVCO is the best approach. In a case where stock gains value while it is 'in- stock' then replacement costing would be more appropriate if you traded in wine that gains value with age. Paintings bought inadvertently could gain value overnight if they were determined to be of vintage quality. For example, an art dealer may buy a painting at a knock down price of £5000 and later find that it belonged to class of highly priced paintings of the 14th Century and its prices could rise 1000 times to £5million. In such a case, it would be erroneous to enter the value of the painting as £5,000.
3. Accounting convention requires that the valuation methods be consistent from period to period. This consistency reduces fluctuations in the profit that are not

caused by the performance of the business and therefore do not reflect the true and fair picture of the business performance.
4. In certain industries, there are generally agreed valuation methods. These allow for easier cross-industrial comparison. In such cases then it would be prudent to use the generally accepted valuation method.

As we shall see later in this book, stock valuation and any other subjective decision to be made about a business would have to be one that reflects the truest and fairest picture of the performance of the business.

4.3.2: Provisions for the depreciation of Assets:

It is important to start by defining the various classes of assets in business:

Fixed Assets refer to those assets in a business that can be used for more than one trading period. This means that a van, furniture, computer systems, productive machinery, fixtures and fittings among other similar assets are fixed because they are used to produce for the business for more than one trading period. Fixed assets are not necessarily expensive purchases. A dealer in prestigious cars holds a stock of cars worth £1million at the end of a trading period these are not fixed assets. However, his fleet of vans worth £50,000 are fixed assets as they are used as productive resources.

Current Assets on the other hand are productive resources that are used during one trading period and what remains is used up in the next period. The stock of prestigious vehicles held by the car dealer is current assets as they are held with a view to selling them within the current or following period of trading. There are many types of current assets, they include stock, cash in bank and hand, prepaid expenses, debtors and anything will be sold or used up during the present or next period.

Tangible and intangible assets as the name suggests, tangible assets are assets that can be touched or felt with one of the other four senses. Examples of tangible assets include cars, buildings, shares held in another company, and so on.

Depreciation is the decline of the value of an asset due to wear and tear or becoming outdated. This decline in value is allocated as a proportion of the total asset value over each accounting period. There are two reasons why the decline in value is included each period; firstly, it is recognition that the value of the asset reduces over the period of time it is used. Secondly, a tax charge is levied against the profits that the business makes. Since profits are the difference between the total revenue and the total expenses then we must recognise that assets are expended in the production of the total revenue. This expense is known as depreciation. Allocating all the cost of an asset to the period when the asset is purchased would overstate the expenses of that period. This would in turn reduce the level of profits during the period, whereas the asset is still available to the business for further production.

To reflect the use of the asset over its lifetime we expense the depreciation in the profit and loss account. Therefore, depreciation is an operating expense. The following section discusses the various methods of calculating the depreciation expense charge also known as provision for depreciation.

For example, a typewriter bought in 1985 would gradually lose value for the next 10 years and depending on various factors could be 1/10th of the original price in 1995, however a typewriter bought in 1994 could also be a 1/10th of its value in 1995 because of obsolescence.

Depreciation is used to reflect the length of time an asset is in use productively within the business. A car bought at the start of a business and used for five years would have given a 1/5th or so of its value each year.

Normally freehold land and property may not depreciate. Freehold land is not chargeable to depreciation, as its value tends to appreciate instead. Accounting standards have however acknowledged the fact that buildings may depreciate over time becoming in need of repair or simply unsuitable for use. For this reason then, the buildings depreciation may be provided for in the books of accounts.

Determining the provision for depreciation:

Generally, there are two widely used methods of depreciation. These are the straight-line depreciation method and the reducing balance depreciation method. The straight-line depreciation method assumes that each year the asset depreciates by the same value. The reducing balance method tries to acknowledge that the older an asset is the less useful it is to the business. In this approach a certain fixed percentage is charged each year on the remaining balance hence the name 'reducing balance'

The following are examples of how these two approaches are used:

Example 4.2:

Jonathan started a business on 1 Jan 2xx1; he bought plant and machinery, which he would use to manufacture tacks, pins and needles. The machine cost £100,000 and he projected that the machine would be useful for a period of ten years. Using the straight-line method determine depreciation chargeable for this machinery.

£

Cost of machine 01/01/2xx1   100,000

Value of depreciation Charge = $\dfrac{100{,}000}{10} = 10{,}000 \; per\, year$

Therefore, each year the business would charge £10,000 to the business account to reflect the usage of the machinery. At the end of the ten years, the machine will be valued at £0

Example 4.2b

Using the information provided about Jonathan's machine use reducing balance to calculate how much value of depreciation for each year beginning 2xx1 to 2xx9 given that 20% will be charged each year.

Reducing Balance Approach

Date		£	£	£
01/01/2xx1	Initial Cost			100,000
Year 1	Provision for depreciation @20% of balance			-20,000
	Asset balance(initial cost - provision for depreciation)			80,000
Year 2				
	Opening Asset balance			80,000
	Provision for depreciation @20% of 80,000			-16,000
	Asset balance			64,000
Year 3				
	Opening Asset Balance			64,000
	Provision for depreciation@20% of 64,000			-12,800
	Asset Balance			51,200
Year 4				
	Opening Asset Balance			51,200
	Provision for depreciation@20% of 51,200			-10,240
	Asset Balance			40,960
Year 5				
	Opening Asset Balance			40,960
	Provision for depreciation@20% of 40,960			-8,192
	Asset Balance			32,768
Year 6				
	Opening Asset Balance			32,768
	Provision for depreciation@20% of 32,768			-6,554
	Asset Balance			26,214
Year 7				
	Opening Asset Balance			26,214
	Provision for depreciation@20% of 26,214			-5,243
	Asset Balance			20,971
Year 8				
	Opening Asset Balance			20,971
	Provision for depreciation@20% of 20,971			-4,194
	Asset Balance			16,777
Year 9				
	Opening Asset Balance			16,777
	Provision for depreciation@20% of 16,777			-3,355
	Asset Balance			13,422
Year 10				
(2x10)	Opening Asset Balance			13,422
	Provision for depreciation@20% of 13,422			-2,684

CHAPTER 4: AN OVERVIEW OF FINANCIAL STATEMENTS

From this example, we notice that the depreciation charged each year reduces as the value of the asset reduces. This could reflect the reducing usefulness of the asset with time. At the end of the tenth year there is still an asset balance known as the residual value of the asset. The residual value is the assumed resale value of the machine after 10 years.

The reducing balance method is a bit more difficult to compute for many years because you would have to work out the balance for each year individually. Another problem is the determination of the appropriate rate of depreciation to apply.

Residual Value is the value that we would expect to resell the asset at the end of the depreciation period. For example, after using a car worth £10,000 for 4 years we may expect to resell it at £2,000, this is its residual value.

In applying the straight-line depreciation with an anticipated residual value, we can use a general formula:

$$\text{Depreciation per year} = \frac{\text{Initial Cost Asset - Residual Value}}{\text{No. Of Years used}}$$

Therefore the car worth £10,000, which is expected to be worth £2,000 at the end of four years, the depreciation per year would be:

$$\text{Depreciation per year} = \frac{10{,}000 - 2{,}000}{4} = £2{,}000$$

The reducing balance is a compounded reduction of depreciation charged each year. The following formula can be used to determine what percentage to charge given a specific residual value.

Rate of Depreciation (R_d) $\qquad R_d = 1 - \sqrt[n]{\dfrac{rv}{c}}$

Where **n** refers to the number of years, we anticipate that we will use the asset
rv refers to the residual value of the asset after the years of use
c is the initial cost of the asset

Therefore our car example rate of depreciation using the reducing balance approach would be:

$$R_d = 1 - \sqrt[4]{\frac{2{,}000}{10{,}000}} = 1 - \frac{6.69}{10} = 1 - 0.669 = 0.331 \text{ therefore in percentages the depreciation}$$

applicable on the remaining balance each year would be 33.1%.

The choice of depreciation method to use is dependent on many factors. These include the type of depreciation that is likely to occur, the repairs and maintenance of the asset, and the nature of the asset. The types of depreciation are dependent on the nature of depreciation; some assets are irreparable and need to be completely replaced once they break down. Such assets would therefore have no residual value or resale value. The straight-line method would be appropriate in these circumstances. Highly specialised equipment that can only be used in that particular business would also be appropriately depreciated using the straight-line approach.

For assets such as cars, that may be resold after a certain period and whose usefulness diminishes due to old age, then the reducing balance method can be used. It is however more appropriate to use one of either methods rather than both methods for depreciating assets in the same business. Some accountants contend that straight-line method is more appropriate, and obviously easier, than reducing balance as a new asset will be attract a higher depreciation charge but less repair costs using the reducing balance approach, whereas in latter years it will incur lower depreciation charges but with higher repair costs. The total cost accruing to the asset will therefore be equal through-out its lifetime. In this case, the straight-line approach seems more appropriate.

4.3.3: Preparing Trading Profit and Loss Accounts

So far, we have looked at the various transactions that occur in a business. We have looked at double entry and at two special items in the trading profit and loss account. Many other items go into a trading profit and loss account depending on the nature and complexity of the business in question.

As we noted earlier, there is a logical progression in preparing accounts. We start by carefully collecting financial information and recording it in the daybooks and ledgers. We then prepare T-accounts, which are then used to populate the trial balance. The trial balance is then used to prepare the trading account and the gross profit from the trading account is used to calculate the net profits after deducting business operation expenses. The net profit or loss is then entered into the balance sheet after distributing drawings or dividends to owners and paying the taxes due to the government.

This section looks at how to prepare a trading, profit and loss account (TP&L account). A trading account is the account used to calculate the Gross profits made by the business. Gross profit is the difference between the total revenue of a business and cost of the sales. We have already looked at the calculations used to determine the costs of sales. Cost of sales usually refers to the expenses that are incurred directly because of the sales. For example, a shoe reseller will consider the cost of buying shoes and bringing them to his premises as the cost of sales. However, though the rent is incurred in the pursuit of the shoe selling business it is not a direct cost to the sale of the shoes, it is an operational cost.

CHAPTER 4: AN OVERVIEW OF FINANCIAL STATEMENTS

Therefore, in a Trading Account you will find the Total sales revenue and the total direct costs of production or purchase of goods that make up the sales.

Example 4.3:

Otieno is a furniture reseller for the period ending 31 December 2xx4, the following information was extracted from his books of accounts.

Particulars	£
Opening Furniture Stock	21,000
Purchases of furniture	33,500
Total Sales for period	78,900
Closing Stock	18,700

Using this information, calculate his gross profit for this period:

Example 4.3

	£	£
Total Sales		78,900
Opening Stock	21,000	
Purchases	33,500	
Less: Closing stock	-18,700	
Cost of goods sold	35,800	-35,800
Gross Profits		43,100

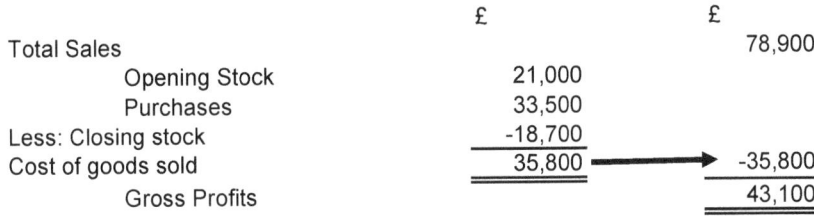

As we can see from the example above, we will need to calculate the cost of the goods sold. The cost of goods sold refers only to those costs that are incurred directly to make sale possible. Note that the account has been arranged in a certain order. This is the conventional and widely used vertical format of preparing final accounts. Figures that are to be subtracted either have a bracket around them or the negative sign. The inner columns show the calculations that are carried out before major calculation is done. For example, you need to calculate the cost of sales; this is shown in the inner column. The result is then transferred horizontally to the outer column where the cost of sales is subtracted from the total sales revenue.

A double underline shows the end of a calculation, whereas a single underline shows that the figures above the line are to be added or subtracted as appropriate. These practices make it easier for all accountants and other stakeholders to understand statements of accounts.

To determine the net profit that we have made in the trading period we use the profit and loss account. This is the account that shows all the expenses that have been incurred in the business' operations but not directly in the sale of the goods or services. The operational expenses are added up then subtracted from the gross profit to give the net profit.

Example 4.3b:

From example 4.3 above: Otieno's other operating expenses were as follows:

Rent and Rates	3,900
Wages to shop assistants	12,000
Telephone and broadband expenses	1,200
Web hosting expenses	140
Interest on start-up loan	90
Stock Insurance premiums	1,090
Sundry expenses	700
Bank Charges	180
Computer repair charges	700
Motor Expenses	2,400

Otieno's TP&L Statement		£	£
Total Sales			78,900
Opening Stock		21,000	
Purchases		33,500	
Less: Closing stock		-18,700	
Cost of goods sold		35,800	-35,800
Gross Profits			43,100
Less Operation Costs			
Rent and Rates		3,900	
Wages to shop assistants		12,000	
Telephone and broadband expenses		1,200	
Web hosting expenses		140	
Interest on start-up loan		90	
Stock Insurance premiums		1,090	
Sundry expenses		700	
Bank Charges		180	
Computer repair charges		700	
Motor Expenses		2,400	-22,400
Net Profit			43,100

The net profit is therefore the difference between the gross profit and the operational expenses.

Given a trial balance we should also be able create a Trading Profit and Loss Account. This is because all the balances at the end of a given period are recorded in the trial balance. Example 4.4 illustrates using a trial balance to prepare a trading profit and loss account.

CHAPTER 4: AN OVERVIEW OF FINANCIAL STATEMENTS

Example 4.4:

Jose' is a runs a successful wine merchant store in Birmingham. The following trial balance was extracted for his business on 31/12/2xx7, the end of his trading period.

Particulars	£
Sales	187,900
Purchases	100,800
Rent and Rates	12,400
Furniture and fixtures	3,600
Vans	31,000
Bank	48,800
Debtors	24,300
Creditors	34,100
Salaries and Wages	32,200
Sundry Expenses	2,500
Capital Account	50,000
Opening Stock	10,000

Note that the closing stock was valued at £16,400 on 31/12/2xx7

Using the information provided, knowing that there was no opening stock for this period, prepare a trial balance for Jose's business. Then using the trial balance, prepare a trading, profit and loss account.

Trial Balance for Jose Wine Business for year ended 31/12/2xx7

Particulars	Debit £	Credit £
Opening Stock	10,000	
Sales		187,900
Purchases	100,800	
Rent and rates	12,400	
Furniture and fixtures	3,600	
Vans	31,000	
Bank	48,800	
Debtors	24,300	
Creditors		34,100
Salaries and Wages	32,200	
Sundry Expenses	2,500	
Capital Account		43,600
	265600	265,600

AN INTRODUCTION TO ACCOUNTING

Once you have established that the trial balance has a balancing figure then you can proceed to use the information in the trial balance to create a trading profit and loss account. Note that the opening balance was the closing balance in the previous period's accounts and constitutes part of the cost of sales in the present period; it is hence part of the trial balance for this period. However, the closing stock will be sold in the next period, which means it had no part to play in the sales in this period and is therefore not included in the trial balance.

Jose's Trading, Profit and Loss Account for the period ended 31/12/2xx7

		£	£
Sales			187,900
Opening Stock		10,000	
Purchases		100,800	
Closing Stock		-16,400	
Cost of goods sold		94,400	-94,400
Gross Profit			93,500
Operating Costs			
Rent and Rates		12,400	
Salaries and Wages		32,200	
Sundry Expenses		2,500	-47,100
			46,400

There are many more operating expenses than those shown in Jose's business. All these expenses are charged against the gross-profit to establish the net profit. Once the trader has determined the profits made from the business then they can decide to pay themselves from the profits. These payments to the owner are known as drawings in a sole-trader and partnerships, in companies, these payments are known as dividends.

Once the net profit has been established then we can prepare the balance sheet. The next section looks at how to do this.

4.4: The Balance Sheet

A balance sheet is a quantitative summary of a company's financial condition at a specific point in time. It includes assets, liabilities and net worth. The first part of a balance sheet shows all the productive assets a company owns, and the second part shows all the financing methods (such as liabilities and shareholders' equity. Another name for a balance sheet is the Statement of Condition.

Each period's balance sheet shows the effects of trading on the Accounting equation.

Assets = Capital + Liabilities

Through trading the three items of the accounting equation change, Assets increase when more are purchased either in cash or in credit, Capital will increase if the income (profits) of the business is not removed from the operations of the business and liabilities may increase if assets have been acquired on credit. These changes are captured each period in the balance sheet. Since businesses change continuously, a balance sheet is reported at a specific point in time rather than over a period. This means that the values of capital, assets and liabilities are determined and this is stated 'as at' a specific date.

Below is an example of a balance sheet:

XYZ Distributors
Balance Sheet at 31 March 2xx9

Item	£	£
ASSETS:		
Fixed assets		
Plant, computers, furniture	xxxx	xxxx
Current assets		
Debtors'	xxxx	
Stock	xxxx	
Cash	xxxx	
Total current assets	xxxx	xxxx
Total Assets		xxxx
LIABILITIES		
Current liabilities		
Trade creditors'	xxxx	
Bank overdrafts	xxxx	
Other short-term liabilities	xxxx	
Total Short-term Liabilities	xxxx	(xxxx)
Net current assets or liabilities		XXXX ....Item (a)
Financed by:		
Capital and reserves		
Profits retained	xxxx	
Share capital	xxxx	
Long-term liabilities	xxxx	xxxx
Shareholders' total/all equity		XXXX....Item (b)

Notes to the balance sheet:

Items 'a' and 'b' should be equal in keeping with the accounting equation: Item 'a' is the net of assets and liabilities of the business, whereas item 'b' is the total capital that has been invested in the business note the effect of profits on capital. Profits retained increase the capital levels, this is to say that the resources available to the business have increased and profits can be used to buy more assets with which to run the business. Losses have the opposite effect.

A balance sheet also shows:

Fixed assets refer to what the business owns that is of a durable nature. Fixed assets are subdivided into either tangible or intangible assets. Tangible assets for example buildings, land, machinery, computers, fixtures and fittings - where relevant are shown at their depreciated or resale value. These assets can be seen or touched. Intangible assets are usually ideas or concepts of value to the business. Intangible assets include goodwill, intellectual property rights, patents, trademarks, website domain names, long-term investments

Current assets include less durable assets as well as what the business is owed also known as accounts receivable. Current assets can be easily and quickly converted into cash, in this category are items such as, Stock, Work-in-progress; money owed by customers, cash-in-hand or at the bank, short-term investments, and pre-payments for example advance rents

Current liabilities refer to what the business owes and must repay in the short term. Current liabilities are amounts owing and due within one year, and these can include; Money owed to suppliers, Short-term loans, overdrafts or other finance, Taxes due within the year - VAT, PAYE, National Insurance, advance corporation tax.

Fixed Assets + Current Assets – Current Liabilities = Net Assets/Net Worth

The Net assets are financed by long-term liabilities. These long-term liabilities include the capital contributed by the owners of the business. Other long-term liabilities are loans; they finance the acquisition of the assets.

Example 4.5:

From example 4.4: Using information from Jose's Wine business we can now prepare a balance sheet to show what has happened to the accounting equation in Jose's business for the period ended 31/12/2xx7:

CHAPTER 4: AN OVERVIEW OF FINANCIAL STATEMENTS

Jose's Balance Sheet for the Period ended 31/12/2xx7

Assets	£	£
Fixed Assets		
Vans	31,000	
Furniture and Fixtures	3,600	
Current Assets		
Bank	48,800	
Debtors	24,300	
Closing Stock	16,400	124,100
Current Liabilities		
Creditors		-34,100
Net Worth		90,000
Financed by		
Capital		43,600
Profits retained for period		46,400
Net Worth		90,000

To solve for the equation of **Assets = Capital + Liabilities** and therefore establish Jose's 'net worth' we prepare a balance sheet. In this case, Jose's net worth is £90,000. This means that if his business were to be sold as a 'going-concern' (Sold as it is with the assumption that the buyer will continue with the same business as Jose) then the buying price would be £90,000.

(Note: usually when businesses are up for sale the simple net worth figure may not be used, as they are also intangible assets such as goodwill: the loyalty that customers have for Jose probably for his friendliness and honesty and so on, this may considerably increase the price of the business).

Example 4.6:

Prepare the trial balance, trading, profit and loss account and a balance sheet as at 31/12/2xx4 for Alexia's Clothes Store using the information provided below:

Particulars	£
Opening Stock	12,300
Sales	121,900
Purchases	66,900
Van Account as at 01/01/2xx4	24,900
Furniture and Fittings 01/01/2xx4	8,000
Closing stock	27,100
Loan Account	12,000

Capital Account	80,000
Returns outwards	5,500
Returns inwards	4,500
Debtors	24,100
Creditors	25,300
Bank	22,300
Cash	14,900
Drawings	9,000
Telephone Expenses	1,200
Loan Interest	2,800
Rent and Rates	9,800
Salaries and Wages	44,000

Alexia's Clothes Store Trial Balance for Period ended 31/12/2xx4

Particulars	Debit £	Credit £
Opening Stock	12,300	
Sales		121,900
Purchases	66,900	
Van Account as at 01/01/2xx4	24,900	
Furniture and Fittings 01/01/2xx4	8,000	
Loan Account		12,000
Capital Account		80,000
Returns outwards		5,500
Returns inwards	4,500	
Debtors	24,100	
Creditors		25,300
Bank	22,300	
Cash	14,900	
Drawings	9,000	
Telephone Expenses	1,200	
Loan Interest	2,800	
Rent and Rates	9,800	
Salaries and Wages	44,000	
	244,700	244700

Alexia's Clothes Store Trading, Profit and Loss Account for the period ended 31/12/2xx4

Trading Account	£	£	£
Sales		121,900	
Less: Returns inwards		-4,500	117,400
Opening Stock		12,300	
Purchases	66,900		
Less: Returns Outwards	-5,500	61,400	
Closing Stock		-27,100	-46,600
			70800
Operating Expenses			
Telephone Expenses		1,200	
Loan Interest		2,800	
Rent and rates		9,800	
Salaries and Wages		44,000	-57,800
			13000

The returns inwards and returns outwards should be removed from the purchases and sales respectively to arrive at the correct cost of goods sold for the period.

Alexia's Clothing Store Balance Sheet for the period ended 31/12/2xx4

Assets	£	£
Fixed Assets		
Van	24,900	
Furniture and Fittings	8,000	32,900
Current Assets		
Bank	22,300	
Cash	14,900	
Closing Stock	27,100	
Debtors	24,100	88,400
		121,300
Current Liabilities		
Creditors		-25,300
Net Worth		96,000
Financed by		
Capital	80,000	
Loan Account	12,000	
Profits	13,000	105,000
Drawings		-9,000
Net Worth		96000

AN INTRODUCTION TO ACCOUNTING

In the balance sheet above, drawings are included under 'Financed by' this shows that money has been withdrawn from the business through drawings by the owners. As already discussed, the net profit increases the value of the business, the opposite would be true for net losses. In a company, a similar withdrawal by the owners (shareholders) would take the form of a dividends issue. We will look at this later in the book.

4.5 Cash Flow Statements

A cash flow statement shows the inflow and outflow of cash in a business. This is very important in ensuring that a business does not run into a cash liquidity crunch - a situation where the demands for cash are more than the money available to pay for those demands. This means that the business has to borrow cash on unfavourable terms due to short notice to meet these demands.

Cash availability should not be confused with profitability. A profitable business might run into a cash liquidity crunch where the demands for cash cannot be met because the cash is not readily available. This may be because of the failure of debtors of the business to pay on time or where the money meant to meet a specific demand is used to pay for something else. The ability to pay for expenses when they arise is an important sign of a business performing well. A business unable to pay for its expenses on time may find it difficult to raise credit or even goods or services on credit. A business must also be able to pay its employees on time. This is because the right of employees to be paid on time is usually enforced by governments in many countries, but more importantly, timely payment of wages and salaries improves the staff morale.

A cash flow statement matches the in flow of cash to the outflow of cash. It shows where the cash came from and where it went. For an ongoing business, cash flows might include items from different periods, for example sales made in the previous period but paid for in the period to which the statement refers. A historical cash flow statement is very important in forecasting the future flow of cash in the business and ensuring that cash is readily available when it is needed. Later in this book Cash Flow, forecasting will be discussed. Below is an example of a cash flow statement:

CHAPTER 4: AN OVERVIEW OF FINANCIAL STATEMENTS

XYZ Distributors:

Cash Flow Statement for the period ended 31st December 2xx9

Item	£	£
Total Cash Revenues:		
Cash Sales	xxxx	
Rent Income	xxxx	
Dividends incomes	xxxx	
Disposal of Asset	xxxx	
Loans	xxxx	
All other cash inflows	xxxx	xxxx
LESS: Total Cash outflow		
(a) Purchases (Merchandise)	xxxx	
(b) Gross Wages (excludes withdrawals)	xxxx	
(c) Payroll Expenses (Taxes, etc)	xxxx	
(d) Outside Services	xxxx	
(e) Supplies (Office and operating)	xxxx	
(f) Repairs and Maintenance	xxxx	
(g) Advertising	xxxx	
(h) Auto, Delivery, and Travel	xxxx	
(i) Accounting and Legal	xxxx	
(j) Rent	xxxx	
(k) Telephone	xxxx	
(l) Utilities	xxxx	
(m) Insurance	xxxx	
(n) Taxes	xxxx	
(o) Interest	xxxx	
(p) Other Expenses [Specify each]	xxxx	(xxxx)
End of period cash position (Cash Surplus/Deficit)		xxxx

The Cash Flow Statement looks like the Profit and Loss Account. However, these statements are different; the Profit and Loss Account includes items that do not involve the flow of cash.

These items include:

Depreciation:
This is the decline of the value of an asset due to wear and tear or becoming outdated. This decline in value is allocated as a proportion of the total asset value over each accounting period. There are two reasons why the decline in value is included each period; firstly, it is recognition that the value of the asset reduces over the period of time it is used. Secondly, a tax charge is levied against the profits that the business makes.

Since profits are the difference between the total revenue and the total expenses then we must recognise that assets are expended in the production of the total revenue. This expense is known as depreciation. Allocating all the cost of an asset to the period when the asset is purchased would overstate the expenses of that period. This would in turn reduce the level of profits during the period, whereas the asset is still available to the business for further production.

Accounts Payable and Accounts Receivable

Accounts payable refers to money, which a company owes to vendors for products and services purchased on credit. This item appears on the company's balance sheet as a current liability, since the expectation is that the liability will be fulfilled in less than a year. When accounts payable are paid off, it represents a negative cash flow for the company

Accounts receivable refer to money, which is owed to a business by a customer for products and services provided on credit. This is treated as a current asset on a balance sheet. A specific sale is generally only treated as an account receivable after the customer is sent an invoice. These two items are non-cash flow items, as they are either expectations of inflow or outflow of cash. In drawing up a Profit and Loss, account we include items of Sale and purchases that may not have necessarily been paid for. The total sales figure includes goods sold on credit to customers that have not been paid for and the purchase figure may include items that have not been paid for by the business.

Bad Debts:

Bad debts are Accounts receivable that will likely remain uncollectible, and will be written off. Bad debts appear as an expense on the businesses Profit and Loss Account, thus reducing net income. In general, businesses make an estimate of bad debt expenses that might be incurred in the current time based on past records as part of the process of estimating earnings. Most businesses make a bad debt allowance since it is unlikely that all of their debtors will pay them in full. Bad debts are also non-cash items that do not appear in cash flow statement but appear on Profit and Loss Account

Items of stock:

Opening and closing stock at the start and at the end of a trading period are also non-cash items that do not appear on the cash flow statement. Though they are used to determine the cost of sales, they do not involve the movement of cash. The item that may involve cash is purchases that have been made during the trading period for which the cash flow statement has been prepared.

Example 4.7

Angela went into business as an IT consultant for the period starting 01/01/2xx6. Following is some of the information collected from her books for the period ended 31/12/2xx6. Using this information, draw up a Cash Flow Statement showing cumulative sales and the final balances for each of the twelve months.

CHAPTER 4: AN OVERVIEW OF FINANCIAL STATEMENTS

Cash Sales

	No. of Hours	Charge per hour £	Total £	Cumulative Sales £
February	20	80	1,600	1,600
March	30	90	2,700	4,300
April	40	90	3,600	7,900
May	50	100	5,000	12,900
June	60	100	6,000	18,900
July	70	100	7,000	25,900
August	80	100	8,000	33,900
September	90	100	10,000	43,900
October	100	100	10,000	53,900
November	100	100	10,000	63,900
December	100	100	10,000	73,900
Total Sales	1060			341,000

Cumulative net cash flow 109672

-
- Angela brought into the business £10,000 as capital and borrowed £5,000 from a close friend payable at the end of two years without interest.
  - During the first month she bought a car on credit paying £2,000 as deposit, she would pay £154 for it for 48 months beginning the first month.
  - In the first month she bought furniture for her home office for £1,800, she also had a computer and printer system installed which was connected to broadband internet through the office network, which cost £2,100.
  - In the first month she started a advertising for clients, the following were her monthly advertising costs:
-

Advertising

Pamphlets and Direct mailing	450
Stationery (business cards/letterheads etc)	230
Search Engine fees	80
Newspaper adverstisement	800

- The following recurrent administrative costs were incurred each month:

Administration costs 600
    web hosting 11
    Telephone and broadband costs 90
    Fuel for car 120

- On the second month, she took out professional indemnity insurance which cost her £45 monthly. She also employed an administrative assistant whom she paid £1,000 per month.
- She took out a £10,000 loan during the seventh month to enable her to move office. The loan repayment was £250 per month beginning on the 8th Month
- On the sixth and twelve month, she took drawings from her business of £6,000 each.
- The rent and rates are calculated as 2/5 of the total monthly cost of her house as the business was initially, for the first six months, run from her residential premises. i.e. (2/5 of rent (700) + council tax (90) + Water, Electricity and gas (64) On the seventh month the business moved to a serviced office at £900 per month

CHAPTER 4: AN OVERVIEW OF FINANCIAL STATEMENTS

Angela's Cash Flow Statement for period ended 31/12/2xx6

MONTH	1	2	3	4	5	6	7	8	9	10	11	12
INFLOW												
Consultancy Fee Income		1,600	2,700	3,600	5,000	6,000	7,000	8,000	10,000	10,000	10,000	10,000
Owner Capital	10,000											
Other Capital	5,000											
Loan capital							10,000					
Opening Cash balance		6,219	3693	-3707	-1707	593	2993	14439	15635	8385	10385	10385
TOTAL CASH INFLOW	15,000	7,819	6,393	-107	3,293	6,593	19,993	22,439	25,635	18,385	20,385	20,385
Capital Expenditure												
Car deposit	2,000											
Furniture	1,800											
Computer and Printer Systems (3)	2,100											
Salaries and Wages												
Administrative Secretary		1,000	1,000	1,000	1,000	1,000	1,000	1,000	1,000	1,000	1,000	1,000
Professional indemnity insurance premiums		45	45	45	45	45	45	45	45	45	45	45
Rent and Rates (1)	346	346	346	346	346	346	900	900	900	900	900	900
Advertising												
Pamphlets and Direct mailing	450	450	450	450	450	450	450	450	450	450	450	450
Stationery (business cards/letterheads etc)	230	230	230	230	230	230	230	230	230	230	230	230
Search Engine fees	80	80	80	80	80	80	80	80	80	80	80	80
Newspaper advertisement	800	800	800	800	800	800	800	800	800	800	800	800
Administration costs												
web hosting	600	600	600	600	600	600	600	600	600	600	600	600
Telephone and broadband costs	11	11	11	11	11	11	11	11	11	11	11	11
Fuel for car	90	90	90	90	90	90	90	90	90	90	90	90
Loan Repayment	120	120	120	120	120	120	120	120	120	120	120	120
Hire Purchase Costs								250	250	250	250	250
Car	154	154	154	154	154	154	154	154	154	154	154	154
Drawings						6,000						6,000
TOTAL CASH OUTFLOW	8,781	3,926	3,926	3,926	3,926	3,926	4,480	4,730	4,730	4,730	4,730	4,730
Net Inflow (Outflow)	6219	3893	2467	-4033	-633	2667	15513	17709	20005	13655	15655	15655
Cumulative in (out) flow	6,219	10,112	12,579	8,546	7,913	10,580	26,093	43,802	64,707	78,362	94,017	109,672

Notes

1. The rent and rates are calculated as 2/5 of the total monthly cost of her house as the business was initially, run from her residential premises. i.e (2/5 of rent (700) + council tax (90) + Water, Electricity and gas (64). On the seventh month the business moved to serviced office at £900 per month
2. The figure for Computer and Printer systems included office networks broadband and other telecommunication system installation which were one off expenses

As we have already noted cash flow statements are important in predicting whether there will be problems in meeting cash financial obligations as they arise. Though a cash flow does not reveal whether or not a business is making a profit, we can tell from the availability of cash if we are making correct financial decisions. For example, a business might be making good business but giving out too much credit to its customers so that they spend their cash on purchases but do not recover it immediately through sales. This is unsound financial decision making.

Rapid expansion of a business could also lead to a cash crunch as more money is tied down in assets that do not immediately create a cash inflow. Note that a cash statement shows how much of the cash has come into the business and how much has gone out. In example 4.7 above, the transactions have been kept simple and easy to understand; later in the book, we will tackle more elaborate cash flow statements.

4.6: Other reports and Statements

4.6.1: Budget

A budget is an itemised summary of estimated or intended expenditures for a given period along with proposals for financing those expenditures. Budgeting refers to planning the use of resources and allocating them among potential activities to achieve the objectives of the organisation. In a business, a budget is the allocation of financial resources to the needs of the business. Budgeting sets out the financial targets for a business. It helps anticipate problems and compare what has actually happened with what was expected.

A budget is a part of the overall planning and provides a benchmark against which the performance of the business can be measured. It also ensures that the resources of the business are correctly allocated as well as serving as a motivating tool for financial management. A budget will also have within it an inbuilt facility to deal with unanticipated demands on resources. A combination of all these advantages means that the management finds it easier to make decisions according to the budget. We will have a closer look at budgets later in the book.

4.6.2: Project or Event Reports

A project is defined as a series of events that lead to the creation of a specific product or service. A project is characterised by a specific start and finish date. An event is a single occurrence or activity within a project.

A project report is a comprehensive appraisal of an ongoing project. It highlights the progress of the project and assesses whether or not the project objectives are being achieved, if there have been deviations from the plan and forms the basis for further plans.

CHAPTER 4: AN OVERVIEW OF FINANCIAL STATEMENTS

A project report will also be used to evaluate the financial performance in implementing and running the project. It will hence include a financial report with Cash flow statements or even an income statement if it is already running.

This initial performance can be used to judge the viability of the project. A project report will also be used be the management to make decisions. Other stakeholders such as banks will use these reports to evaluate the viability of the project as well as whether they can lend money to the business to complete the project.

All these statements therefore serve as important documents of communication between a business and its stakeholders.

Revision Questions:

1. Define the following financial statements and state their purposes in a business:
    - Trading, Profit and Loss Account
    - Balance Sheet
    - Cash Flow statement
    - Trial Balance

   Differentiate between a Trading, Profit and Loss Account and a Cash Flow statement.

2. The valuation of stock is very important for all businesses: discuss the effects of rapid inflation and deflation of purchase prices on the following methods of valuation:
    - FIFO
    - LIFO
    - AVCO
    - Replacement Value

3. A medium sized retailer trade does not use the same method consistently to value his stock. Discuss the various effects this could have on his net profit and balance sheet and how failure to have a consistent valuation approach can be used fraudulently.

4. Define depreciation and explain why we make a provision in the books for it. Show how you would record a provision for depreciation in a cash flow statement, balance sheet and a profit and loss account.

5. Why would a profitable business find itself in a cash crunch situation? Discuss how to avoid this situation from arising in a business.

6. The following information was extracted from Harold's books of accounts for a 12 month period. Use this information to determine value of the stock at the end of each month using both FIFO and AVCO

Month	Purchases	Sales/Issued
April	3,000 units @ £6	1,800 units
May	4,500 units @ £5	2,200 units
June		
July	1,600 units @ £8	
August		2,500 units
September	3,650 @ £7	2,700 units
October		1,200 units
November		
December	2,000 units@£6	
January		
February		1,900 units

7. Oaten bought plant and machinery at the beginning of the year 01/01/2xx1 for £120,000. He anticipates that he will use the machine for six years then sell it off at its residual value of £30,000. Calculate the rate at which he needs to depreciate this asset on a reducing balance basis and show the value of the asset at the end of each year to the sixth year. Using the same information calculate the straight-line depreciation value (note: you only need one calculation for this)

8. The following trial balance was extracted from Leroy's books of accounts for the period ended 31/08/2xx9:

Particulars	Dr. £	Cr. £
Sales		36,000
Purchases	16,600	
Opening stock for the period	4,500	
Salaries and Wages	12,000	
Returns inwards	800	
Returns outwards		1,200
Capital Account		30,000
Debtors	4,000	
Creditors		3,500
Furniture & Fittings	2,000	
Rent and rates	9,400	
Telephone charges	1,500	
Sundry Expenses	1,500	
Transport expenses	1,800	
Vehicles	12,000	
Cash	2,700	
Bank	1,900	
	70700	70,700

- Using the information in the trial balance prepare a Trading, Profit and Loss Account for Leroy's business for the period ended 31/08/2xx9, given that the closing stock on 31/08/2xx9 was 3,800
- Prepare a balance sheet for Leroy's business

9. The following information was extracted from Sue's books of accounts.
    - Started a business on 01/04/2xx7 depositing £25,000 in her bank account, she also borrowed £10,000 from her bank towards the business. The annual interest on this loan was to £100 per year, the loan and interest repayment totalled £378 per month.
    - She purchased a business van on hire purchase at £18,000; she put down a deposit of 3,000, the hire purchase agreement stated that she pays £350 per month for 48 months.
    - She incurred the following monthly expenses:

Rent and rates	750
Salaries and wages	1,500
Insurance premiums	100
Transport costs	180
Telephone charges	120
Advertising costs	250
Sundry Expenses	300
Legal costs	80
Purchases	700

Purchases refer to the cost of the goods that were resold during this period

- She adopted a straight-line depreciation for the car anticipating that the car will be used for 5 years and will have no residual value.
- During the year the following month-by-month sales occurred.

Month	£
April	2,500
May	1,800
June	3,600
July	4,000
August	7,800
September	6,900
October	8,800
November	7,300
December	10,800
January	9,850
February	7,000
March	5,200
Total	75,550

- The closing stock of the business at the end of the trading period 31/03/2xx8 was £1,400

Using the information provided, prepare a cash flow statement and a trading, profit and loss account for the period.

CHAPTER 4: AN OVERVIEW OF FINANCIAL STATEMENTS

10. The following trial balance was extracted from the financial records of Franklin's business.

Trial Balance for the period ended 31/07/2xx1

Particulars	Dr. £	Cr. £
Capital		40,000
Loan		10,000
Drawings	9,000	
Vehicles	18,000	
Plant and Machinery	31,000	
Computer System	2,300	
Opening Stock	14,500	
Prepaid Rent and Rates	2,000	
Debtors	7,700	
Cash in hand	5,690	
Bank	8,100	
Creditors		11,600
Accrued telephone expenses		1,200
Sales		84,210
Purchases	22,800	
Return inwards	1,200	
Return outwards		1,960
Loan interest	1,540	
Transport costs	3,100	
Rent and rates	9,230	
Telephone Expenses	2,750	
Sundry expenses	1,800	
Advertising	4,340	
Salaries and Wages	16,800	
	161850	148,970

Closing stock for the period £16,980

Using the trial balance prepare Franklin's Trading, Profit and Loss Account and a Balance Sheet

Part 2:
Accounting Conventions

Chapter 5: Recording Financial Transactions

At the end of this chapter, the learner will be able to describe:

1. The Cash and Accrual Accounting Systems
2. The nature, purpose and limitations of Accounting conventions
3. International Accounting Standards
4. Legal Considerations in Accounting conventions
5. Accounting and economic Concepts of income
6. Conceptual Framework of accounting

5.1: Introduction

Accounting information is used by many stakeholders for different reasons. These reasons range from making decisions on whether the business in question is robust to how much it owes in taxes. Different stakeholders will for this reason require different reports covering the information that they want. However, this would lead to many different reports for the same business. Many different reports, in turn would mean that there are different views for the same business. It would therefore be impossible to compare the performance of that business against other businesses or over time. The solution to this problem would be to prepare accounts that provide all the requisite information for all the stakeholders. This information should also mean the same thing to different people at different times.

The important question would therefore be how we achieve this with one set of accounts. How do we ensure that the one set of account meets the needs of all the stakeholders? The best way of ensuring that these needs are all met by the one set of accounts is to produce guidelines and formats in which the accounts should be prepared. This is known as the accounting standards. Accounting standards are principles and guidelines that are used by all businesses preparing final statements of accounts to ensure that these accounts are easy to understand and useful to all stakeholders.

Accounts are prepared to allow for comparison of the performance of a business with other businesses in the same sector as well as over time. It is for these reasons that there are accounting standards and conventions. In the United Kingdom, the formalisation of accounting standards started as early as 1960s. The first accounting body to standardise accounting practices was the Accounting Standards Committee that issued Statements of Standards of Accounting Practice (SSAPs). ASC was in 1990 replaced by Accounting Standards Board that issued FRS (Financial Reporting Standards). A larger umbrella body now exists this is the Financial Reporting Council. This organisation is made up of operating bodies, one of which is the Accounting Standards Board, others include; Auditing Practices Board, Professional Oversight Board for Accountancy, Financial Reporting Review Panel and Accountancy Investigation and Discipline Board. These five operating bodies ensure that not only are there accounting standards, but that they are adhered to and any misconduct in their application is dealt with.

The ASB is concerned with the establishing and improving standards of financial accounting and reporting, for the benefit of users, preparers, and auditors of financial information. By creating and maintaining the standards the FRC ensures that, the interests of the public and other stakeholders are protected. It also ensures that financial information is objective, comparable and represents business entities as correctly as possible.

Following are accounting conventions that have not been expressly included in the statements of standards or the Financial Reporting Standards but nonetheless are adhered to by accountants. They include:

5.2: The Cash and Accrual Accounting Systems

An important concept in accounting relates to the recognition of revenues, expenses, transfers and related assets and liabilities in the books of accounts. This is known as the 'basis of accounting'.

This section provides an overview of the accounting principles and basis of accounting. There are two distinct basis of accounting: cash and accrual accounting.

5.2.1: Cash accounting

Cash accounting is the most elementary form of accounting and is typically used by individuals, small businesses. Under the cash basis, revenues are recorded when received and expenditures are recorded when monies are paid. The virtue of cash accounting is its simplicity. As accounting is not performed until monies are received or spent, the relationship of revenues and expenses to the accounting period in question is dependent on the actual flow of cash.

This system makes no provision for non-cash transactions; therefore, the accounting reports may provide inadequate information for control purposes and may limit analysis of the financial condition of the business.

5.2.2: Accrual Accounting

Accrual accounting is a system where revenues are recognized when earned and expenditures are recognized in the period incurred, without regard to the time of receipt or payment of cash. This method of accounting allows a more accurate evaluation of operations during a given fiscal period. A fiscal period refers to a period within which financial transactions are considered. Ordinary businesses and other commercial entities consider a fiscal year. A fiscal year is a period of twelve calendar months without regard to the first calendar month being the first fiscal month of the period. This means that a business' fiscal year could start on 1 November and end on 31 October the next year.

However, using the accrual method does not reveal the real cash position of a business and this may lead to liquidity problems. As we have already seen in our consideration of the cash flow statement, profitability is not synonymous with liquidity. Where liquidity is the ability of a business to meet its financial obligations as they arise, profitability is its ability to have higher revenue than total operating expenses. Since the accrual basis only deals with the time when a transaction occurs and not with the time when cash is received in payment or used to pay for expenses, then it is easy to assume that high profitability is equivalent to high liquidity. If debtors do not pay in time and creditors require their payments then a profitable business may find that it is unable to meet its financial obligations. A cash flow statement therefore becomes important in ensuring that this situation does not creep up on the business.

It is important to understand the basics of the two principal methods of keeping track of a business's income and expenses: cash method and accrual method (sometimes called cash basis and accrual basis). Concisely, these methods differ only in the timing of when transactions, including sales and purchases, are credited or debited to a business's accounts. The accrual method is the more commonly used method of accounting.

Under the accrual method, transactions are counted when the order is made, the item is delivered, or the services occur, regardless of when the money for them (receivables) is actually received or paid. In other words, income is counted when the sale occurs, and expenses are counted when the business receives the goods or services. The business does not have to wait until it receives the money, or until money is actually paid for goods and services received.

Under the cash method, income is not counted until cash (or a cheque) is actually received, and expenses are not counted until actually paid. A business that has stock, sales and purchases on credit will find it more practicable to use the accrual method to ensure that the statements prepared reflect all the transactions that occur in a given period.

If the delivery of a good or a service is over a period, the good of service is deemed delivered at the end of the delivery.

For example, a business that installs computer systems for huge pervasive organisations may take two to three months to complete a contract. We recognise the delivery of such a system at the end of the period. Therefore, if a system started on 1 April 2xx8 and ended on 10 August 2xx8 and the organisation paid for such a system on 31 December 2xx8. Then the following would be done under the different systems.

Under the Accrual basis, the transaction would be recorded as occurring on 10 of August 2xx8; under the cash basis, the transaction would have been recorded as occurring on 31

AN INTRODUCTION TO ACCOUNTING

December 2xx8. This would have no real effect if all the three events occurred within the same fiscal year, say for example the business' year started on 1 March 2xx8, and ended on 28 February 2xx9 the next year. However, if the fiscal year began on the 1 October and ended on the 30 September the next year, under the accrual method, the transaction would be shown to have occurred during the fiscal year 2xx7/2xx8 and the organisation would be shown as a debtor in the balance at the end of the year. Under the cash accounting, approach the transaction would not be recorded until 31 December 2xx8 and in the fiscal year 2xx8/2xx9. This is obviously erroneous as it shows that the transaction has not occurred and debtors are not recognised therefore the picture presented in the financial statements of 2xx7/2xx8 would be wrong, just as 2xx8/2xx9 would be wrong.

5.2: The Nature, Purpose and Limitations of accounting conventions

Accounting conventions refer to the established "codes" of basic principles and procedures that apply in recording and reporting financial information. These conventions are important because they ensure that financial information can be used by different stakeholders.

Academic writers on accountancy have identified many accounting concepts, which could be regarded as forming part of the accounting conceptual framework. Accounting conventions are different from the accounting conceptual framework because they are codified and are derived from the conceptual framework. A conceptual framework is the body of knowledge that forms the basis and the thinking applied in a certain discipline. These are the basic assumptions; the accounting conceptual framework can be regarded in the same light as the laws of motion or relativity in physics. That is to say, they are the basis upon which practices, ideas and applications of the discipline are based. For example, 'what is the best stock valuation approach and why?' Accounting as a discipline has only just started to take seriously the need for a theoretical conceptual framework that would guide the profession towards a more coherent body of knowledge. Unlike many other disciplines accounting has been for centuries, a matter of necessity rather than a discipline developed from theoretical discourse. This is bound to change as organisations become more complex and accounting becomes more complicated as they attempt to cover all possible scenarios. Valuation of assets, determination of depreciation and other such provisions have meant that a coherent body of accounting knowledge has had to be created to cater for the many subjective interpretations that can arise. These will form the basis of reasonable assumptions that can be made while interpreting financial information.

The fundamental accounting concepts are defined in SSAP 2, these include:

5.2.1: Realisation:

A transaction and any profits arising from such a transaction is recognised when the good is delivered to the buyer rather than when they pay for it. This means that goods delivered to a buyer are deemed sold and the profits made at the time of delivery rather than at the time when it is paid for. The same applies for the provision of services. The realisation concept is especially important in cases of credit sales. Credit sales are paid for after the goods or services are delivered. Realisation is a concept that is at the heart of many other fundamental principles; the accrual accounting is consistent with realisation in that the sale or purchase of goods and services is recognised at the time when the sale is made. Later we shall look at matching which refers to ensuring that transactions are related to the time they occur rather than to when they paid for.

5.2.2: Materiality:

In accounting, it is important to decide which items are both relevant and consequential; As we can see from the application of accounting standards and accounting policies, the preparation of accounts involves a high degree of judgement. Where decisions are required about the appropriateness of a particular accounting judgement, the "materiality" convention suggests that this should only be an issue if the judgement is "significant" or "material" to a user of the accounts. This convention might be used to overrule a strict interpretation of other conventions. It is used to determine the appropriateness of conventions.

For example, the repainting of machinery worth £5,000,000 might cost £20, this will increase the value of the machinery to £5,000,020, however this amount is immaterial compared to the value of the machinery and it is not appropriate to include it in the depreciation account. Instead, it will be included as part of the revenue expenditure. The same would apply to items of office stationery that would be included as capital and accounted for as stock but their value may be so immaterial that it is only sensible to include such items as revenue expenditure. This convention thus lends flexibility to accounting. Materiality therefore seeks to make sense to accounting conventions and prevent inappropriate or mischievous application of the other conventions.

5.2.3: Going concern

The assumption that when accountants prepare accounts for a business, that the business will continue. This has an important implication in the valuation of resources of the business. If we assume that the business is being closed down then we value the assets at cost or at the going market price. Certain highly specific assets might not even fetch the cost price. However if we assume that the business is a going concern then assets are valued at the going concern rate which might be either the depreciated value or the market price. For example, if a business that extracts minerals uses s a highly specialised drilling machine that costs millions of pounds, for so long as we assume that the business will continue then this machine will appear in the balance sheet valued in millions. However, if the minerals run out and we know that the business will not be in operation in the next financial period then we can attach a market value to it, but in such cases the machine could have only been suitable for that particular mine and no one else in the mining industry wants to buy it. If the owners then decide to disassemble it and sell it off as scrap, its value could fall to a few thousand pounds.

5.2.4: Consistency:

Where there is a subjective judgement made in the preparation of account then that subjective decision must be consistently applied year after year so that users of accounts can make meaningful comparisons from period to period. For example, the depreciated values of assets must be determined in the same way period after period. A more important example is the valuation of stock at the end of each period. As we saw earlier in the determination of stock values, the methods adopted may have a profound effect on profits for a given period, especially during high inflation or deflation. Accountants must therefore adopt the most representative method for stock valuation and consistently use that valuation method unless there is a material change in the circumstances that prompted the accountants to use that method in the first place. For example, if a business, which has been using FIFO for the last five years, buys stock and it gains value while in their hands, it may be more appropriate for them to use the replacement approach to value the stock. The stakeholders who use these statements must be informed that this change in the valuation has occurred.

5.2.5: Prudence:

Accountants recognise an anticipated loss as soon as they become aware of it and make provisions for such a loss even before it is realised. On the other hand, they never recognise a profit or income until such a profit is realised. Prudence however dictates that accountants anticipate a loss but never a profit; this would have the effect of having the business always prepared for adverse outcomes. This seems to be the opposite of realisation where a profit is recognised at the point of sale. However, these two conventions can be reconciled if the accountant will recognise a sale at the time it occurs, rather than when it is paid for. The accountant, using his/her judgement will decide whether the sale will be realised. Thus, an accountant may recognise a sale and the profits thereof if there is a reasonable certainty that it will be paid for. The principle of prudence demands that accountants ensure that sales made on credit will be paid for, if they receive information that a credit agreement will not be honoured then they should make a provision for bad debts. The provision recognises that the sale might not be realised and the business might incur the cost of the goods or services provided to the defaulting customer.

On the other hand, incomes are only recognised when they are received. This means that profits may not be recognised before the sales have been paid for. It prevents businesses from planning for future expenditure on income they have not received. This would not be 'prudent'.

CHAPTER 5: RECORDING FINANCIAL TRANSACTIONS

5.2.6: Matching:

Incomes should be correctly matched to the expenses of a given period. This means that all expenses of a given period should be matched to the incomes they generate. This agrees with the principal of accrual, which states that all goods and services are recognised at the point of sale rather than at the point of payment. Adhering to this convention ensures that profits or losses of a given period are assigned to that period rather than a previous or future period. A fiscal year is a basic period over which the performance of a business can be assessed. By matching expenses to incomes, we are able to determine whether the business is being efficient and productive during the relevant period. Without this basic period we would be unable to determine how one business is performing compared to the rest of the industry.

5.2.7: Capital and revenue expenditure:

A capital expenditure is one where there is residual value after the accounting period during which the expenditure was incurred. As such, an expenditure that remains of value to the business for more than one accounting period is taken as a capital expenditure. Revenue expenditure is one, which is spent by the end of the accounting period and has no residual value. The distinction between these two types of expenditure is important when drawing up a balance sheet where we need to determine, which assets are fixed and which assets are current. It is also important in the calculation of profits. Profits or losses are the difference between total revenue and total revenue expenditure. An expenditure incurred during a certain period only and used to produce part of the total revenue for that period is taken to be an operating expense. An expenditure that is used for more than the period when it was incurred gives rise to a fixed or current asset.

5.2.8: Depreciation:

Depreciation refers to the part of a capital expenditure apportioned to the profit and loss account during each accounting period. This is meant to capture the gradual wear and tear of such an asset. It also ensures that the period during which such an asset is bought is not overcharged with the value of the asset since the usefulness of the asset does not end with the end of that period. The determination of how much to charge to the depreciation account in relation to a given asset is subjective. Depreciation charges depend on what the business believes will be the length of the usefulness of the asset and its residual value. This is open to abuse, as different businesses will have different perceptions regarding these two aspects of depreciation. A business that chooses to depreciate its asset over a shorter period of time and claim to anticipate no residual value for it will be left with a relatively new asset with a high residual value while having charged the expense account with high depreciation values and therefore reducing profits in those period and subsequently taxes payable.

AN INTRODUCTION TO ACCOUNTING

For example, Ketan is an accomplished businessperson; on 01/01/2xx1, he bought plant and machinery worth £60,000 and decided that the machine would be useful for three years without a residual value after those three years. He applied the straight-line depreciation approach to it.

Each year he deducted £20,000 from his profit and loss account. The industrial average depreciation policy is that the plant and machinery would last for 5years and its residual value would be at least £20,000. Therefore under the straight-line depreciation the yearly charge would have been:

$$Depreciation Value = \frac{£60,0000 - £20,000}{5} = £8,000 \, per year$$

However, Ketan understated his profits by £12,000 each year for three years, and after three years, the machinery written-off as fully depreciated was worth £36,000.

The following are basic accounting conventions; these have not been included in the legislation however, they are widely agreed upon by accountants.

5.2.9: Historical Cost Convention:

The most commonly encountered convention is the "historical cost convention". This requires transactions to be recorded at the price ruling at the time, and for assets to be valued at their original cost.

Under the "historical cost convention", therefore, no account is taken of changing prices in the economy. This might present an incorrect picture because the value of currencies changes over time due to inflation and other economic factors. Assets valued at cost may be an objective valuation but it is erroneous because the value of assets reduces with time (depreciation). Transactions are recorded at the prevailing prices at the time they occur. This is advantageous in that traders do not have to renegotiate credit agreements because of prices that have changed between the time of transaction and the time of payment. While the concept of valuing assets at cost may be misleading that of recording prices at the time of transactions may well form the firm foundation on which business is based. It is even protected in the Sales of Act Goods Act (1979) which states that, a contract of sale of goods is a contract by which the seller transfers or agrees to transfer the property in goods to the buyer for a money consideration, called the price. This means that the seller has accepted to transfer the value in the good to a buyer for a price. In this case the price is known as a 'money consideration' this means that so long as the buyer and seller agree without being under undue pressure then the price will be binding for the goods they have exchanged. This agrees with the historical convention. If, therefore, John had reason to believe that he would die soon and would no longer need his Mercedes Benz worth £50,000 and sells it for £100 to Megan and they both agree to exchange the good for this 'money consideration' and then John found out that he would not be dying soon. The law protects Megan, she can

CHAPTER 5: RECORDING FINANCIAL TRANSACTIONS

reject £100 from John to return his car as there was a money consideration that was offered and accepted. However, if John made a gift of the car to Megan then he may recover it.

The historical approach has uses that are more practical, once a transaction has been made then it cannot be broken because of changes in the economy. This allows businesses to go about their business and plan based on completed transactions.

5.2.10: Separate entity:

This convention holds that a business is the affairs of a business should be held separate from any other business or even individual even if such individuals own the business. This enables accountants to measure the performance of each business. The separate entity principle is further reinforced by the separate determination principle where each transaction's effect on the business is determined separately from all the other transactions. It simply means that for us to arrive at the aggregate effect of all the transactions in a business we must treat each transaction separately and the net effect of each transaction is then aggregated with other net effects of other transactions and the overall effect determined. This separate treatment of each transaction ensures that we can trace and understand the implication of each transaction. For example, a business bought a machine for £10,000; after three months, they found that it was unsuitable for the purposes it was intended. They therefore sold it for £3,000 making a loss of £7,000, and then they bought a suitable machine for £12,000. These transactions while in fact have gained the business a machine worth £12,000 cannot be cancelled off to show that the new machine cost £19,000 because of the loss incurred in the disposal of the wrong machine. Each transaction must be shown individually.

5.2.11: Monetary terms:

The accountants only account for those items that can be measured in terms of money. All accounting items must thus be quantified in monetary terms. Other items may be quantified if someone is willing to pay money for them for example workforce skill, morale, market leadership, brand recognition, quality of management etc.

These other items are quantified subjectively. They are known as intangible assets, for example goodwill, which is the 'feel-good' factor and reputation of a business. This is observable all around us, businesses whose names are easily recognisable and associated with a certain characteristic. This is known as branding, where the name Coca-cola does not simply refer to a cola drink, but to a drink that brings people closer together. Successful brand names are one of the most important intangible assets; Goodwill represents the excess of the purchase cost over the fair value of assets less liabilities of acquired companies. If a business were to purchase Coca-cola they would pay more for the company than the fair value of the business assets less any liabilities. This difference arises as a business becomes more successful and is known as the goodwill. Other intangible assets include patents, copyrights, and royalties and so on.

AN INTRODUCTION TO ACCOUNTING

5.2.12: Double Entry:

Double entry is the convention of recognising the dual effect of financial transactions. This is where each transaction affects two different accounts in a business. This convention shows how resources flow from one part of the business to another part.

5.2.13: Objectivity:

This implies that accounting information should be prepared in an unbiased and neutral manner and should not be seen serve the purposes of any one party.

5.2.14: Substance over form:

The many provisions that are set out by the various principles may create a problem in reporting financial information such that in keeping with them the information, to be conveyed to the users of the accounts, is lost. The substance of a transaction is the actual economic effect that it has on the business, whereas the form is the manner in which this information is recorded in the books. A classic example is the purchase of assets on hire purchase, such as an asset is entered in the balance sheet at its full value as legally it belongs to the business. However, the business has not paid for it so in actual sense they owe the value of the asset to the vendor of the asset. This information must be expressed both in accordance to the principles of accounting which is recognising the who value of asset in the statements, but users of the accounts must be informed that the asset has not been paid, through notes or supplementary accounts showing this information.

There is general agreement that, before it can be regarded as useful in satisfying the needs of various user groups, accounting information should satisfy the following criteria:

Relevance this implies that, to be useful, accounting information must assist a user to form, confirm or maybe revise a view - usually in the context of making a decision
Consistency that implies consistent treatment of similar items and application of accounting policies
Comparability; should be able to compare different businesses using the financial information provided by the accountants.
Reliability; accounts should be presented in a truthful, accurate and complete manner. Such accounts should be verifiable and nothing significant should be left out of the accounts.
A regular time interval, which implies that accounts will be after a specific period. This ensures that accounts for different periods are comparable.

5.3: International Accounting Standards

Today there are many international businesses. There are also many businesses in different countries that have the same operations. International accounting standards have been

CHAPTER 5: RECORDING FINANCIAL TRANSACTIONS

established to allow businesses to be compared across countries. It also aims to give guidelines to businesses that have operations in different countries where the accounting standards may be different. By standardising the accounting conventions across many countries, accounts can be easily compared and used to make financial decisions.

The International Accounting Standards Board (IASB) replaced the Board of the International Accounting Standards Committee (IASC), which operated from 1973 until 2001.

IASC was founded in June 1973 because of an agreement by accountancy bodies in Australia, Canada, France, Germany, Japan, Mexico, the Netherlands, the United Kingdom and Ireland and the United States, and these countries constituted the Board of IASC at that time.

The international professional activities of the accountancy bodies were organised under the International Federation of Accountants (IFAC) in 1977. In 1981, IASC and IFAC agreed that IASC would have full and complete autonomy in setting international accounting standards and in publishing discussion documents on international accounting issues. At the same time, all members of IFAC became members of IASC. This membership link was discontinued in May 2000 when IASC's Constitution was changed as part of the reorganisation of IASC.

5.3: Legal Considerations in Accounting Conventions

5.3.1: Stewardship and Accountability

Most businesses in the United Kingdom and elsewhere are Limited companies. A limited company refers to a business that is owned through shares. Shares are equal unit divisions of the total value of the business. Such a business also has limited liability; limited liability means that an investor cannot lose more than the amount invested. Thus, the investor is not personally responsible for the debts and obligations of the company in the event that these are not fulfilled. This is the reinforced by the provision that a company is an 'artificial person' with its own obligations, duties, which can own property as well as sell it, sue or be sued. It is also consistent with the accounting convention of 'separate entity' – where the activities of the owner are separate from those of the business for the purposes of accounting.

There are two types of companies; these are Public and Private Limited Companies. As we will see later in this book, public companies are those companies whose shares can be owned by any member of the public. Usually such companies are quoted in the stock market. Being quoted in the stock market means that their shares can be traded in the stock market and anyone who has money can buy or sell those shares in the stock market. A public company has at least two shareholders and no limit to the number of people who can own its shares.

AN INTRODUCTION TO ACCOUNTING

Private companies shares on the other hand may not be traded in the stock market and the sale of shares to the public is restricted. Such shares are rarely traded and the membership of shareholders usually a few people. A private company may also have a lower limit of two shareholders and no upper limit. Private companies are characteristically smaller than public companies and the shareholders are usually the managers of the day-to-day activities.

Since the public company has so many members it may not be possible for them to be directly involved in the management of the business. This means that other people may need to be appointed as stewards of such a business. Stewardship refers to the delegated responsibility of the day-to-day running of a business entity by the shareholders to the managers of such business.

Another important characteristic of a company is that its shareholders and stewards enjoy a limited liability. While the shareholders may lose their investment in the business, the stewards are protected by the Limited liability clause.

The stewards are hence legally bound to report to the shareholders and the public that might be interested in the business the true and fair position of the business. Stewards are therefore expected to be accountable; the collapse of companies in the EU and USA makes this all the more urgent.

5.3.2: Sources of financial regulations in the United Kingdom

Regulations for the accounting profession in the United Kingdom come from the government and public sector as well as the private sector and accountants self-regulation bodies. Some of the private organisations include the aforementioned *Financial Reporting Council, ASB* and *IASB*. Others are the *Stock Exchange*, which produces regulations on the financial regulations of listed companies, these are companies listed and traded on such a stock exchange. *Financial Reporting Review Panel* examines the accounts of companies that do not seem to comply with the regulation to present a true and fair view of the financial performance and position.

The Parliament through the companies act effect legislation that hence is legally enforceable against companies that fail to comply with the regulations. The government through the department of Trade and Industry also regulates the accounting procedures of businesses.

5.4: Conceptual Framework of Accounting

5.4.1: Background

ASB has published its *Statement of Principles for Financial Reporting*. The Statement sets out the principles that the ASB believes should underlie the preparation and presentation of company accounts. This statement ensures that ASB prepares its standards in a consistent manner and in keeping with a clear conceptual framework.

When the ASB was created, in 1990, its founders recommended that it should carry out work on a conceptual framework to help ensure that its standards had a consistent manner of preparation. The ASB agreed and therefore developed an informal frame of reference to guide it in its work. This was agreed on informally and a lot of discussion went into formalising it. In 1999, ASB issued a formal statement of Principles for financial reporting.

The key principles that were contained in the ASB's initial informal frame of reference have been examined closely over the years during the development of new accounting standards and the revision of existing ones. Many of those key principles now play a prominent role in company reporting and form a basis for the standards that have been discussed earlier in this chapter.

An accounting conceptual framework can be defined as:

A coherent system of inter-related objectives and fundamentals that should lead to consistent standards that prescribes the nature, function and limits of financial accounting and financial statements. Such a framework would serve as the basis on which further accounting standards can be set. These basic tenets are the general ideas derived or inferred from specific instances or occurrences that can then be used to create an acceptable standard of operation.

However, it is easier to state what a conceptual framework should be, than to precisely define it.

The main reasons for developing an agreed conceptual framework are that it provides:

1. a framework for setting accounting standards;
2. a basis for resolving accounting disputes;
3. Fundamental principles, which then do not have to be repeated in accounting standards

However, the main problem would be that such a conceptual framework would present very general ideas, which would not be useful in specific cases and may create room for disagreements thus defeating the purpose of being a coherent system.

5.4.2: Purpose and scope of the Statement of Principles

The purpose of the draft Statement of Principles is to define the principles that should underlie the preparation and presentation of general-purpose financial statements. It also provides the conceptual underpinnings for preparing future accounting standards. The Statement comprises of the following eight chapters:

1. The Objective of Financial Statements
2. The Reporting Entity
3. The Qualitative Characteristics of Financial Information
4. The Elements of Financial Statements
5. Recognition in Financial Statements
6. Measurement in Financial Statements
7. Presentation of Financial Information
8. Accounting for Interests in Other Entities

The ASB believe that the draft statement will assist preparers and users of financial statements, as well as auditors and others, to understand its approach to formulating accounting standards. It should also help them understand the general nature and function of information reported in financial statements.

It is important to remember that the Statement of Principles is not an accounting standard and, therefore, does not prescribe how financial statements should be prepared or presented.

The draft statement focuses on the financial statements that either are intended to give a true and fair view of the organisation's financial performance and financial position or are intended to be consistent with financial statements that give such a view. This includes annual and interim financial statements, as well as preliminary announcements and summary financial statements.

5.4.3: Relevance of the Statement

The draft Statement is primarily designed to be relevant to the financial statements of profit-oriented organisations including those in the public sector, regardless of their size. However, it could also be relevant to not-for-profit organisations if some of the principles are re-expressed or their emphasis changed. A separate paper on not-for-profit entities and the Statement of Principles is to be issued in due course.

The draft Statement recognises that the concept of a true and fair view is fundamental to the whole system of financial reporting. An example of this is its insistence on relevance and reliability as the main indicators of the quality of financial information. The concept of a true and fair view is considered the 'ultimate' and lies at the core of all-financial reporting. It is regarded as the ultimate test for financial statements and, as such, has a direct effect on accounting practice.

Financial statements will not give a true and fair view unless the information they contain is sufficient in quantity and quality to satisfy the reasonable expectations of the readers to whom they are addressed. These expectations change over time and the ASB seeks, through its accounting standards and other pronouncements, to respond to these expectations.

The key principle contained in the Statement of Principles defines the objective of financial statements as:

"To provide information about the reporting entity's financial performance and financial position that is useful to a wide range of users for assessing the stewardship of management and for making economic decisions."

This definition provides the basis for developing all the subsequent principles within the Statement. Fundamentally, the Statement assumes that it can achieve this objective by focusing on the information needs of present and potential investors. This is because they need information about the organisations' financial performance and financial position that is useful to them in evaluating its ability to generate cash, and in assessing its financial adaptability.

Fundamental to the preparation of financial statements is the need to provide relevant, reliable, comparable and understandable information. In deciding which information to include in financial statements as well as how to present it, the aim should be to ensure that they provide information that is useful. The materiality test is used to determine whether the information's usefulness is of such significance as to require it to be given in the financial statements. An item of information is considered material to the financial statements if its misstatement or omission might reasonably be expected to influence the economic decisions of the users of those financial statements.

Like other disciplines, the development of a conceptual framework for accounting is on going. New financial requirements and situations give accountants and other developers room for further thought and development of the conceptual framework.

5.5: Accounting and Economic Concepts of Income:

5.5.1: Accounting Concept

Income refers to the wealth created through a business activity. There are however two ways of determining these incomes, these are the accounting and economic concepts of income. While in accounting we consider the difference between total revenue and total expenditure as income (otherwise known as profit), in economics income is the opportunity cost of employing resources in the business in question. This means that the good forgone so that resources can be employed in the business is the economic income. It therefore refers to the money available to the owners of the business once all those who have contributed have been compensated for their contribution. It means that if £1,000 is made from a business, which incurred a cost of £1,000 to run, then the economic income is zero as the income is equal to the opportunity cost.

Income, generally defined, is the money that is received because of the normal business activities of an individual or a business. Income in a business is also the profit from that business. It is the difference between expenditure and revenues. Hence, as an accounting concept income is the profit generated from a business activity.

Profit = Income = Revenues - Expenses

This income is considered before the returns on the contributors of capital such as shareholders. Under accounting, there are various types of profits; Gross profit is the difference between total revenue and the cost of goods sold or manufactured for sale. The net profit is the difference between the Gross profit and the operating costs of the business such as rent and rates and so on. As we shall see later in this section as we examine Economic income further, accounting income does not take into account whether the profits generated by this business are the best use to which the resources employed were put. Economists ask what the best way to employ the resources is, or is the current employment the most efficient employment. Therefore, in defining economic profits/income we use opportunity cost.

5.5.2: Economic Concept of Income

Economics is a discipline concerned with the optimum allocation of resources. This means that economists are concerned with whether the resources, which are by their nature scarce, are efficiently allocated between the unlimited wants.

For example, imagine you had £24 and make a list of things that you could do with this money: The list may look like this:
- Buy a snack worth £4.55
- Take a train to Oxford University to attend an economics seminar £11
- Buy a polo shirt £12
- Buy a pair of jeans trousers £22
- Spend the night out with your friends in a local club £24

Evidently, £24 is not enough to meet all these 'wants' and you will have to forego some of the 'wants' so that you can fulfil others. You therefore have to make a choice; there are various choices in the list above you could decide to buy a snack for £4.55, buy a return ticket on the train £11 and save £4.45. Another option would be to buy a pair of jeans and a polo shirt with all the money, or even go out to a local club in the evening.

Economists now consider your decisions and see how efficient they may be for the £24 you have. They ask; is it better to go to the seminar where you may learn new things, meet important contacts and may be even be offered a position in a project (these events not being given) or is it better to buy clothes? Economists assume that human beings are rational and they make the choices that maximise their returns and reduce what they have to forgo. From the example above, if you decide to go to Oxford and have a snack on the journey you will forgo the evening out and the clothes. In economics the best decision is the one where the returns from the choice made are the highest possible with the resources available and the one with the least opportunity cost.

Resources used in a business should therefore used in the most efficient manner possible. It follows then that if the income generated from the resources is higher than the opportunity cost then the business is making a profit and vice-versa is true. Therefore the total cost of a business includes operating costs, charge for using resources (for example, interest charged for capital, rent charged for land, wages charged for labour and so on). It therefore means that if the business has made more than this then it has a positive economic income. In accounting, income is shown before charges on capital and distribution of dividends.

There are different types of economic incomes:

Normal income/profit, this is the income where the cost of producing one more unit of a certain good is equal to the average cost of producing that good. For example, in a shoemaking business, the total cost of producing 100 shoes is £700. Therefore, the average cost is £7. Normal profit occurs when the cost of producing one additional shoe is also £7. This means that resources are perfectly allocated in such a business. Resources would not be thought of as well allocated if additional shoes cost more because it means that the production of subsequent shoes will be expensive, may be because they require more workers or more workspace, which would in turn mean that there is need for more resources. If the price of producing one more shoe kept falling with additional shoes, then the business has not reached the optimal production level and has inefficiently allocated available resources. Assuming all the other production factors to be constant, normal profits are achieved in an industry where there is fair competition when the marginal cost equals the average unit cost of production and the resources are therefore most efficiently allocated. It also means that the business is able to cover all the costs that are incurred in the usage of the resources employed in the business.

Supernormal profits/incomes are profits earned over and above the total costs of using the resources used in business. Supernormal profits mean that the business is able to compensate all the owners of the resources (workers for labour, shareholders for capital, landowners for land, entrepreneurs for entrepreneurial skill and so on). A supernormal profit refers to profit that exceeds the normal returns for the resources employed. This can occur where the providers of the resources are being paid less than they should or the industry is not sufficiently developed to meet the demand for its products and the businesses in that industry can charge higher prices for the goods therefore being paid more than they would be paid if there were more producers.

A common type of supernormal profit is the super-profit of a monopoly. A monopoly is a business that operates in a business environment where there is no conceivable competition. It means that a business, which is a monopoly, provides goods or services that have no viable substitutes and no economic competition can challenge this position.

Subnormal profits are profits that are earned below the normal profits level. A business that consistently makes subnormal profits finds that it cannot pay for the resources used in the business, and resource owners are no longer willing to offer their resources. Such a business eventually exits the industry where it is making subnormal profits.

An Alternative economic view to income

Income can also be perceived as a constraint to unlimited consumer spending. This view is derived from the definition of economics: Economics is the study of how households (individuals) and firms (businesses) make choices when they are faced with unlimited wants yet having limited resources. In this case, income is viewed as a resource. Economics looks at ways of allocating resources optimally in a situation of unlimited wants that cannot be met with the resources available.

This choice between unlimited wants is represented by the following simple equation:

$$I = P_x X + P_y Y$$

Where: P_x is the price of good X, X is the quantity of good X, and I is the total available income (P_y and Y are similar to P_x and x). If you need to examine more than two goods, you can add more on to the equation.

The above equation represents the constraint of choice, that if a person had an income 'I' then he or she would need to allocate it between good 'X' and good 'Y'. This allocation would depend on the prices of the goods as well as the quantities of goods required. If one requires more of 'Y' goods then they have to forfeit some of good 'X' and vice versa. In economics income is a constraint of consumption. Economists assume that households and firms have fixed incomes; therefore, they have to make a choice between the different wants that they face.

At a national level, income is also seen as a constraint of consumption but the choice is not between two goods 'X' and 'Y' but between three distinct items, these are Consumption of the nation, Investment and government expenditure. This can be represented as:

$$Y = C + I + G$$
Where: Y is the total national income,
        C is the consumption
        G is the government expenditure

National income, measured by statistics such as the Net National Income (NNI), measures the total income of all individuals in the economy. This total income can be allocated between the three items stated. A choice of allocation must be made between the three.

CHAPTER 5: RECORDING FINANCIAL TRANSACTIONS

The income concepts of accounting and economics are therefore based on the basic tenets of these two disciplines. To an economist resources are scarce, which necessitates the foregoing of certain other wants so that the more important wants can be fulfilled. The best business activity is one where the resources are employed in the most efficient manner and that allows for the highest return. The one way to ascertain whether a business is really producing, as it should is to compare its produce with the alternatives to which those resources would have been employed. This is known as the opportunity cost.

Accounting is however concerned with the 'profit-motive' this is whether a business is producing more than it is using up in terms of resources. This sounds like the same concept as the economic profit concept. The fundamental difference is that cost to the accountant is actually just the operating costs rather than the total costs of setting up a business. Where economists determine whether the business has met reimbursed all the resources employed including the capital and whether this is the best use the resources could have been put to, accountants want to ascertain whether the total revenues exceed the direct and indirect cost of the goods sold. A more controversial definition of economic income is that income is the constraint placed on a consumer as to what he or she can consumer due to its limited or fixed value. This economic definition is extended to countries and looks at the allocation of resources between consumption of the country, investment and government expenditure.

Revision Questions

1. Define the Accounting Conceptual framework, why is it important that accounting as a discipline develop this framework?
2. Explain the concept of substance over form. How important would this be in ensuring that the correct information is conveyed by the books of accounts?
3. Distinguish between the accruals and the cash accounting systems, what are their advantages and disadvantages? Why is it important that we develop international accounting conventions?
4. The principle of realisation states that transactions should be recognised when the goods or services are provided, whereas the prudence principle states that losses should be recognised at the earliest possible time and profits only after they have been paid for. Using your knowledge in accounting and supporting your arguments with the other principles of accounting provide reconciliation for the two principles.
5. Stock and other asset valuation is a subjective accounting decision. State when it would be appropriate to use the following methods of stock valuation:
    i. LIFO
    ii. FIFO
    iii. Replacement Value

6. Explain the money measurement concept. Why do you think it is important to have accounting information expressed in monetary terms?

7. The concept of materiality guides accountants on what is important and what is unimportant to the stakeholders, on the other hand, substance over form embodies the practice of including the actual economic effect of a transaction over the preparation of accounts in the correct form. Reconcile the two principles giving examples where appropriate.
8. Distinguish between the economic concept of income and the accounting concept of income
9. Income can be viewed as a constraint using individual choice equations and national income equation, explain how income can be viewed as a constraint
10. Discuss the importance of accounting principles to stewardship and accountability in businesses.

Chapter 6: Auditing

NATURE OF AUDITING AND FUNDAMENTAL AUDIT PRINCIPLES

At the end of this chapter, the learner will be able to describe:
- *Nature of auditing*
- *Fundamental auditing principles*

LEARNING OBJECTIVES
At the end of this session, you should be able to:
- *Define the meaning of the term 'audit'*
- *Define the concept of the 'true and fair view'*
- *Describe the different types of audit*
- *Differentiate between external and internal audit*
- *Define the concept of 'independence'*
- *Describe the qualities and skills auditors should possess.*

6.1: Introduction to the concepts of auditing

An audit can be defined as the inspection and verification of financial accounts, records and accounting procedures. It involves the professional examination and verification of businesses' accounting documents and supporting dates for rendering an opinion as to their fairness, consistency, and conformity with Generally Accepted Accounting Principles (GAAPs).

Some businesses are required by the law to carry out comprehensive audits. This applies to all companies that are not classified either as 'dormant' (not operating during the year in question) and those considered 'small' in the Company's Act of the UK. Small companies are those whose turnover does not exceed £5.6million per financial year, a balance sheet total of not more than £2.8 million and less than 50 employees. However, companies below these thresholds may carry out voluntary non-statutory audits. There are a number of advantages in doing this:

Firstly, a company that has audited results can present a 'true and fair' picture to third parties it would like to do business with , for example banks, suppliers, people interested in purchasing the business and so on. An audited set of accounts is widely accepted as authentic and reliable for third parties to make financial decisions on. Secondly, the government's tax department, which requires returns from a business, will be satisfied with audited reports. The authenticity of the tax returns is enhanced by presenting an audited set of accounts. Audited accounts may also be used to give a true picture to shareholders and partners and this may reduce mistrust and disputes between partners and shareholders as well as with the management. A further use of audited statements is that it alerts the management and those responsible for ensuring that the accounting process in the business is free of loopholes which can be fraudulently exploited or where errors may inadvertently occur. Therefore, an audit is an important health check facility for the accounting systems of the business. For partnerships, audited reports are useful in periods of transition where a partner may be leaving, it is only fair that he or she is reimbursed the fair share of the business, at the same time partners who join the partnership would want to be certain of the situation they are getting themselves into.

There are two broad types of audits: internal audit and External audits.

Internal audits refers to audits carried out within the business by employees of the business. The purpose of such audits is to ensure that the preparation of financial statements and reports within the business is done according to the accounting standards and that such information presents a true and fair view of the business. This is especially important for managerial decision-making processes and resource allocation. The internal audits form an important part of internal controls. Internal controls are systems within a business that ensure that the rules and procedures that provide the necessary checks and balances against fraud and errors are maintained and adhered to.

External auditing on the other hand is aimed at providing unbiased information to stakeholders other than managers and other stewards of the business. External auditing is a mechanism that ensures that accounts prepared for interested third parties. It presents the third parties with a true and fair picture of the financial position and performance of that business. An audit is thus a process of verifying that the information given in the accounts is the truth. It also ensures that it presents a fair opinion of the business' performance. An external auditor is required to give a fair opinion on the financial reports that he/ she audits.

An auditor is charged with the responsibility validating financial information that is presented by the business to various stakeholders. It is assumed that an auditor involved in auditing a businesses' account has nothing to gain from such accounts apart from his/her fees for the auditing services. This has become a very important issue in auditing today due to the increased scandals in the USA and Europe, where the auditor fails to present the true picture regarding the financial position of a business because his or her independence to the business presenting the accounts has been compromised.

Auditing is also an important business activity due to stewardship. Stewardship refers to where the day-to-day activities are not carried out by the owners of the business but by people appointed on behalf of the owners. Such people are known as stewards. Stewards have a duty to report to the owners of the business and other stakeholders the true and fair financial position of the business. Auditors verify that the stewards have presented the true and fair position regarding the operation of a given business.

Once the auditors verify the accounts that have been presented by the stewards; in this case the management through its accountants, they have to give their opinion as to the state of the financial reports that have been presented. So auditing is a two-stage process, firstly the auditor has to verify the financial information to be true and then give his/her opinion on the reports that have been produced from the financial information. This opinion must be fair.

A commonly held misconception is that the auditor is responsible for detecting all instances of fraud in the company being reported on. The primary responsibility for the prevention and detection of fraud and error rests with management. The auditor should plan the audit so that there is a reasonable expectation of detecting material misstatements resulting from fraud and error. The auditor should carry out additional procedures when he or she has an indication that fraud or error may exist. However, the auditor does not have a general duty to uncover all fraudulent activity – it would not be possible or cost-effective to give absolute assurance that all material misstatements will be detected.

6.2: True and fair

The objective of an audit of financial statements is to enable the auditor to express an opinion on whether those statements give a true and fair view (or are presented fairly, in all material respects), in accordance with an identified accounting framework.

The auditor performs certain tests of the transactions and balances underlying the financial statements, and evaluates their overall presentation. In the same way as accounts are prepared in accordance with a specified framework, such as International Financial Reporting Standards (IFRS), auditors conduct their work in accordance with a framework of auditing standards. The auditing standards most commonly associated with IFRS financial statements are the International Standards on Auditing.

The external auditor's report is normally included with the published financial statements. The statutory requirements regarding which entities should be subject to audit, and the precise matters on which the auditor should report, are determined by national governments. In addition, the rules regarding training and education of auditors and regulation of the profession vary from country to country.

6.3: Auditing regulatory bodies

The International Auditing and Assurance Standards Board (IAASB) sets international auditing standards, The IAASB is a committee of a wider body known as the International Federation of Accountants (IFAC). IFAC was founded in 1977 as a non-profit making, non-governmental representative organisation for the world's professional accountancy bodies. Over 150 accountancy bodies in more than 110 countries are members of IFAC.

The IAASB (formerly the International Auditing Practices Committee – IAPC) develops standards and pronouncements on auditing and reporting practices. The due process includes the issue of exposure drafts, which allows the public a period in which to comment on them. The final pronouncements require the affirmative vote of at least three-quarters of the members.

IAPC issues authoritative guidance on specific industry and audit issues known as International Audit Practice Statements (IAPSs) in addition to the standards. These include guidance on auditing banks, small enterprises, information systems and derivative financial instruments.

IAPC standards and guidance are set at the level that experienced accountants view as best practice. ISAs are not overly prescriptive, reflecting the intended worldwide audience.

IFAC itself has no enforcement authority. National regulators (and in some cases regional regulators such as the European Commission) exert influence over which audit standards should be used in a particular country. At the same time, national professional accountancy bodies require that their members conduct work in accordance with appropriate auditing and ethical standards. IFAC's member bodies are expected to use their best endeavours to incorporate the International Standards on Auditing into national auditing standards. In some countries, ISAs have been adopted as the national standards.

The International Organisation of Securities Commissions (IOSCO) began reviewing the ISAs in 2001 with a view to endorsing these to its members for use for cross-border listing purposes. The process of examination is similar to that which resulted in endorsement of the International Accounting Standards in 2000. Obtaining this endorsement is important for the capital markets, as it means that stock exchanges worldwide will accept audits of financial statements from other countries that are audited in accordance with the International Standards on Auditing.

IFAC also sets ethical and independence standards for the international profession through its Ethics Committee. It is implicit that an auditor performing work in accordance with International Standards on Auditing also abides by the IFAC Code of Ethics for Professional Accountants.

6.4 Fundamental Principles of an Auditor

The International Federation of Accountants, through its Ethics committee has set out a code of practice for professional accountants. An auditor is an accountant by profession; he or she is expected to adhere to these ethical principles in the execution of his/her duty. However, as an auditor the principle of independence is very important as it forms the basis for a true and fair reporting of the audited accounts. The code has the following eight specific provisions:

1. **Integrity;** an accountant is expected to uphold honesty in the execution of his/her duties

2. **Objectivity;** he/she should execute his/her duties without being influenced by his/her emotions or personal prejudices. He or she should strive to stick to the truth and use only information in preparing his/her accounts.
3. **Professional competence;** an accountant should display adequate skills, knowledge and ability in the execution of his duties. This means that not only should he or she be adequately qualified but also he/she should have sufficient experience and with it skill in the execution of his/her duties.
4. **Due care:** in legal terms due care refers to the care that a reasonable person would exercise under the circumstances. This means that given the circumstances and the assumed skill of an accountant, he or she will be held to certain standards expectations and be expected to act reasonably, as far as his/her accounting work is concerned.
5. **Confidentiality;** the accountant has a responsibility of ensuring that information is accessible only to those who have authorised access. This means that the accountant is not expected to discuss any issues pertaining to his/her work that would ordinarily be considered confidential.
6. **Professional behaviour** an accountant should be seen to conform to standards prescribed for an accounting professional.
7. **Technical standards**, this principle relates to professional competence and means almost the same thing. An accountant should have special skill or practical knowledge pertaining to his/her profession.
8. **Objective and independent**: An auditor should be able to maintain his/her objectivity as well as independence to ensure that he or she arrives at a fair opinion at the end of an audit process. The independence requirements in the Code state that the auditor should be independent in fact and in appearance. Detailed guidance is given about situations that impair independence, such as financial involvement with the client; appointments to managerial positions in the client; the provision of other services (such as consulting or bookkeeping) and personal relationships.

These general principles were developed in 2001 as a way of creating a principle based approach to auditing that would cover all the possible outcomes rather than rules and regulation. Rules and regulations cannot possibly cover all the outcomes; they can be easily abused, which means that it is important that safeguards be implemented.

6.5: The Audit process

The main steps of the audit process are set out in the standards. The large firms of auditors also have their own internally developed methodologies for conducting audits, but these are generally consistent with the ISAs. The four main stages of the audit process are:

- Defining the terms of engagement;
- Planning, including assessment of audit risk and materiality;
- Gathering audit evidence; and

- Reporting

6.5.1: Defining the terms of engagement

The terms of engagement are normally set out in an engagement letter, drafted by the auditor and signed for agreement by the client. The engagement letter is designed to document and confirm the client's understanding of the auditor's appointment, responsibilities, scope of work, and the form of any reports to be issued. The engagement letter sets out the respective responsibilities of management and the auditors.

This is an important part of the auditing process as it informs both the auditor and the management of the scope of their responsibilities. The scope of the audit also defines the liability of the auditor to the owners and any other third party stakeholders that can reasonably be expected to use the audit results to evaluate the business.

6.5.2: The Audit Plan

The audit plan outlines the expected scope and conduct of the audit. It is good practice for the overall plan to be discussed and agreed with the client, for instance with an audit committee. However, the auditor ultimately decides the amount and timing of work that has to be performed to provide the basis on which an audit report can be issued.

The concepts of materiality and audit risk, their interrelationship and their application are critical to the audit. They are used when planning and conducting an audit and when evaluating the results of the procedures.

Information is material if its omission or misstatement could influence the economic decisions that users might take based on the financial statements. The assessment of materiality is a matter of the auditor's professional judgement, and is considered at both the overall financial statement level and in relation to individual account balances and disclosures.

Audit risk is the risk that the auditor gives an inappropriate opinion when the financial statements are materially misstated. It has three components: inherent risk (the risk that there is an error), control risk (the risk that internal control procedures do not discover the error), and detection risk (the risk that the auditor fails to detect an error). The quality of the control systems of the entity being audited, as confirmed by the auditor's tests on the controls, will affect the assessment of control risk. Detection risk is determined by the amount of other audit work the auditor performs, taking account of the nature of the item. The auditor will also consider his/her cumulative knowledge and experience of the entity being audited when assessing risk.

Audit risk and materiality are inversely related – the higher the materiality threshold set by the auditor, the lower the audit risk. The auditor must use judgement in assessing the appropriate materiality level taking into account what the users of financial statements would view as relevant information. The higher the inherent risk and control risk, the more audit work that must be performed in order to reduce the detection risk and thus provide the level of audit risk acceptable for the assessed level of materiality. Disclosure guidelines in reporting frameworks such as IFRS may help in forming this judgement.

6.5.3: Gathering auditing material

The planning stage of the audit, including the assessment of audit risk, culminates in a detailed work programme. A work programme must aim to be efficient and time – effective due to disruptions that the client might suffer in certain key areas of the business as auditors seek to collect information regarding the business. Tests of controls are tests performed to obtain audit evidence about the design and operation of the accounting and internal control systems. Substantive tests are generally of two types:
(a) Analytical procedures, or
(b) Tests of detail of transactions and balances, for which sampling can be used.

Analytical procedures consist of the analysis of significant ratios and trends, including the resulting investigation of relationships and fluctuations that are inconsistent with other relevant information or deviate from predicted amounts. Relationships can be very stable (for example between cost of sales and sales if there is a fixed margin) and may therefore be powerful tools for the auditor.

The audit of accounting estimates can be a difficult and highly sensitive area. Management is responsible for making accounting estimates based on its judgement of the uncertain outcome of events that have occurred or are likely to occur. The auditor evaluates the reasonableness of those estimates.

6.5.4: Reporting the audit outcome

The Auditor's Report on the financial statements is often the only visible and publicly available output from the audit process. It is, however, not necessarily the only report issued by the auditors. Depending on legal requirements or the terms of the individual engagement, the auditor may issue additional reports to management, to the audit committee or to a supervisory board and to regulatory authorities.

International Standard on Auditing ISA 700 provides guidance on the form and content of the auditor's report issued in connection with the independent audit of general-purpose financial statements. The 'unqualified opinion' is when the auditor concludes that the financial statements give a true and fair view (or are 'presented fairly, in all material respects') in accordance with the identified financial reporting framework. An unqualified opinion also indicates implicitly that any material changes in accounting principles or in the method of their application, and the effects thereof, have been properly determined and disclosed in the financial statements.

An auditor can also express a qualified opinion. Following are instances of qualified opinions:

a) **Adverse opinion:** this is where the auditors state that the accounts do not give a true and fair view of the business' financial position and performance. This would mean that relying on such statements would be seriously misleading.
b) **Disagreement:** here the auditor disagrees with the treatment or disclosure of a matter in the financial statements
c) **Except for limitation of scope:** here the auditors state that they can only give a opinion for a limited scope of reports and not the others as they do not have sufficient evidence regarding the material out of this defined scope.
d) **Disclaimer of opinion:** In this case, the auditors are unable to express their opinion on such a large section of the accounts that they opt not to present any opinion.

6.5.6: Reference to the accounting framework

Financial statements must be prepared using a comprehensive basis of accounting (IFRS or other national GAAP) in order for the auditor to express a true and fair view. The auditor's opinion must refer explicitly to the basis of accounting or framework.

The date of the auditor's report normally sets the boundary for the auditor's responsibility in relation to subsequent events, such as events that provide further evidence of conditions that existed at the period-end (adjusting events under IAS 10), and significant events that occurred after the period-end date (non-adjusting events). The auditor generally performs specific steps to identify subsequent events until the date of the auditor's report. The auditor does not date the audit report earlier than the date that management approves the financial statements.

It is the auditor's responsibility to consider the process management has undertaken to assess the appropriateness of the going concern assumption as a basis for the preparation of the financial statements. Management and the auditors would normally consider the 'foreseeable future' – usually taken to be a period of not less than one year after the balance sheet date.

The general presumption is that an entity's continuance as a going concern is assumed in the absence of information to the contrary. Where there are significant uncertainties over going concern, management should adequately disclose the relevant facts in the notes to the financial statements. Even where disclosure is satisfactory, the auditor normally draws attention to the matter in an emphasis of matter paragraph in the audit report.

The financial information included in the financial statements includes at least one-year's worth of comparative information. The opinion given in the auditor's report may refer to the current year results only, which is known as the corresponding approach. However, the auditor's opinion refers to both the current and comparative years' results when the comparative approach is adopted.

Use of the comparative approach or the corresponding approach should be consistent throughout a country. The only exception expected is for entities that have a foreign stock exchange listing, where that exchange requires one approach and the convention in the entity's home country is the other approach. The use of the same approach for the domestic and foreign filings is preferable.

An audit provides a high, but not absolute, level of assurance on the financial statements being reported on. Auditors can also be engaged to provide other types of assurance services, which are distinguished from audits in the IFAC framework as shown below:

IFAC Framework for Auditing and Related Services

6.6: Other forms of financial information inspection and verification

A **'review'** is an engagement in which an auditor is asked to carry out procedures that provide a moderate level of assurance on financial information – a lower level of assurance than that provided by an audit. The procedures, consisting primarily of inquiry and analytical review, are performed to provide auditors with a reasonable basis for stating whether anything has come to their attention that causes them to believe that the financial statements do not give a true and fair view in accordance with the identified basis of accounting.

Auditors are often engaged to perform reviews of interim (for example half-yearly or quarterly) financial statements prepared under IAS 34. One of the options available under IAS 34 is to provide condensed interim financial information, rather than full interim financial statements. Condensed information, by its nature, does not provide all the information necessary to gain a full understanding of the financial position and results. It is therefore not normally possible for the auditor to report that such condensed information gives a true and fair view. The auditor instead reports that the information has been properly prepared in accordance with IAS 34.

'Agreed-upon procedures' refers to the situation in which an auditor is engaged to apply procedures that the auditor and client have agreed on financial information. The auditor's report lists the factual findings from applying these procedures, but provides no general assurance on whether the information complies with an accounting framework. Examples of this type of service are due diligence reports in the context of mergers and acquisition activity and reviews of compliance with contractual arrangements.

A **'compilation'** engagement involves the professional accountant in collecting, classifying and summarising financial information. No audit procedures are undertaken and no assurance is expressed in the report.

Revision Questions

1. Define auditing and explaining why it is important to have an audit.
2. Explain what is meant by a 'true and fair view'.
3. Why do the principles of auditing maintain that the auditor is not expected to detect all errors and frauds? Who is responsible for maintaining an accounting system that is free of errors and frauds?
4. An auditor is supposed to be independent in carrying out his audit. Discuss the eight provisions set out by the International Federation of Accountants and discuss how each maintains the independence of the auditors.
5. Explain the auditing process and discuss the importance of each of the four stages of an auditing process.
6. Explain the four possible opinions that an auditor may express in his or her report at the end of an audit process.
7. Discuss at least two other forms of financial inspection and verification that a business can undergo.
8. Why is it important that an auditor refer to the specific conceptual frameworks that he or she has used to arrive at his or her opinion?
9. Using your knowledge on 'stewardship and accountability' explain why auditors are appointed by shareholders.
10. What are the advantages of having an audit carried out?

Part 3: Nature and capital structure of Limited Companies

Chapter 7: Limited Liability Companies

Learning outcomes: At the end of this chapter, the learner should be able to describe:

7.1: Nature of Companies
7.2: Private and Public Companies
7.3: Accountability and stewardship
7.4: Regulation and supervision
7.5: Capital Structure of Companies

7.1: Introduction

A business can be owned in different ways, these types of ownership are also known as the legal structures. Legal structures define the relationship between the business and other entities within and without the business. The legal structure also defines the ownership of the business, how many people own the business and how they own it. Therefore, the legal structure is the basis by which a business is defined. There are four basic legal structures:

- Sole trader/proprietorship: a sole trader is a business that is owned by one person this does not mean that there is only person working at the business, but that there is a sole owner of the business who has a right to all the profits and also makes final decisions about the business. The sole trader is liable to all the debts incurred by the business and may even lose his personal private property if the debts exceed the value of his business. This is known as unlimited liability.
- A partnership is a business started by a minimum of two people and maximum of twenty people in the United Kingdom. These people jointly own the business, make decisions together and have a right to participate in the profits generated from their business. The partners are also exposed to unlimited liability, they share the losses and their private property may be taken to satisfy the debts incurred in the business. A partnership is governed by the Partnership Agreement, this document sets out the management structure, the proportions of profits and losses that the partners may share, who can and cannot be a partner and even who is responsible for what part of the business. Partners are jointly and severally liable for the activities of any one of the other partners carried out in the name of the business. This is known as vicarious liability, if a partner engages in illegal trade the other partners become liable if that partner is charged in court, regardless of whether they knew what he or she was up to.
- A company is a business owned by 'shareholders' through equal parts of the capital known as 'shares'. There are two types of companies: private and public companies. A company is formed when at least two people (promoters) apply to the registrar of companies to be formed into a company. Once they have been formed into a company, they are referred to as 'shareholders'. Shareholders enjoy limited liability; this means that they are only liable insofar as they have invested in the company and no more. If the company incurs debts it cannot satisfy then they will lose only

that which they have invested in the company and no more, in other words the shares they hold for the company. It is the nature of a company that it is an 'artificial person' this means that a company has its legal rights, obligations and duties like normal human beings. A company can own property and therefore even insure the property in its own name. A company can sue another person, artificial or natural and it can be similarly sued. This may seem confusing but is consistent with the principle of separate entity we saw in the previous chapter. This makes companies a very attractive legal structure as its owners are protected from the fall-out that may ensue from the business activities of the company. This provision has safeguards known in law as 'lifting the veil' where a the owners of a company construe to defraud third parties through the company then the limited liability 'veil' may be lifted and the guilty persons prosecuted.

A private company is one, which is owned by at least two people up to a maximum of fifty people. The shareholding in a private company is not open to the public and for one to be a shareholder he or she must receive the consent of the existing shareholders. The share capital is divided into shares and the more shares one owns the more of the company they own. Shareholders are compensated for risking their funds in capital through annual or biannual payments of 'dividends'.

A public company is one where the shareholding is open to the public, the shares of a public company are available in the secondary trading markets such as the stock market and anyone without restrictions can acquire these shares. The public company has at least two shareholders and no upper limit to the number of shareholders that it may have. The main aim of a company going public is to raise funds. By offering shares to the public, a company is in effect offering people to buy it and in return offer their money as capital to the company.

- Cooperatives are businesses formed when a group of people with a shared interest form an enterprise to fulfil that interest. The group runs such a business collectively and they share the profits or losses equally.

7.2: The Nature of Companies

A company is a business owned through shares. This means that the owners of the company contribute capital and share profits according to the number of shares they own. All shares have the same value; this value is the face or the par value. The par value is the amount that each share is worth at the start of the business. The par value does not change throughout the life of the business. However, the market value of the share, which is the value at which the share of a business can be sold at a point in time if it was offered to the market, keeps fluctuating. . This is the value commonly quoted as the value of the share.

A share is one of a finite number of equal portions in the capital of a company, entitling the owner to a proportion of distributed (not reinvested) profits known as dividends and to a portion of the value of the company in case of liquidation. Shares can be voting or non-voting, meaning they either do or do not carry the right to vote on who will be a member of the board of directors and corporate policy

An investor who buys shares of a company becomes an owner of the company. He or she is entitled to share in the profits or losses of the company. Such an investor is known as a shareholder. A shareholder is protected by a certain characteristic of a company that is known as a limited liability. Limited liability means that a shareholder cannot lose more than he or she invested into a company. Unlike the other legal structures where personal belongings of the owners of the business can be sold off to settle debts, a shareholder only loses the amount he or she paid to acquire the shares he or she holds.

A company is regarded as a separate artificial legal person with a separate identity from its members. All those connected to a company are connected to it through a series of contracts these include:
1. Shareholders, these are people or other legal entities that have bought shares from the company and are hence the legal owners of the artificial legal entity as stated in company documents known as Articles of Association.
2. Directors are appointed as managers or overseers of the activities of the company. They are appointed to act on behalf of the shareholders the legal owners of the company. They are therefore obliged to adhere to the contractual agreement between them and the shareholders.
3. Employees have contracts of employment with the company.

Being a legal entity gives a company rights and obligations just as a natural person enjoys. Thus, a company can sue other people, artificial or natural. Other people can sue it. A company can also own property and it has rights to that property, protected by the law. A company will enter into contracts in its own name and such contracts are binding between the company and those with whom it enters into contracts with.

Since a company is a separate person, if any of its members dies or ceases for some other reason to exist the company will continue existing. As such, a company is treated as completely separate from its owners or any other members.

The difference between legal persons and natural person is that whereas legal persons exist only where the law recognises their existence, natural persons are regarded as persons everywhere they go. The natural persons also have entitlements that a legal person does not. For example, the members can decide to wind-up companies, whereas no one is allowed to kill a natural person.

7.3 Articles of Association and Memorandums of Association:

Articles of Association refer to documents that govern the relationships within the company such as the relationships between directors, managers and directors, auditors and shareholders and so on. They are the guidelines that explain the internal organization of the company which are filed along with the memorandum of association when registering a company. They constitute the regulations for governing the rights and duties of the members of a company among themselves. Articles deal with internal matters such as general meetings, appointment of directors, issue and transfer of shares, dividends, accounts and audits.

On the other hand, a memorandum of association governs the relationship between a business and the external world. It contains the name of the business, the address of its registered office, the objects of the association and its powers. It also contains provisions requiring that the income of the association is used for the objects of the association (except on termination), and states that the liability of its members is limited or guaranteed. The memorandum includes the authorised share capital and details on the issued share capital. A public limited company has a clause stating that it is a public company.

These two documents must be delivered to the registrar of companies at the point of registration of the company as they define what the company stands for and how it is defined.

7.4: Public and Private Companies

Private companies and public companies are owned through shares. Both have a minimum of two members and the upper limit is fifty members for the private company and undefined for the public company in the UK. However, private company's membership is restricted to the private members. No one can buy shares in a company without the consent of the existing members and hence membership in a private company is restricted to members that the existing shareholders approve of.

Public companies on the other hand are owned through shares that are available to anyone to purchase. As such, the ownership of the public companies is constantly changing as shares move from one person to another. Shares of public company are traded publicly in the stock market. A company whose shares can be traded freely in the stock market is said to have its shares 'floated' or 'quoted'. Not all the public companies in the United Kingdom are quoted or listed.

Companies are subject to regulation of the laws that create them. In the United Kingdom, companies are registered by the Registrar of Companies in the Companies House and are subject to the Company's Act. Listed companies are also subject to the regulation by the Stock Market Authorities. This close regulation is aimed at protecting members of the public who might be in business with private or public companies.

Public companies are generally designated in the UK with a PLC at the end of their names. This means 'Public Limited Company', whereas private companies are designated with an

'Ltd' at the end of their names. These designations are meant to alert those doing business with the company that they are dealing with a separate legal entity and that the natural persons they are in contact with are simply representatives.

Public companies are usually huge entities with millions of pounds in capital. However, to be registered in the London Stock Exchange a company needs paid up capital of £50,000. Companies choose to become listed or quoted to raise capital from the public through additional issue of shares. Shares sold through the stock market gain market value that is dependent on the perception of the market traders of the performance of the company that has been listed. This market value could also depend on the expectations of the public for the future performance of the company.

Floating a companies shares, which refers to changing a private company to a public company, means that the ownership of the company changes and includes any member of the public who chooses to buy those shares. This vast number of owners means that they have to appoint representatives to run the company on their behalf. These appointees are known in accounting as stewards. They include the management and employees of the company. Usually the day-to-day running of the business is left to the management of the company whereas certain owners, usually elected by those with a substantial shareholding of the company's shares, are appointed as directors. Directors are overseers of the operations of the business and are often the planners of the direction that the business is to take. They make final decisions on the operations of the company. They are expected to act on behalf and in the interests of the shareholders.

In the next section, we explore the concepts of stewardship and regulation of such stewardship.

7.5: Stewardship

A steward is a person entrusted with another person's resources, financial and other matters. A steward is expected to act in the best interests of the owners of the resources. The management of a company are the stewards of that company. The shareholders appoint from among themselves a board of directors. These individuals are expected to represent the interests of the shareholders in the day-to-day running of the company. There are two types of directors: Executive directors and non-executive directors. Executive directors are involved on a full-time running of the company. Non-executive directors work on a part-time capacity and may not be directly involved with the day-to-day operations.

The board of directors must regularly, usually over a financial year, report to the shareholders on the performance of their company. This reporting takes the form of financial statements and reports showing the financial performance and position of the company. The law requires that these duties be carried out in an honest and professional manner. The information provided must be accurate and true to the best knowledge of the directors.

This is especially important due to the moral hazards that may arise in a relationship based purely on trust but also involving a vast amount of resources. The management is also protected by the limited liability clause that protects the owners and stewards of the company. However, as happened with Enron, a deliberate act or omission to defraud either the shareholders or the public can lead to the persons behind the 'veil of incorporation' being held personally liable to crimes 'committed' by the company.

The regulation of the activities of the stewards becomes even more important where members of the public are involved. This means that public companies come under more scrutiny and regulations than the private companies do.

7.6: Particular areas of Regulation

The relationship between the company owners and the management is dependent on accurate information. Misinformation may result in what is known as 'adverse selection' as in the case of Enron where the public perceived the future of Enron as USA's 7th largest company as good due to misreported shortages of energy and fraudulent reporting of the financial position and performance. Members of the public made adverse decisions due to the fraudulent reporting of Enron's financial information and due to Enron's influence on California's Energy supplies making their prospects look rosy while they were not. This led to an inflation of the share value and in turn to an adverse selection. If the public knew about Enron's activities then they would have made a different decision regarding the company's shares, which they did when the truth became available.

To safeguard shareholder value there are three areas that are regulated very closely. These are:
1. Disclosure of material information: The information that has an implication to the shareholders value at present or in the future
2. The format on which such information is to be disclosed: This means that all the financial information to be presented to shareholders is clear and understandable for all who use it. Different formats may lead to different interpretations.
3. The measurement and valuation of the information: Due to constantly changing values of assets or liabilities it is important that the method of valuation employed is clear.

7.7: Capital Structure of Companies

The capital structure of a company refers to how a company chooses to finance itself. It is important that an optimal structure be selected. A company can finance itself in different ways; these include owners' contributions also known as equity, loans, bonds, options.

The owner's contribution is known as equity, it refers to the initial contribution of shareholders. Further capital can be raised by issuing more shares to shareholders. In a public company, new shares can be floated in the stock market to provide further capital. This type of capital implies that holders of shares have a control of the company's affairs and participate in the profits after taxes. Shares of a public company can be transferred by the shareholder to another person without consent of the other shareholders. Such a transfer in a private company needs the consent of other shareholders.

Loans are another way of financing companies operations. The company initially receives an amount of money from the lender, which they pay back, usually but not always in regular instalments, to the lender. This service is generally provided at a cost, referred to as interest on the debt. A lender does not have any rights of ownership of the company. However, unlike the shareholders his/her interest is guaranteed and must be paid by the company for as long as the loan is outstanding. Dividends are however not always payable to the shareholders, sometimes the company may not be in a position to pay dividends to shareholders or it may wish to retain the profits for investment purposes.

A company can issue bonds to the market. These are essentially debts owed to the bondholders. They also earn an interest for as long as they are outstanding. While the principal of a loan is paid back to the lender in instalments over time, a bond earns an interest and at the end of the agreed period is redeemed or repaid in whole to the lender. A bond may be secured to a specific asset in the company so that in case of default the bond lender can be paid through the sale of that asset.

A debenture is a bond that is not secured to any asset. In case the company goes into liquidation then the owner of the debenture will be treated like any other creditor and will be paid from the assets. A debenture is advantageous as it leaves the assets of the company available for further borrowing.

Options are protective instruments in business that a company can use to finance fluctuations of their asset values in future. If a company takes out a loan but expects the economy to grow rapidly, pushing prices up and hence the cost of borrowing money, they can buy an option to ensure that they will pay in future the same interest as they would if there was no rise in the interest rates. An option is defined as the right to buy or sell property at an agreed price; the right is purchased and if it is not exercised by a stated date, the money is forfeited.

All companies must choose an optimal capital structure to ensure that they do not pay too much to finance their operations. An optimal capital structure would mean that the management constantly alters the structure of capital to capture changes in the capital market. For example when the interest on bonds rises the company may decide to convert its bonds into loans, by taking loans and paying off the bonds.

7.8: Share Capital

As we have already seen, the share capital is raised from the shareholders through the sale of shares. The 'authorised share capital' is the maximum number of shares that a company is allowed to issue and has paid duty on. The issued share capital on the other hand is the total number of shares that have been offered and such offer accepted by the public. They are shares that have been subscribed for and that have been fully or partially paid for by shareholders. The 'paid up' share capital refers to the shares that have been fully paid for.
When a company decides to become a public company and therefore issue shares to the public to raise funds, it has to ascertain the Authorised Share Capital available to it. It then determines how much of the authorised share capital will be issued. The issued share capital may be fully paid or partially paid.

The total amount already paid for is referred to as the 'Called-up' capital, whereas the part of the Issued share capital unpaid for is known as the 'Uncalled Capital'.

Example 7.1:

Blueberry Industries have decided to go public and have paid stamp duty of an authorised capital of 1 million shares each costing £10. It decides to issue 500,000 shares during the first issue at £10 per share, the call up £6 of this shares and the remaining amount would be paid later.

Show the effect of these transactions in a balance sheet.

Blueberry Industries

Financed by	£	£
Authorised Share Capital		10,000,000
Issued Share Capital		5,000,000
Called up		3,000,000 (£6x500,000)
Uncalled Capital		2,000,000 (£4x500,000)

For Blueberry industries, though they have issued 500,000 shares, they have only received £3,000,000 of the expected £5,000,000. This information must be clearly disclosed in the balance sheet.

7.8.1: Types of shares
There are generally two types of shares; these are ordinary shares and preferential shares.
Ordinary shares

These are the most common types of share class. Most companies, which have only one type of share, would normally just have ordinary shares. These shares convey no extraordinary privileges or restrictions.

Preference shares

Preference shares, as the name suggests, bear a preferential treatment to ordinary shares, though the shares do not confer the right to vote, dividends are paid first to the preference shareholders and then to the ordinary shareholders. Preference shares are less risky compared to ordinary shares. Though preference shareholders receive dividends before ordinary shareholders, the amount received is normally restricted and would be largely unaffected if the company made substantial profits.

Many classes of shares can be created in a company's memorandum or articles of association, so long as they are within the law they are allowable. Redeemable shares can either be ordinary or preferential shares. Redeemable shares are shares that can be bought back from the shareholders, this practice is now restricted as it reduces the capital of the contributed by the shareholders. In addition, shares can also be convertible. Convertible shares have options for the holder to transfer the shares for either a predetermined amount of cash for a number of ordinary shares.

The next chapter looks at how financial information is represented in the financial statements for interested parties.

7.8.2: Debentures and bonds

A debenture is a long-term liability that is unsecured on an asset and is offered on the credit rating of the company and its potential for future earnings. A debenture is like a loan but is secured generally on the assets of a business; therefore, no specific asset of the business is attached as the security for a debenture. A debenture receives a fixed interest amount just like a loan.

A bond, on the other hand, is a debt, which is secured on the company and may have certain obligations of disclosure of the issuer. This means that a company that issues bonds does may have to inform those who hold bonds if circumstances change significantly to affect the bond held. A bond has a fixed period of maturity and the bond issuer (the company) has to pay the holder a fixed interest amount for so long as the bond is outstanding once the bond and at the end of the maturity period the whole bond is redeemed by the company (or bought back from the bondholder).

Revision Questions

1. Name and describe three legal structures.

2. What do you understand by the concept of limited liability?

3. Name four characteristics of an artificial person, why is this principle important in the preparation of accounts for a company?

4. 'Without the limited liability clause, most big businesses that exist today would not exist' discuss this statement giving examples.

5. What are the advantages and disadvantages of being in a partnership?

6. Discuss three areas that are essential in safeguarding shareholder value and how their implementation can be effective in safeguarding such value.

7. Discuss the concept of stewardship and why it is important that safeguards be put in place to ensure that the relationship between stewards and shareholders is not abused

8. Define the following terms and show how they may be similar in application

    - Vicarious liability
    - Lifting the veil of incorporation

9. Why is it important that a company choose the right capital structure? Discuss the advantages and disadvantages of a company issuing ordinary shares, preference shares, debentures and bonds
10. What are the differences between the Articles of association and the memorandum of association?

Chapter 8: Company Accounts

At the end of this chapter, the learner should be able to describe, interpret and prepare:
1. Profit and Loss Accounts
2. Balance Sheet presentations
3. Cash flow statements

8.1: Introduction

Chapter Four in this book discusses the preparation of accounting statements. Public Companies must publish their accounts periodically. These accounts are published in a standardised manner for three reasons. Firstly, a standardised approach ensures that all companies treat similar items in the statements in the same way. For example, it is important that the assets be valued in a similar manner since their values change over time due to depreciation, appreciation, obsolescence, repairs and so on. Different companies in the absence of standardised conventions will report the values of their assets differently. This would mean that those using the statements have different reports for the same items that have undergone the same treatment.

Secondly, reports are an important tool of evaluating performance of a business within an industry, and over time. This requires that the same standards be observed by all the businesses and that they are observed consistently over time. Thirdly, certain issues in the statements must be expressly stated. These items help shareholders and third parties evaluate the performance of the stewards who have been entrusted with the day-to-day operations of the business, for example the director's remunerations and audit fees. For tax purposes, the final accounts must clearly state the profits made from the operations of the business.

Sources of disclosure standards and information include:
1. Company's Act
2. Financial Reporting standards
3. The supervisory requirements imposed by the Council of the Stock Exchange.

8.2: Profit and loss account

The profit and loss account shows the financial performance of a business in a given period. This performance is determined by comparing the income and the expenditure incurred in the realisation of the revenue. There are two formats of presenting profit and loss statements: the vertical format and the double-sided format. The double-sided format looks like the double entry where the items of income are on the right hand side and the expenses on the left hand side. The double-sided format is rarely used nowadays. The vertical format is more popular as it is easier to follow through and produce year on year comparisons for similar items.

As stated above the standards for the preparation of statements are derived from three sources.

Company's Act requires that the following three items be expressly disclosed:
- The amount of the company's profits or losses from ordinary activities before tax
- The amount of any transfers to or withdrawals from the company reserves both proposed and completed. This requirement safeguards the investments of the shareholders. Transfers or withdrawals from the company's reserves reduce the investment of the shareholders and as such they must be expressly informed
- The aggregate amounts of the dividends

The Financial Reporting Standards (FRS 3) changed significantly the way in which financial performance is reported. Its objective is to require businesses to highlight the components and concepts of financial performance to aid a wide range of users in understanding the performance achieved by the business in a financial period, and to assist the users in forming a basis for their assessment of both future results and cash flows. The standard gives guidelines on:

1. How much flexibility can be adopted in reporting financial information especially in combining items that are not material on the face of the profit and loss accounts? This guideline is adopted in deciding what is and what is not material in the profit and loss statement and can be combined with a material item.
2. The disclosure of exceptional items in the business, exceptional items refer to significant deviations in the ordinary operations of a business. These could be either positive resulting in exceptional gain or negative resulting in exceptional loss.
3. The format of the profit and loss account, states that the profit and loss account be set out in a vertical format to show the following components of financial performance:

- Results of continuing operations, which includes the results of acquisitions during an accounting period
- Results of discontinued operations
- Profits or losses on the sale or termination of an operation; costs of a fundamental reorganisation or restructuring and profits or losses on the disposal of the fixed assets
- Extraordinary items

Below is a recommended format for a profit and loss statement. Shown below is the format of the profit and loss account (this is a simplified version of that illustrated in FRS 3).

CHAPTER 8: COMPANY ACCOUNTS

Profit and loss account for the period ended: 31 Dec 2XXX	£m
Turnover:	
Continuing operations	x
Acquisitions	x
	x
Discontinued operations	x
	x
Cost of sales	x
Gross profit	x
Net operating expenses	x
Operating profit:	x
Continuing operations	x
Acquisitions	x
	x
Discontinued operations	x
	x
Profit on sale of properties in continuing operations	x
Loss on disposal of discontinued operation	x
Profit on ordinary activities before interest	x
Interest payable	x
Profit on ordinary activities before taxation	x
Tax on profit on ordinary activities	x
Profit on ordinary activities after taxation	x
Minority interests	x
Profit before extraordinary items	x
(Extraordinary items included only to show position)	x
Profit for financial year	x
Dividends	x
Retained profit for financial year	x

The statement above shows items in a profit and loss statement for presentation to shareholders and interested third parties. The standard further stipulates that the items included should be divided into two, these are, those relating to continuing activities of the business and those relating to activities of the business that have been discontinued. This differentiation ensures that those interested in the business understand and can make predictions on the performance of the business. Discontinued activities would hence mean, to the users of the accounts, that they will no longer have an effect on the future of the business. They would only consider those items included in the continuing activities column.

AN INTRODUCTION TO ACCOUNTING

The standard stipulates that the profit and loss account be set out in a layered format to show the following components of financial performance:

- Results of continuing operations (including the results of acquisitions during the relevant period)
- Results of discontinued operations
- Profits or losses on the sale or termination of an operation; costs of a fundamental reorganisation or restructuring and profits or losses on the disposal of the fixed assets
- Extraordinary items

Continuing operations	**Discontinued operations**
Normal operations	Normal operations
Profits or losses on the sale or termination of an operation; costs of a fundamental reorganisation or restructuring and profits or losses on the disposal of the fixed assets	Profits or losses on the sale or termination of an operation; costs of a fundamental reorganisation or restructuring and profits or losses on the disposal of the fixed assets
Extraordinary items – being unusual items outside ordinary activities	

A profit and loss account included in the financial report will usually have a vertical format. The vertical format has become more popular than the side-by-side presentation as it makes it easier to relate items and compare them period-to-period.

It is important to differentiate exceptional items from extraordinary items. Exceptional items are those that occur on a one-off basis in the ordinary course of the business for example the disposal of an asset. If not expressly disclosed such an item may distort the actual revenues of the business. This inclusion may give the impression that the business is doing better than it actually is. The standard requires that exceptional items be related to the actual item they affect. Categories of exceptional items include:

1. Those that are reported under the item they relate to
2. Those that are reported after profits and losses have been arrived at but before interest is deducted these are:

    - Costs of fundamental reorganisation or restructuring that will not recur
    - Profits or losses on sale or termination of an asset or operation respectively

Extraordinary items are "material items possessing a high degree of abnormality which arise from events or transactions that fall outside the ordinary activities of the reporting entity and which are not expected to occur". The standard does not give examples of extraordinary items but has extended the definition of ordinary activities to include virtually anything that an entity might undertake, thus effectively ruling out the use of extraordinary items.

The statement above only shows the basic entries of a profit and loss account. This statement is what would be required for disclosure by the Company's Act. However, the information on the profit and loss statement is also used by the shareholders and other interested parties to evaluate the performance of the business. This means that there is need for more information. The flexibility to include more information is contained in the FRS 3 Stipulations. These would result in a more detailed profit and loss account as shown below:

Item	Value £: Year 1	Value £: Year 2
Turnover	xxxx	Xxxx
Cost of Sales	Xxxx	Xxxx
Gross Profits or Loss	Xxxx	Xxxx
Distribution Costs	Xxxx	Xxxx
Administrative expenses	Xxxx	Xxxx
Other operating income	Xxxx	Xxxx
Income from shares in group undertakings	Xxxx	Xxxx
Income from participating interests	Xxxx	Xxxx
Income from other fixed asset investments	Xxxx	Xxxx
Other interest receivable and similar income	Xxxx	Xxxx
Amounts written off investments	Xxxx	Xxxx
Interest payable and similar charges	Xxxx	Xxxx
Profit or loss on ordinary activities before taxation	Xxxx	Xxxx
Tax on profit on ordinary activities		
Minority interests that are included only in group accounts	Xxxx	Xxxx
Extraordinary income	Xxxx	Xxxx
Extraordinary charges	Xxxx	Xxxx
Extraordinary profit or loss	Xxxx	Xxxx
Tax on extraordinary profits or losses	Xxxx	Xxxx
Tax on extraordinary profits or losses in minority interests	Xxxx	Xxxx
Other taxes not shown under the above items	Xxxx	Xxxx

Following is an item-by-item description for the profit and loss statement shown above:

8.2.1: Turnover refers to the total income from the ordinary activities of the business. These are reported for continuing operations, discontinued operations and for operations acquired during the period in question. These must be expressly distinguished in the profit and loss account.

Turnover may also be reported according to its geographical origin. If revenue is generated from two different regions then it can be reported separately as deriving from those different regions. The same treatment applies to revenues that are generated from business activities that are significantly different from other business activities. This treatment is known as segmental reporting: For example, ABC is a car-manufacturing company that also produces hi-tech household appliances. It has a worldwide market for its products. The diagram below shows what a segmental reporting of its activities would look like:

Region/product	Car-manufacture £s '000	Household appliances £s '000	Banking institution £s '000	Budget airlines £s '000
Africa	35,000	1,000	0	0
Americas	965,000	56,000	120,000	700,000
Europe	103,000	9,000	5,000	0
Asia	112,000	25,000	450,000	0
Total turnover	1,215,000	91,000	575,000	700,000

The above table shows the revenues from different countries and from different activities. This type of reporting is useful as it allows users to assess the performance of each segment, its risk and its future prospects.

8.2.2: Cost of Sales is expenses that relate directly to the acquisition, manufacturing or processing of the final product that is sold by the business. It includes:

1. The opening stock for the business
2. The work in progress at the time of preparation of the profit and loss statement
3. Direct material purchased for the production of the final product
4. Other charges related with the direct production
5. Fixed and variable production overheads
6. Depreciation of productive assets
7. Research and development costs

Apart from the above expenses, all the other expenses that can be related directly to the production of the final product are also regarded as costs of sales.

8.2.3: Distribution costs refer to the costs incurred in the movement and storage of the goods for sale. It also refers to the promotion, advertising and selling costs of those goods and services.

Other costs referred to as distribution costs are costs incurred in transferring goods to customers. Costs related to the salaries, wages and bonuses for the sales personnel and the costs of operating sales outlets. Sales discounts are also put down as distribution costs.

8.2.4: Administrative Costs include salaries and wages of administrative staff and other wage related expenses for example pensions and social security contributions.

Costs related to office and other administrative buildings, these include repayment on loans or mortgages, depreciation, professional fees incurred in the general activities of the business and so on.

Administrative costs also include fees paid to business professionals for any services provided for example auditing, business consultancy or any other services provided by professionals contracted in to perform those services but who are not in the employ of the business.

Amounts written off as bad debts are also included in the administrative costs

8.2.5: Directors fees and emoluments must be reported separately. This enables the shareholders to review the performance of the management as the stewards of the business. This information also ensures that the management is not overcompensating themselves using the resources of the business.

8.2.6: Research and development costs these expenses must also be revealed to the shareholders due to their highly speculative nature. Research and development in most businesses is very expensive and may not always succeed even after expending many resources on it. This item is hence expressly revealed to the users of the accounts.

8.2.7: Other operating expenses are also expressly stated if they are significant. In this case the convention of materiality is applied. Significant values in different businesses could vary as widely as the as their revenues vary.

8.2.8: Income from shares within the group of companies is also expressly revealed. Where one company is seen to have control over the activities of another company then a group relationship is said to exist. A group is made up of a parent company and a subsidiary or subsidiaries. A company that owns more than 50% of another company is expected to have a controlling influence and regarded as a parent company. In preparing financial reports hence, the results of the subsidiary are included in the parent company's accounts and the two treated as one entity.

8.2.9: Other investments are also expressly reported to the users of the accounts they include:

1. Where the company has a participating interest, this means that the company exercises some control over the day-to-day activities of another company. However, it does not own over 50% of that other company.
2. Joint ventures with other business or otherwise entities are also expressly revealed in the profit and loss account
3. If the company owns 20% or more of another company then an associate's relationship is created. An associate's relationship is one in which a company owns less then 50% of another company but still has a significant influence over the other company.

4. Interests from other investments for example bonds or loans to other entities
5. Dividends earned from listed companies

8.2.10: Interests payable and similar charges are also stated expressly. They include any interest payable for money that has been borrowed say from banks or other places. It could also be interest related to leasing agreements or other recognisable obligations for example interests payable on leased assets. Commitment and procurement fees for loans are also seen as interest charges. These are fees payable to those arranging a certain form of financing for example lawyers.

The amortisation of discounts or premium on bills, debentures and so on are also classed as interest payments. Amortisation of these items refers to the spreading over a period of time expenses incurred in the issuing of instruments such as debentures. Debentures are issued at a discount; this discount is an expense to the company. A debenture is a long-term obligation and charges relating to its acquisition for example the discount on issue should be spread through the life of the debenture. This is done through the amortisation of the charges over the lifetime of the debenture. This amortisation must be expressly revealed.

8.2.11: Profit and loss on ordinary activities is expressly required by the company's act. The profit or loss reported is the balance of all the items mentioned above. Exceptional items under the items mentioned so far are included along with the items in particular. For example if there was an exceptional item within the administrative costs item then that item is reported with the administrative costs but expressly stated.

8.2.12: Taxation is also revealed as per the provisions of the Company's Act 1985 (as amended). These provisions include:

- Tax on profits or loss on ordinary activities
- Tax on extraordinary profits and losses
- Other taxes not shown under the above two categories

8.2.13: Minority interests refer to other shareholders of a partially owned company who represent the lesser amount of shares. These are called minority interests. For example if company A owns 86% of a company B and 14% will be referred to as minority interests. Since companies are required to report 100% on the companies in which they are majority shareholders. Then they must also show how the operations of the company affected the minority shareholders. The profit and loss results of the minority interests are shown separately after the consolidated group accounts.

8.2.14: Dividends are also stated expressly as required by the Company's Act 1985 (as amended). It requires that the aggregate amounts paid and proposed be shown in the reported profit and loss account.

CHAPTER 8: COMPANY ACCOUNTS

8.2.15: Other information that is required includes:

- **Employees Information:** this information includes the total average number of employees for the year and related costs. These costs are broken into salaries and wages, pensions and social security contributions
- **Comparative information:** this is information relating to the previous 2 or 3 years. Items in these years are also divided into continuing and discontinued activities. It also shows acquisitions in those years, which if retained, are continuing operations. All exceptional items are included under the items they relate to, except the sale of an asset at a profit or loss, or the costs of substantial restructuring or reorganisation of the entity.
- **Earnings per share:** for companies that are traded publicly the company financial reports must show on the face of the profit and loss account. Earnings per share, is defined as the portion of a company's profit allocated to each outstanding share of common stock. Calculated as:

$$= \frac{\text{Net Income} - \text{Dividends on Preferred Stock}}{\text{Average Outstanding Shares}}$$

Earnings per share are related to the profits attributable to the shareholders contribution. By subtracting the dividends payable to preferred stock for example we are left with the amounts to which the shareholders are entitled to. Shareholders are the owners of the company; the EPS shows how much of the returns are related to the shareholders investment per share.

Example 8.1:

Patrick Group, a multi-national company prepares two sets of accounts, one for internal use and one for external use. The following trading profit and loss account was prepared for internal use. Prepare a statement for external purposes.

Patrick Industries Trading Profit and Loss Account for the period ended 31/12/2xx1

		£	£	£
Turnover				123,500
Less: Cost of Sales				
Opening Stock			14,700	
Purchases			69,000	
Closing Stock			-21,000	-62,700
				60,800
Less: Distribution Costs				
Salaries and Wages			28,800	
Motor distribution costs				
Fuel and maintenance		9,800		
Depreciation of Motors		2,200		
Depreciation of Machinery		1,600	13,600	
Sundry distribution expenses			4,500	
Less: Administrative Expenses				
Salaries and wages			15,500	
Motor Administration expenses				
Fuel and maintenance		2,100		
Depreciation		1,000		
Depreciation administrative equip		1,200	4,300	-66,700
				-5,900
Other Operating incomes				2,000
Income from participating interests			10,000	
Income from participating interests			2,300	
Income from other fixed asset investments			5,400	
Other interest receivable and similar income			2,000	19,700
Amounts written off investments			1,500	
Interest payable and similar charges				
Loans payable in 5 years			3,000	-4,500
Profits on ordinary activities before taxation				11,300
Tax on profit on ordinary activity				-930
Profits on ordinary activities after taxation				10,370
Retained profits brought forward				64,300
Transfer to the general reserve				74,670
Proposed ordinary dividends				-30,000
Retained profits for the year				44,670

Using the information provided in the statement above we can produce a statement intended for external stakeholders. You will notice that each entry has a number assigned to it. These numbers show that further explanation is available for each of these items. Instead of including all the details about the distribution costs, the statement shows the final figure, if any of the stakeholders using the statement needs more information then they can read about it in the notes that have been made regarding that item.

Patrick Industries

Statement of Trading, Profit and Loss Account for period ending 31/12/2xx1

		£	£
1	Turnover	123,500	
2	Cost of Sales	-62,700	
3	Gross Profit	60,800	
4	Distribution Costs	-46,900	
5	Administration Costs	-19,800	
6	Other Operating incomes	2,000	
7	Income from participating interests	10,000	
8	Income from participating interests	2,300	
9	Income from other fixed asset investments	5,400	
10	Other interest receivable and similar income	2,000	
		15800	
11	Amounts written off investments	-1,500	
		14300	
		14300	
12	Interest payable and similar charges	-3,000	
13	Profits on ordinary activities before taxation	11300	
14	Tax on profit on ordinary activity	-930	
15	Profits on ordinary activities after taxation	10370	
16	Retained profits brought forward	64300	
17	Transfer to the general reserve	74670	
18	Proposed ordinary dividends	-30000	
19	Retained profits for the year	44670	

The statement above is derived from the one that had been prepared for internal use, note that the two statements are similar, this is because accountants are aware that after producing the internal document then an external document will have to be produced. Making the two statements very differently would result in unnecessary duplicate work.

The columnar entries make it possible for values of different years to be compared. In this case, the year 2xx0 figures could have been entered in the second column this would have made it possible for each item to be compared with an equivalent item in the previous year.

Example 8.2:

The following transactions were derived from Robert's Haulers for the period ending on the 31/12/2xx8.

AN INTRODUCTION TO ACCOUNTING

Particulars of Robert Haulers for the period ending 31/12/2xx8

Particulars	£
Opening Stock	345,000
Purchase	650,500
Sales	1,630,700
Capital Account	3,495,000
Accounts receivable	135,000
Accounts payable	231,000
Rent and rates: Administration	67,800
Salaries and wages: Distribution	179,500
Salaries and wages: Administration	115,000
Depreciation: Distribution	120,000
Delivery Vans and Trucks accounts	1,200,000
Depreciation: Administration	54,000
Retained profits 01/01/2xx8	34,700
Furniture and Fittings	15,400
Computer and RFID tracking system	78,900
RFID research expenses	54,000
Other Administration Expenses	37,500
Other distribution expenses	98,500
Income from participating interests	23,400
Interest on bank deposits	11,000

Notes:
1. The closing stock for the period was £243,600
2. The tax liability for ordinary activities profits was £69,650
3. Directors fees were included in the Administration's Salaries and wages and stood at £50,000
4. Auditors who audited the year's accounts were not paid by the end of the period the cost was £7,800

Use this information to create a trading, profit and loss account for the management of business and then enter this information in a statement meant for external use.

A Trading, Profit and Loss account prepared for internal use is detailed as various departments within the organisation, refer to it to see the relationship between costs and output. For example, in calculating the gross profits generated in the period, we show how the cost of goods sold have been arrived at. This is because the 'Stocks and purchasing' department may wish to know how efficient they are in ordering the necessary stock and that the levels that remain at the end of a trading period are optimal. Compare the internal statement shown here and the accounts prepared for publication for the same company. Note the differences.

Robert Haulers
Trading. Profit and Loss Account for the period ended 31/12/2xx8 for internal use

Turnover:			1,630,700
Less: Cost of Sales			
Opening Stock	345,000		
Purchases	650,500		
Closing Stock	-243,600		-751,900
Gross Profits			878,800
Operating Expenses			
Rent and rates	67,800		
Salaries and Wages	244,500		
Directors' fees	50,000		
Depreciation	174,000		
RFID research exp	54,000		
Auditors	7,800		
Other Admin exp.	37,500		
Other Distrib. exp	98,500		-734,100
			144,700
Other incomes			
Income from participatin interests		23,400	
Interest on bank deposits		11,000	34,400
Profits on ordinary activities before tax			179,100
Tax on profits on ordinary activities			-69,650
Profits after tax on ordinary activties			109,450
Retained profits brought forward			34,700
Retained profits 31/12/2xx8			144,150

You will notice in the published accounts the research expenses, auditors' remuneration and director's fees are explicitly stated. These three items are very sensitive; the research expenses should be stated because research is highly speculative, as much as a breakthrough in research can lead to astronomical profits, most researches turn out to be a waste of money. Since such money belongs to the shareholders then they must be made aware of any research that is being done using their money.

Auditors are contracted by shareholders to inspect the books of accounts of a business and report to the shareholders truthfully and fairly. For this service the auditors must be paid a fair amount of money, too much money may lead to the auditor's independence being compromised and on the other hand poor pay may lead to shoddy work.

Lastly, the directors, who are entrusted with resources by the shareholders, must not be seen to allocate themselves huge parts of those resources in remunerating themselves. Therefore, this figure must also be expressly stated in the accounts.

Published Statements of Trading, Profits and Loss for Robert's Haulers for the period ended 31/12/2xx8

		£
Turnover		1,630,700
Less: Costs of Sale		-751,900
Gross Profits		878,800
Administration costs	224,300	
Distribution costs	398,000	-622,300
RFID research expenses	54,000	
Auditors remuneration	7,800	
Directors' Fees	50,000	-111,800
Income from participating int.	23,400	
Income from bank deposits	11,000	34,400
Profits on ordinary activities before taxes		179,100
Tax on profits on ordinary activities		-69,650
Profits on ordinary activities after taxes		109,450
Retained profits brought forward		34,700
Retained profits 31/12/2xx8		144,150

8.3: Balance Sheet

A balance sheet is a statement showing the performance of a business as at a given date. It shows the total value of the business. By comparing a previous period balance sheet with a current balance sheet, investors can tell whether the net worth of their company has increased.

It also shows the ratio of equity, the amount that has been contributed by the shareholders of the business less the obligations of the company, and the debt. The debt-equity ratio is a measure of a how much the company has borrowed to finance its growth also known as Capital leverage. It is calculated by dividing long-term debt by shareholders equity. It indicates what proportion of equity and debt the company is using to finance its assets.

$$\frac{\text{Total Liabilities}}{\text{Shareholders Equity}}$$

A higher debt/equity ratio generally means that a company has financed most of its growth with debt. This means that users of the accounts should anticipate increased interests and erratic growth as this debt is repaid.

On the balance sheet, assets and equities are listed under classifications according to their general characteristics. It is a relatively simple matter to make a comparison of one classification with another or to make comparisons within a classification because similar assets or similar equities are listed together.

Assets usually represent what the capital has been used to buy as well as the liabilities that have arisen in the acquisition of those assets. Balance sheets start from the top with assets. Assets less liabilities equal capital. This is the accounting equation represented by the balance sheet, the balance sheet is supposed to 'balance' this means that assets less liabilities will always be equal to the capital that has been invested in the business. A balance sheet also shows how the investment has been distributed between various assets and liabilities.

The order of items on the balance sheet is prescribed by the Company's Act (1985) and must be adhered to, generally there are two formats the vertical format and the T-format. Once a company chooses the format to adopt, then it has to be consistent over the years and any change of format must be justified. There are headings that must be shown and in the prescribed manner, however items within those headings may enjoy more flexibility. Below is a sample Balance Sheet:

XYZ Limited: Balance Sheet as at 31 Dec 2xxx

Called-up share capital not paid
FIXED ASSETS
- Intangible Assets
- Tangible Assets
- Investments

CURRENT ASSETS
- Stock
- Debtors
- Investments
- Cash at hand and in bank

Prepayments and accrued income
Creditors for amounts due within the year
Net Current assets or liabilities
Total assets less current liabilities
Creditors: amounts falling due after/ over one year
Provisions for liabilities and charges
Accruals and deferred incomes
CAPITAL AND RESERVES:
- Called up share capital
- Share premium account revaluation reserves
- Other reserves
- Profit and Loss accounts

Minority Interests

The following is an item-by-item description of the components of the balance sheet above:

8.3.1: Called-up share capital not paid refers to the share capital that has been issued and now the company requires that it be paid for. These shares represent capital owed to the company; they are therefore regarded as assets.

8.3.2: Fixed assets are those assets that are not to be converted into cash in the present fiscal period. Assets are generally defined as items of economic value that can be used to produce further wealth. A fiscal period is conventionally one year. The classification of assets into either fixed assets or current assets is dependent on the operating cycle. This is the length of time it would take money to be converted into an asset and back into money. Fixed assets are generally regarded to be those assets that are not likely to be converted into money within one operating cycle. Current assets on the other hand are conventionally converted from cash to assets and back into cash within the operating cycle.

Fixed assets for the purposes of financial reports include:

- Intangible assets, which lack a physical substance, are used to produce revenue. For example, brand names, patents, licences, goodwill, copyrights and trademarks.
- Tangible assets refer to assets that have a physical substance used for production of wealth. They include land, buildings, motor vehicles, computer systems and so on
- Investments refer to property or other possessions acquired for a future financial gain or benefit. An investment in the balance sheet represents money used by the business to increase wealth through investing in another business or another area other than that in which it ordinarily does business.

8.3.3: Current Assets

Current assets include cash and other assets that in the normal course of events are converted into cash within the operating cycle. For example, a manufacturing enterprise will use cash to acquire inventories of materials. These inventories of materials are converted into finished products and then sold to customers. Cash is collected from the customers. Current assets are usually listed in the order of their liquidity; frequently consist of cash, temporary investments, accounts receivable, inventories and prepaid expenses. Inventories refer to at the end of the trading period, work in progress, finished goods or goods acquired for resale. Current assets are discussed in detail in the following section

- **Cash**

Cash is simply the money on hand and/or on deposit that is available for general business purposes. It is always listed first on a balance sheet. Cash held for some designated purpose, such as the cash held in a fund for eventual retirement of a bond issue, is excluded from current assets. Therefore the cash asset recorded in a balance sheet is one, which refers to money held generally in the business to meet unspecified business needs.

- **Marketable Securities**

These investments are temporary and are made from excess funds that are not needed immediately to conduct operations. Until these funds are needed, they are invested to earn a return. These investments in securities can be converted into cash easily; usually short-term government obligations, company bonds or company shares in the stock market. These are obviously less available for the needs of a business than cash and some time may be needed before they are converted into cash for the business.

- **Accounts Receivable or debtors**

Accounts receivable are the amounts owed to the business and are evidenced on the balance sheet by promissory notes. Accounts receivable are the amounts billed to customers and owed to the business on the balance sheet's date. All other accounts receivable should be labelled appropriately and show them apart from the accounts receivable arising in the course of trade. If these other amounts are currently collectible, they may be classified as current assets.

- **Inventories**

Inventories are goods that are available for sale, products that are in a partial stage of completion, and the materials that the business will use to create products. The costs of purchasing merchandise and materials and the costs of manufacturing various product lines are accumulated in the accounting records and are identified with either the cost of the goods sold during the fiscal period or as the cost of the inventories remaining at the end of the period.

- **Prepaid expenses**

These expenses are payments made for services that will be received in the near future. Strictly speaking, prepaid expenses will not be converted to current assets in order to avoid penalising companies that choose to pay current operating costs in advance rather than to hold cash. Often your insurance premiums or rentals are paid in advance.

8.3.4 Current Liabilities

On the equity side of the balance sheet, as on the asset side, a distinction between current and long-term items is also made. Current liabilities are obligations that will be discharged within the normal operating cycle of the business. In most circumstances, current liabilities will be paid within the next year by using the assets classified as current. The amount owed under current liabilities often arises because of acquiring current assets such as inventory or services that will be used in current operations. These are shown as the amounts owed to trade creditors that arise from the purchase of materials or merchandise as accounts payable. If the business is obliged under promissory notes that support bank loans or other amounts owed, the liability is shown as notes payable. Other current liabilities may include the estimated amount payable for income taxes and the various amounts owed for wages and salaries of employees, utility bills, payroll taxes, local property taxes and other services.

8.3.5: Long-Term Liabilities

Debts that are not due until more than a year from the balance sheet date are generally classified as long-term liabilities. Notes, bonds and mortgages are often listed under this heading. If a portion of the long-term debt is due within the next year, it should be removed from the long-term debt classification and shown under current liabilities.

8.3.6: Deferred Revenues

Customers may make advance payments for merchandise or services. The obligation to the customer will be settled, as a rule, by delivery of the products or services and not by cash payment. Advance collections received from customers are classified as deferred revenues, pending delivery of the products or services. That means that the business owes the person who paid for goods in advance the amount paid for goods that he or she anticipates will be delivered in the future

8.3.7: Owner's Equity

The owner's equity must be subdivided on the balance sheet: One portion represents the amount invested directly by shareholders, plus any portion of retained earnings converted into paid-in capital. The other portion represents the net earnings that are retained. This rigid distinction is necessary because of the nature of any company. Ordinarily, shareholders, or owners, are not personally liable for the debts contracted by a company. A shareholder may lose his investment, but creditors usually cannot look to his personal assets for satisfaction of their claims. Under normal circumstances, the shareholders may withdraw as cash dividends an amount measured by the company earnings. The distinction in this rule gives the creditors some assurance that a certain portion of the assets equivalent to the owner's investment cannot be arbitrarily withdrawn. Of course, this portion could be depleted from your balance sheet because of operating losses. The owner's equity in an unincorporated business is shown more simply. The interest of each owner is given in total, usually with no distinction being made between the portion invested and the accumulated net earnings. The creditors are not concerned about the amount invested. If necessary, creditors can attach the personal assets of the owners.

To safeguard the interests of creditors the shareholders equity cannot be withdrawn as dividends or for any other purpose.

CHAPTER 8: COMPANY ACCOUNTS

Valuing at Cost

Cost is conventionally used as the basis for valuing assets. Assets, when acquired under normal circumstances, are recorded at the price negotiated between two independent parties dealing at arm's length. Simply stated, the cost of an asset to the purchaser is the price that he or she must pay now or later in order to obtain it. The fair value of the asset is not relevant in recording the transaction on your balance sheet. A purchaser may acquire an asset at a cost that is greater or less than the fair value determined in the marketplace. If the asset is acquired, the purchaser accounts for the assets at his cost, value notwithstanding. A simple formula to remember in determining cost is Assets = Liability + Equity or Equity = Assets – Liability. For example, if you bought a car worth £20,000 at £10,000 then the value to appear in your balance in relation to the car would be £10,000 even if the car were clearly worth more.

Example 8.3:

Study the following list of balances extracted from Mark Merchandisers.

Mark Merchandisers Company Limited balances as at 31/10/2xx9

		£	£
Capital Accounts			
	Ordinary Share Capital @£5 per share		1,350,000
	Called up share capital not paid	500,000	
	Preference Share account		640,000
Share premium revaluation reserves			56,000
Reserve Account			950,000
Profit and Loss Account			740,000
Patents and Trademarks		158,400	
Land and buildings at cost		1,180,000	
Vehicles at cost		480,000	
Factory Machinery		840,000	
Depreciation provisions	Vehicles		168,000
	Factory machinery		84,000
Closing stock:	Work in Progress	150,000	
	Goods for resale	160,000	
	Complete goods	240,500	
Accounts receivable	Trade debtors	108,000	
Investments		85,000	
Shares in businesses where the company has a participating interest		289,000	
Prepayments and other accrued incomes		36,000	
Provision for doubtful debts			32,600
Bank Overdraft			49,000
Accounts payable	Trade creditors		145,000
	Accrued expenses		12,300
		4226900	4226900

Using the information provided above produce a publishable balance sheet for Mark Merchandiser's Company Limited as at 31/10/2xx9

Published Statements of Accounts for Mark Merchandisers
Balance Sheet as at 31/10/2xx9

	£	£	£
Called up share capital not paid			500,000
Fixed Assets			
Intangible Assets Patents and Trademarks	158,400		
Tangible Assets Land and Buildings	1,180,000		
Vehicles	312,000		
Factory Machinery	756,000	2,406,400	
Shares in businesses where the company has a participating interest		289,000	
General investments		85,000	
Current Assets			
Stock Work in progress	150,000		
Goods for resale	160,000		
Complete Goods	240,500		
Accounts receivable			
Trade Debtors	108,000		
Prepayments and accrued incomes	36,000	694,500	
Current Liabilities			
Provision for doubtful debts	32,600		
Bank overdraft	49,000		
Accounts payable			
Trade creditors	145,000		
Accrued Expenses	12,300	-238,900	3,236,000
Total Assets less current liabilities			3,736,000
Capital and Reserves			
Capital			
Ordinary Share capital @£5 per share		1,350,000	
Preference share capital		640,000	
Share premium revaluation account		56,000	
Reserve Accounts		950,000	
Profit and Loss Account		740,000	3,736,000
			3,736,000

Publishable statements of account generally follow the structure outlined above; however, they vary in complexity depending on activities of the business that is preparing the statements. The conventional structures adopted are aimed at ensuring that even shareholders with limited knowledge in accounting can make sense of the accounts prepared by different businesses. It also enables stakeholders to compare statements from different companies.

Notes to the statements may be added to further explain the items included in the financial statement. This allows for flexibility in reporting and how much can be included in the reports. Extraordinary items must be reported as such and further explained with notes.

CHAPTER 8: COMPANY ACCOUNTS

Extraordinary items could be items not within the normal operational activities of the company and must therefore be expressly communicated to the stakeholders.

Note that the reserve accounts and the profit and loss account reserves are not company assets, they are monies owed to the shareholders and are not available to pay for expenses and therefore appear on the same side with the capital of the company.

8.4: Cash flow Statements

Cash flow statements are used to assess the ability of a business to generate cash and use the cash generated to meet obligations as they arise. All businesses are required to provide a cash flow statement regardless of their size and the industry they operate in. No exemptions are made for subsidiaries whose parents have also published a cash flow statement

Only the cash flows of transactions are reported in the cash flow statement. Adjustment is required for a transaction for which income and expenses are recognized in one period but cash flows occur in another. A cash flow statement is useful in predicting the cash needs that will arise during a given operating year.

8.4.1: Cash flow Classifications:

1. **Operating cash flows**, which refer to cash flows relating to the normal activities of a business in the relevant accounting period. These are all other cash flows other than the investing or financing cash flows. These can be arrived at either directly or indirectly by removing the non–cash items from the income and expenditure statement. Interest paid is often classified as an operating activity, even though it arises on a financing balance. It is argued that interest costs must be covered by operations and is included in determination of net income/expense, and should therefore be classified as an operating cash flow.

2. **Investing cash flow** refers to investing activities that include cash payments to acquire property, plant and equipment and other long-term assets. Investing activities also include cash payments and cash receipts relating to acquisition and disposal of debt and equity interests in other businesses and interests in joint ventures (except for those relating to dealing or trading activity) Loans or advances made to other parties are classified as investing activities.

3. **Financing Cash flows** are all those cash related flows relating to obtaining, servicing and redeeming sources of finance. Those sources can include loans, debentures and share capital. This includes dividends paid by the business to its shareholders.

Different businesses can classify cash flow information differently. For example, a financial institution carries out in its ordinary course of business will be classified as operating activities, even though for other entities the same activity would likely be classified as investing or financing.

Loans and advances a financial institution makes should be classified as operating, as should the interest paid and received on those balances. Likewise, dividends received should be classified as operating cash flows.

8.4.2: Classification of tax cash flows

Tax cash flows are normally classified as operating cash flows. However, where specific cash flows can be identified with either investing activities or financing activities, then it is appropriate to classify that element of the tax cash flows as investing or financing respectively where the tax cash flows are included in investing or financing categories, disclosure of the total tax cash flows should also be given.

8.4.3: Foreign currency cash flows

Foreign currency cash flows should be translated into the reporting currency at the rate of exchange on the date of the transaction. This translation should be consistent with the translation of the transaction in the income statement.

A foreign subsidiary's cash flows should also be translated at the exchange rates relevant to the underlying transactions however; a rate that approximates to the actual rate, for example a weighted average rate may be used.

The period-end rate cannot be used to translate foreign currency cash flows. However, residual balances arising because of a foreign currency transaction will be included in the balance sheet at the period-end rate. Consequently, a reconciling difference will arise between the changes in cash, cash equivalents reported in the cash flow statement, and the equivalent amounts obtained from the balance sheet. This reconciling difference is not a cash flow but is reported separately in the cash flow statement.

8.4.5: Treatment of overdrafts

A bank overdraft may be used as part of a business' day-to-day cash management tools rather than as financing arrangements. Normally, such overdraft accounts will regularly fluctuate between a positive and a negative balance. The overdraft balance should be included in the balance of cash and cash equivalents where overdrafts are used for such cash management purposes. In all other circumstances, an overdraft balance is treated as part of the business' financing.

8.4.6: Classification of short-term investments

Investments with an original maturity of less than three months should not be considered a cash equivalent if there is any doubt that the obligated entity will fully redeem the security at maturity.

8.4.7: Acquisitions and disposals

The cash flows in respect of each major acquisition or disposal should be separately disclosed and classified as an investing cash flow. The amount reported is net of any cash included in the business or asset acquired or disposed of.

The amount of cash in the businesses or assets acquired or disposed of should be disclosed in the notes. This can be given in aggregate. The amount paid for or received should also be disclosed in the notes.
Subsidiaries' cash flows are consolidated into the cash flow statement from the date of acquisition. The cash flows of other investments accounted for using the equity method or the cost-dividend method are recognized as dividend income.

8.4.8: Discontinuing operations

The net cash flows relating to discontinuing operations should be disclosed, generally in a note. The cash flows should be classified between operating, investing and financing.

8.4.9: Barter and other non-cash transactions

The cash flow statement should not include transactions that do not include the transfer of cash. The same applies to the non-cash element of consideration, for example, in a barter transaction.

However, relevant information concerning non-cash transactions should be disclosed in the notes. The information should be classified between operating, investing and financing transactions.

8.4.10: Extraordinary items

Items that qualify as extraordinary should continue to be classified as either, operating, investing or financing according to the nature of the transaction However, separate disclosure of the extraordinary item's cash flows should be made on the face of the cash flow statement.

AN INTRODUCTION TO ACCOUNTING

8.4.11: Segmental analysis

Businesses are encouraged, but not required, to give a summary analysis of cash flows by segment. This would be at the level of operating, investing and financing cash flows. Segmental analysis is also relevant to the profit and loss account discussed earlier.

8.4.12: Preparing Cash flow statements

The statement below shows how to prepare a cash flow statement indirectly. This is where the non-cash flow items are subtracted from the net income to reveal the cash flow items.

As already discussed, the statement has three headings these are, operating activities, investing cash flow and financing cash flow.

Statement of Cash Flows XYZ Ltd for the period ended 31 Dec 2xx0
Items
Cash Flows from Operating Activities
Net Income
Adjustments
Depreciation Expense
Amortization Expense
Gain on Sale of Equipment
Increase in Accounts Receivable
Decrease in Unearned Rent Revenue
Decrease in Inventories
Increase in Accounts Payable
Increase in Prepaid Expenses
Increase in Income Taxes Payable
Net Cash Provided by Operating Activities
Cash Flows from Investing Activities
Purchase of Securities
Sale of Equipment
Purchase of property, plant and equipment
Net Cash Used in Investing Activities
Cash Flows from Financing Activities
Borrowings from Banks

Issuance of Common Stock
Payment of Cash Dividends
Net Cash Used in Financing Activities
Net Increase/Decrease in Cash and Cash Equivalents
Cash and Cash Equivalents, January 1, 2xx1
Cash and Cash Equivalents, December 31, 2xx0

Depreciation and amortisation expenses are notional rather than real cash flows. Depreciation and amortization are considered as expenses and are listed in an income statement under expenses. They represent the gradual wear and tear of assets. They however are not cash flows.

Gains on the sale of equipment or other assets are cash inflow; however, it is not included in the income account. In this case, the gain is added to the net income. However, a loss in the sale of equipment is not subtracted from the net income, as it is not a cash flow. The loss on the disposal of an asset is calculated by removing the value arrived at through depreciation from the price at which the plants, property or equipment was sold, it does not involve money flowing out of the business.

Other adjustments in the net income to arrive at the cash inflow for the period being considered include prepaid expenses, which are added back to the net income as they relate to a future period. Accounts receivable are not removed from the net income as they represent goods sold to customers on credit and hence no cash inflow has been realized.

Unearned rent revenue is also an anticipated income for the period to which the cash flow statement refers, which has not been received as cash. Taxes payable are also added back to the net income as there might have been a provision for them in the income statement but they have not been paid for yet, hence there has been no cash outflow.

As already discussed the cash flow statement can be prepared in two ways; it can be prepared from a record of cash transactions that occur in a given period (refer to example 4.7) or it can be prepared from existing balance sheet and profit & loss statements as has been discussed in this section.

Example 8.4

The following information was collected from Francesca Company Limited books of accounts for the period ended 30/04/2xx4.

Francesca's Transactions

	£
Gross profits	45,600
Operating Expenses	19,000
Depreciation: Motor Vehicles	6,700
Plant and machinery	12,000
Furniture and Fittings	4,800

The following balance sheets were also extracted from her books of accounts

- During the period, the company purchased machinery worth £15,000 and used £13,500 to invest in securities in an upstart business.
- The balance sheets presented below shows the performance of the business for the years 2xx4 and 2xx5

CHAPTER 8: COMPANY ACCOUNTS

Francesca Company Limited Balance sheet for the as at 31/12/2xx5 and 31/12/2xx4

	31/12/2xx5 £	31/12/2xx4 £
Fixed Assets		
Plant and Machinery	35,500	32,500
Vehicles	38,300	45,000
Furniture and Fittings	9,900	14,700
Current Assets		
Trade Debtors	6,800	4,800
Stock	10,000	11,600
Investments	13,500	
Cash in Bank	12,300	15,000
Current Liabilities		
Trade Creditors	-16,000	-15,000
	110,300	108,600
Financed by:		
Capital		
Ordinary Shares	50,000	50,000
Preferential shares	20,000	20,000
General Revenue reserves	40,300	38,600
	110,300	108,600

Net income calculation

Gross Profits	45,600
Operating Expenses	-19,000
Total Depreciation	-23,500
Net Income	3,100

Francesca Company Limited Statements of Cash Flow at end of the period 31/12/2xx5

	£	£
Net Income		3,100
Add: Depreciation charges	23,500	
Add: Decrease in stocks	1,600	
Add: Decrease in debtors	2,000	
Add: Increase in creditors	1,000	28,100
Net Cash inflow from operating activities		31,200
Cash Flows from investing		
Purchase of plant and machinery	15,000	
Cash used in investing activities	13,500	-28,500
Increase in the cash flow during the period		2,700

You will notice that the increase in the cash flow during the period is equal to the difference between the cash in bank balance for the year 2xx4 and 2xx5. This can be used as a test of accuracy of statements that you have prepared.

AN INTRODUCTION TO ACCOUNTING

Revision Questions:

1. Discuss the reasons why company accounts are prepared in standardised manner and the problems that would arise if these standards and formats were not adhered to.
2. Discuss the importance of the application of FRS (3) in the preparation of Statements of Accounts.
3. Certain items must be expressly disclosed in the published statements, discuss why the following items must be disclosed
    - Director's remuneration
    - Auditor's remuneration
    - Research and Development costs
    - Extraordinary items or transactions
4. A cash flow statement is useful in predicting liquidity of a business, what would large amounts of cash available indicate about the performance of the business? What should a business that finds it has too much cash available do?
5. Revenue reserves and profits and loss account balances are generated within the business yet are included as items of the financing side, explain the rationale behind the inclusion of these reserves on the capital side of the balance sheet.
6. The following trial balance was obtained from Hajinda's Car Resale Company Limited, using this information prepare a trading profit and loss account for external use and a balance sheet to be published:

Hajindas Car Resale Company Limited trial balance for the period ended 30/06/2xx3

Items	£	£
Capital Account		150,000
General reserves		89,000
Sales		307,550
Purchases	32,600	
Opening Stock	69,000	
Motor Vehicles	43,000	
Plant and machinery	24,400	
Patents and trademarks	65,700	
Bank	46,700	
Debtors	16,900	
Creditors		17,850
Salaries and Wages	128,800	
Rent and Rates	36,000	
Provisions for depreciation		
Motor vehicles		4,300
Plant and Machinery		1,240
Administration costs	21,400	
Transport expenses	34,500	
Loan interest	2,100	
Tax for period	5,690	
Director's remuneration	28,000	
Auditor's fees	15,150	
	569940	569,940

Notes: The closing stock was 83,700

The following Trading, Profit and Loss Account and balance sheet have been prepared from the trial balance above:

Trading, Profit and Loss Account for the period ended 30/06/2xx3

	£	£
Sales		307,550
Opening stock	69,000	
Purchases	32,600	
Closing stock	-83,700	-17,900
		289,650
Less: Operating Costs		
Salaries and Wages	128,800	
Rent and rates	36,000	
Provisions for Dep'n	5,540	
Administration costs	21,400	
Transport expenses	34,500	
loan interest	2,100	
Director's Fees	28,000	
Auditor's Fees	15,150	-271,490
Net Profit before tax		18,160
Tax payable		-5,690
Net profit after tax		12,470

Hajinda's Balance Sheet for the period ended 30/06/2xx3

	£	£
Fixed Assets		
Patents and trademarks	65,700	
Motor vehicles	38,700	
plant and machinery	23,160	127,560
Current Assets		
Bank	46,700	
Stock	83,700	
Debtors	16,900	147,300
Current Liabilities		
Creditors	17,700	
Provision for taxation	5,690	-23,390
Total assets less current liabilities		251,470
Financed by		
Capital	150,000	
General reserves	89,000	
Profit and Loss	12,470	251,470
		251,470

7. The following balances were collected from Jairo's Distributors Company Limited as at 31/12/2xx1. Using this information prepare a Trading, Profit and Loss Account and a Balance Sheet statement for publication

Jairo's Trial Balance as at 31/12/2xx1

Item	£	£
Issued Share Capital		
500,000 Ordinary Shares @£ 1 per share		500,000
Share Premium Account		200,000
Profit and Loss Account		450,000
Long-term loan		750,000
Land and Buildings at cost	1,100,000	
Plant and Machinery at cost	125,000	
Motor Vehicles	89,000	
Trade Debtors	134,500	
Cash in Bank	164,500	
Stock	150,000	
Provision for doubtful debts		45,000
Trade Creditors		139,200
Accumulated depreciation to date		
Plant and Machinery		50,000
Motor Vehicles		26,700
Director's remuneration	100,400	
Auditor's fees	25,000	
Administration Expenses	540,000	
Selling and Distribution Expenses	345,000	
Loan interest	12,500	
Cost of Sales	980,000	
Sales		1,605,000
	3765900	3,765,900

Notes

1. Depreciation on Plant and machinery and motor-vehicles is provided at 10% of cost
2. The land and buildings are not to be depreciated as the latest valuation showed that they have actually appreciated

8. Pepa Industries Company Limited had the following balances as at 31/12/2xx5, using this information, prepare a trading profit and loss account for publication.

Pepa industries balances as at 31/12/2xx5

Particulars	£
Profit and Loss Account at 31/12/2xx4	78,900
Sales	234,500
Purchases	132,400
Stock as at 01/01/2xx5	18,500
Returns inwards	23,000
Returns outwards	16,500
Wages and salaries	48,200
Rent and rates	24,000
Distribution Expenses	56,700
Administration Expenses	39,900
Bad Debts	3,400
Interest from bank deposit	2,000
Income from Investments	12,500
Plant and Machinery at cost	
Administrative	18,000
Distribution	4,500
Vehicles Administrative	24,000
Distribution	17,600
Taxation for the period	6,200
Accrued Auditor's fees	4,000

Notes
1. Stock as at 31/12/2xx5 was £10,300
2. 40% of the wages & salaries and Rent & rates were apportioned to Administration
3. Depreciation on all plant and machinery should be applied at 15% of the cost while vehicles attract a depreciation charge of 20%

9. The Balance Sheet of Ace Plc for the years ended 31/08/2xx1 and 31/08/2xx2 were as follows:

Ace Plc Balance Sheets for the periods ended 31/08/2xx1 and 31/08/2xx2

	£ 31/08/2xx2	£ 31/08/2xx1
Fixed Assets		
Land and Buildings	1,150,000	1,150,000
Motor vehicles at cost	106,000	106,000
Accumulated depn Vehicles	-31,800	-21,200
Current Assets		
Stock	23,000	29,000
Trade debtors	16,400	21,000
Bank	13,400	4,500
Current Liabilities		
Accrued auditors fees	-6,000	0
Trade creditors	-18,900	-14,100
	1,252,100	1,275,200
Financed by:		
Issued Share capital	1,200,000	1,200,000
Profit and Loss Account	52,100	75,200
	1,252,100	1,275,200

Using the information provided prepare a cash flow statement for Ace Plc.

10. The following information has been extracted from Churchill Plc on 31/05/2xx0

Profit and Loss Account for the period ended 31/05/2xx0

	£	£
Sales		112,200
Operating Expenses	75,600	
Depreciation Motor Vehicles	6,250	
Amortised goodwill	20,000	-101,850
Net Profit before taxation		10,350
Tax payable		-3,000
Net profit after taxation		7,350
Retained Profit		

Balance Sheets for as at 31/05/2xx9 and 31/05/2xx0

	£ 31/05/2xx0	£ 31/05/2xx9
Fixed Assets		
Intangible Assets		
Goodwill	0	20,000
Land and Buildings	70,000	70,000
Motor vehicles: Cost	50,000	50,000
Accumulated depreciation	-25,000	-18,750
Current Assets		
Stock	14,600	7,100
Debtors	21,000	9,800
Bank	19,500	7,600
Current Liabilities		
Creditors	-9,600	-11,600
Taxation	-3,000	-4,000
	137500	130,150
Financed by:		
Issued share Capital	100,000	100,000
Retained profits	37,500	30,150
	137,500	130,150

Using the information provided prepare a cash flow statement.

Chapter 9: Ratios for Financial Statement Analysis

Learning outcomes: At the end of this chapter, the learner should be able to:
1. *Calculate various financial ratios*
2. *Use the results of the ratios to interpret financial performance*

9.1: Introduction

Financial ratios are important tools in evaluating the performance of a business and hence predicting its future performance. Ratios are important tools that can be used to break down the large amount of information presented in financial statements. Ratios can be used as tests over time as well as across the industry. They are aimed at providing information on the business at a glance. However, ratios may have a number of limitations, these include; lack of uniformity in the preparation of accounts. Later in this chapter as each ratio is discussed the learner will note that the ratios are derived from financial statements, and so long as there are no strict conventions on issues such as inventories valuation or asset valuations then there is a possibility that two businesses in the same industry cannot be compared.

A second problem is that there is no conceptual framework. The accounting conceptual framework is in its early stages of development. The information required from the financial statement is mandatory and all companies falling under the accounting regulations must, with slight flexibility, present this information in the stated manner. A conceptual accounting framework has already been discussed in this book. This conceptual framework however does not extend to the ratios thus reducing their reliability

A third problem is the increase in multi-national companies that are also members of a group of companies. This leads to aggregated accounts. Aggregated accounts if used to calculate ratios have a 'smoothing over' effect where weaknesses in certain parts of the group are compensated for by strengths in other parts of the same group thus giving a distorted overall picture.

Ratios are used to compare different figures across the industry known as 'cross-sectional analyses and over time, which is known as 'time-series analyses'. In cross sectional analyses the business' performance is compared with other businesses across the industry. Ratios will for example compare the profitability of two businesses in the industry. If business 1 made a profit of £100,000, and business 2 made a profit of £500,000 in the same period. It may appear as though business 2 was performing better than business 1 if we do not take into consideration other aspects of the business for example the investment of capital.

If business 2 invested £5million to produce the £500,000 whereas the business 1 £500,000 to make a profit of £100,000; a simple ratio of profits to investments will show that business 1 is more profitable than business 2 even if in absolute terms business 2 seems to be performing better as shown below:

$$\text{General Ratio} = \frac{\text{Profit}}{\text{Investment}}$$

$$\text{Bus1} = \frac{100{,}000}{500{,}000} = 0.2 \text{ in percentages } 20\%$$

$$\text{Bus2} = \frac{500{,}000}{5{,}000{,}000} = 0.1 \text{ in percentage } 10\%$$

This means that there is a lot of information that can be derived from the absolute figures that appear in statements of profit and loss as well as balance sheet need to be interpreted further to be useful to various stakeholders. Many qualities of a business can be determined from different ratios. These can be categorised as follows:

- Profitability ratios are used to measure the efficiency and the performance of a business and its management. How good is the business in converting their resources to profits?
- Activity ratios measure how efficient the business in moving stock, note that stock must be held for an appropriate length of time, this time should be neither too long nor too short. A business must therefore retain the right amount of stock at all times; too much stock would increase the opportunity cost of holding the stock as well as the storage costs. If stock is not adequate or available when it is needed then the business might grind to a halt incurring further cost such as idle workers. Other types of turnover include asset turnover, account receivable turnover,
- Capital structure analyses are used to determine whether a business has over-committed itself to debt in its operations and how much of it is still financed by the shareholders.
- Capital Market analyses indicate the performance of the business in the stock market if its shares are listed. This performance may also indicate how the market perceives the business and its future prospects.

The following section looks at the particular ratios in each category.

9.3: Profitability Analysis Ratios

Though the financial statements, and in particular the profit and loss account, gives absolute profit values, it does not give a clear picture of the performance of the business. Absolute figures in the profit and loss statement fail to show a relationship to other

CHAPTER 9: RATIOS FOR FINANCIAL STATEMENT ANALYSIS

important factors in the business. Profitability ratios hence help users of the accounts to evaluate the performance of the business in relation to other factors within the business.

9.3.1: Return on Assets (ROA): the return in total assets is the relationship between the assets employed during the relevant period and the returns gained from those assets. It shows the profitability in terms of the assets held throughout the year.

$$\text{Return on Assets (ROA)} = \frac{\text{Net Income}}{\text{Average Total Assets}}$$

Where:

$$\text{Average Total Assets} = \frac{\text{(Beginning Total Assets + Ending Total Assets)}}{2}$$

9.3.2: Return on Equity (ROE): this refers to the profitability derived from the investment of the shareholders known as equity. In this case, net income refers to profits after interest and payment of preference dividends but before tax.

$$\text{Return on Equity (ROE)} = \frac{\text{Net Income after interest}}{\text{Average Stockholders' Equity}} \times 100\%$$

$$\text{Average Stockholder's Equity} = \frac{\text{Beginning Equity + Ending Stockholders' Equity}}{2}$$

9.3.3: Return on Capital Employed this, like the ROA above, is a measure of the returns to capital employed in the company. Capital employed refers to the contributions of the shareholders plus the retained earnings less the dividends payable. The net income refers to profits after interest and payment of dividends to preference shareholders but before taxes

$$\text{Return on Capital Employed} = \frac{\text{Net Income}}{\text{Capital Employed}} \times 100\%$$

9.3.4: Profit Margin is the simplest of measures of profits to sale. In themselves, these ratios reveal little regarding the performance of the business. A high ratio means that the business is making more out of each £1 of sales meaning that the cost of sales is low compared to the sale prices or the indirect operating expenses are low. This is information that can be deduced by simply evaluating the statement.

AN INTRODUCTION TO ACCOUNTING

$$\text{Profit Margin} = \frac{\text{Net Income}}{\text{Sales}} \times 100\%$$

9.3.5: Earnings per Share (EPS): the EPS is regarded as a more efficient measure of profitability as in this case the net income refers to profits after all interests and taxes. The amount is available to the ordinary shareholders and is net of all the exceptional and extraordinary items.

$$\text{Earning per share} = \frac{\text{Net Income}}{\text{Outstanding issued shares}}$$

The EPS is also an important ratio in the capital market's analysis, as we will see later on this section.

Example 9.1:

The following balance sheet and Trading, Profit and Loss Accounts and Balance Sheet were prepared from Polly Company Limited books of Accounts. Using the information provided calculate the following profitability ratios

- Return on Assets,
- Return on Equity,
- Return on Capital Employed,
- Gross Profits Margin and
- Net Profit Margin

CHAPTER 9: RATIOS FOR FINANCIAL STATEMENT ANALYSIS

Polly's Trading, Profit and Loss Account for the period ended 30/11/2xx3

	£	£
Sale		340,000
Opening Stock	90,400	
Purchases	101,700	
Closing Stock	-77,900	-114,200
		225,800
Operating Expenses		
Salaries and Wages	48,000	
Rent and Rates	18,000	
Administration Expenses	24,900	
Distribution Expenses	21,300	-112,200
Net Profit before taxes		113,600
Tax on profits		-16,000
Net proift after taxes		97,600
Dividends payable		-26,000
Retained Profits		71,600

Polly's Company Ltd as at 30/11/2xx3

	£	£
Fixed Assets		
Motor Vehicles	48,000	
Plant and Machinery	28,100	
Current Assets		
Trade debtors	12,800	
Stock	11,200	
Bank	9,900	
Current Liabilities		
Trade creditors	-7,800	102,200
		102,200
Financed by		
Issued share capital	30,600	
Retained profits	71,600	102,200
		102,200

$$\text{Return on Assets (ROA)} = \frac{\text{Net income}}{\text{Average Total Assets}}$$

$$\text{Average Total Assets (ATA)} = \frac{\text{Total Assets at Start} + \text{Total Assets at end}}{2}$$

$$\text{ATA} = \frac{109{,}800 + 131{,}000}{2} = 120{,}400$$

$$\text{ROA} = \frac{113600}{120{,}400} = 0.94$$

The ROA shown above can also be converted to a percentage by multiplying by 100%. This would mean that the ROA is 94%, which is a very high return on the assets employed. ROA is used to measure how efficiently a business employs the assets available to it. A high ROA means that the business is very efficient in converting assets to profits. We use the average asset level because assets may fluctuate over the financial period being considered. To smooth this effect we average the assets by dividing the sum of the assets at the beginning of the period and the assets at the end of the same period and dividing by two to find the average asset level of the year.

$$\text{Return on Equity (ROE)} = \frac{\text{Net Income after interest charges}}{\text{Average Stockholders Equity}} \times 100\%$$

$$\text{Average Stock holders equity} = \frac{\text{Stock Holders Equity at Start} + \text{Equity at end}}{2}$$

$$\frac{30,600 + 30,600}{2} = 30,600$$

$$\text{ROE} = \frac{113,600}{30,600} = 3.71$$

In Polly's business there are no interest charges and therefore the net income, which ordinarily would have been taken as the income after interest but before taxation remains simply as profit before tax. There has been no change in the equity levels and therefore the average stockholder's equity remains as £30,600. The return on equity measures how efficiently the equity contributed by the owners is being employed to produce a profit.

$$\text{Return on Capital Employed (ROCE)} = \frac{\text{Net Income} \times 100\%}{\text{Capital Employed}}$$

Capital Employed = Shareholder's capital + Retained Earnings - Dividends payable

$$\text{ROCE} = \frac{113,600}{30,600 + 71,600 - 26,000} = 1.49$$

Returns on the capital employed is a ratio that shows how efficiently all the resources that were used in the business were used. If Polly Company Limited had debentures, preference shares, loans and so on, then these would also be included in the computation to arrive at the capital employed. It is noteworthy that different companies may include or exclude items that they deem to be or not to be relevant to this computation. Therefore in considering the ROCE values calculated by different businesses we have to be sure we know what is within the computation.

CHAPTER 9: RATIOS FOR FINANCIAL STATEMENT ANALYSIS

$$\text{Profit Margin} = \frac{\text{Net Income}}{\text{Sales}} \times 100\%$$

$$\text{Net Profit Margin} = \frac{\text{Net Profit}}{\text{Sales}} \times 100\% = \frac{113600}{340,000} = 33.41\%$$

$$\text{Gross Profit Margin} = \frac{\text{Gross Profit}}{\text{Sales}} \times 100\% = \frac{225,800}{340,000} = 66.41\%$$

The profit margins are used to relate the sales activity to profitability. The gross profit margin in a business that manufactures or adds value rather than merely reselling what it buys indicates the efficiency of that business in its production activities. The net profit margin may be used to indicate the operating efficiency of the business. It is important however to realise that ratios cannot be interpreted in exclusion of other ratios and a qualitative review of the business.

9.4: Activity Efficiency Analysis Ratios

These are ratios aimed at evaluating the performance of the management in a company. The movement of inventory for example is because of efficient organization that is directly linked to efficient and effective management. Turnover is also important as it shows whether or not the business is incurring excessive storage costs due to excessive stock or losing better investment opportunities by holding a lot of stock where less stock would have been adequate and the funds in the stock could have been used more profitably.

9.4.1: Assets Turnover Ratio: this is a simple measure of how efficiently the average assets in the year are being converted into sales. It is noteworthy that there should be a direct correlation between the average assets total assets and the sales level. This is because there are more assets available to the business to increase sales.

$$\text{Assets Turnover Ratio} = \frac{\text{Sales}}{\text{Average Total Assets}}$$

$$\text{Average Total Assets} = \frac{\text{Beginning Total Assets} + \text{Ending Total Assets}}{2}$$

9.4.2: Accounts Receivable Turnover Ratio: this is a measure of how efficiently the business is converting its credit sales into cash. The higher the ratio the better for the business as it means there are a lower proportion of debtors to the business at the end of a trading period.

AN INTRODUCTION TO ACCOUNTING

The average accounts receivable figure captures the movement of debt levels throughout the year. This ratio can be used to give a rough estimate of the length of time it takes to collect debts by relating the ratio to time periods. This is given as:

$$\text{Average Collection period (in days)} = \frac{\text{Sales} \times 365 \text{ days}}{\text{Accounts receivable}}$$

$$\text{Accounts Receivable Turnover Ratio} = \frac{\text{Sales}}{\text{Average Accounts Receivable}}$$

$$\text{Average Accounts Receivable} = \frac{\text{Start accounts receivable} + \text{ending accounts receivable}}{2}$$

9.4.3: Inventory Turnover Ratio: this measures the length of time that stock is held in the business, if stock is held for too long then the costs of holding such stock might rise. On the other hand, stock must be readily available for supply to customers or for manufacturing. An optimal stock level must thus be maintained in the business at all times. These values can also be used to estimate the length of time stock is held in the business. Generally, the shorter the period the better it is for the business. However, it must be noted that different businesses will have different times depending on their needs:

$$\text{Average length of time stock is held in the business} = \frac{\text{Stock}}{\text{Cost of goods sold}} \times 365 \text{ days}$$

$$\text{Inventory Turnover Ratio} = \frac{\text{Cost of Goods Sold}}{\text{Average Inventories}}$$

$$\text{Average Inventories} = \frac{\text{Beginning Inventories} + \text{Ending Inventories}}{2}$$

Example 9.2

The following balance sheets and trading, profit and loss accounts were prepared at the end of year 31/12/2xx5 as well as 31/12/2xx4 for Tina's Entertainment Business. Using this information to calculate:
- Assets turnover ratio
- Accounts Receivable Turnover ratio
- Inventory Turnover ratio

CHAPTER 9: RATIOS FOR FINANCIAL STATEMENT ANALYSIS

Tina's Entertainment Business Balance Sheet for the period ended 31/12/2xx5 and 31/12/2xx4

	£ 31/12/2xx5	£ 31/12/2xx4
Fixed Assets		
Furniture and Fittings	17,800	19,000
Vehicles	43,000	30,400
Current Assets		
Stock	24,500	21,900
Debtors	11,400	9,800
Bank	9,600	6,700
Total Assets	106,300	87,800
Current Liabilities		
Creditors	-7,600	-8,800
Accrued expenses	-2,100	-1,700
	202,900	165,100
Financed by:		
Capital	50,000	50,000
Retained Profits	26,600	7,300
Loan	20,000	20,000
	96,600	77,300

Tina's Entertainment Business Profit and Loss Account for the periods ended 31/12/2xx5 and 31/12/2xx4

	31/12/2xx5 £	31/12/2xx4 £
Sales	180,000	224,100
Cost of Sales	-102,400	-131,200
Gross Profit	77,600	92,900
Operating Costs	-58,300	85,600
Net Profits	19,300	7,300

Assets Turnover Ratio = $\dfrac{\text{Sales}}{\text{Average Total Assets}}$

$\dfrac{180,000}{97,050} = 1.85$

Accounts Receivable Turnover Ratio = $\dfrac{\text{Sales}}{\text{Average Accounts Receivable}}$

$\dfrac{180,000}{10,600} = 16.98$

Inventory Turnover Ratio = $\dfrac{\text{Cost of Goods Sold}}{\text{Average Inventories}}$

$\dfrac{102400}{23,200} = 4.41$

Using the balances from the two years we can calculate the average of any balance for example the average inventories are the average of the inventories for 2xx5 and 2xx4. The higher a turnover ratio is the more that asset turns over in the business. The Assets turnover ratio shows how efficiently the assets are being used. A very low ratio may indicate that there are many assets not being used efficiently, in Tina's case above its takes an average of £97,050 in terms of assets to produce a sales of £180,000. This is a very low ratio, which may mean that the assets are not being utilised properly. However, as already stated elsewhere no ratio should be used by itself and the quantitative analyses must be accompanied by qualitative analyses.

It is in the interest of the business to collect its debts efficiently and as soon as possible, failure to recover debts on time will lead to cash liquidity problems where the business is not in a position to meet its maturing expenses. Therefore, the accounts receivable ratios coupled with the average collection period in days can be used to determine how efficient the business is in collecting amounts outstanding.

Inventory turnover is used to calculate how efficiently the stock is being ordered, used and converted into sales or other products. The ratio refers to how many times new stock has been ordered in a given trading period. Excessive orders of say in our example 30 or 40 would be very expensive to the associated costs of ordering and transportation. If the ratio is say 1 then it means that there was only one order made for the whole year, which could mean that the business is holding too much stock, which is again not optimal.

9.5: Capital Structure Analysis Ratios

The long-term stability of a company is dependent on the capital structure it has adopted. A company must finance its operations; there are many ways of financing these operations. They include contributions by shareholders also known equity, loans, preferential shares, debentures, bonds and so on. Each of these instruments has a different effect on the long-term stability of a company. Loans, bonds, debentures and preference shares require regular payments regardless of the performance of the business. Equity on the other hand does not have this requirement. It is important hence to determine how much a company is dependent on other sources of finance other than equity, and hence determine its stability.

9.5.1: Debt to Equity Ratio: this is the ratio between long-term debt and the funds contributed by the shareholders. Long-term debts are loans, preference shares, and all other long-term liabilities that enjoy a preferential participation in the profits. This means all long-term liabilities that have their interests paid or dividends distributed before profits are distributed as dividends to ordinary shareholders.

This ratio provides an important evaluation for the long-term stability of the company.

CHAPTER 9: RATIOS FOR FINANCIAL STATEMENT ANALYSIS

$$\text{Debt to Equity Ratio} = \frac{\text{Total Long-term Liabilities}}{\text{Total Stockholders' Equity}}$$

9.5.2: Interest Coverage Ratio: is the ratio that shows the number of times interest on long-term financing instruments is covered by the profits.

$$\text{Interest Coverage Ratio} = \frac{\text{Income before Interest and Income Tax Expenses}}{\text{Gross Interest Expense}}$$

9.6: Capital Market Analysis Ratios

These ratios compare the market's perception of the business shares with their actual values in their books of accounts. The market perception maybe partially derived from the actual book value; however, this is rarely the case. In a stock market, other forces come into play, predominantly the force of demand and supply. Long-term speculators on the stock market might find these ratios useful, as they are interested in the real value of the company. Shareholders will also be interested with this comparison. Short-term speculators are however, predominantly interested in the forces of demand and supply for a particular share.

9.6.1: Price Earnings (PE) Ratio is the ratio between the market price for a given share in and its earning per share. The higher this value is the less the company earns per share. It could also mean that the value of the share in the market is not driven by how much the company earns but by other factors for example future prospects of the company.

$$\text{Price Earnings (PE) Ratio} = \frac{\text{Market Price of Common Stock per Share}}{\text{Earnings per Share}}$$

9.6.2: Market to Book Ratio: the PE ratio compares the price in the market with the earnings attributable to that share. The market to book ratio on the other hand compares the price that each share represents in the statements of accounts to what the market perceives its true value to be. Ideally, this ratio should be one meaning that the market can see the share at its actual value. Values greater than one mean that the market has overvalued the share and vice versa.

$$\text{Market to Book Ratio} = \frac{\text{Market Price of Common Stock per Share}}{\text{Book Value of Equity per Common Share}}$$

$$\text{Book Value of Equity per Common Share} = \frac{\text{Book Value of Equity for Common Stock}}{\text{Number of Common Shares}}$$

9.6.3: Dividend Yield: refers to the proportion of the market price that can be attributed to dividends expected by buying or owning the share. Whereas the dividend payout ratio is, the amount of dividend paid in proportion to the net income of the company.

$$\text{Dividend Yield} = \frac{\text{Annual Dividends per Common Share}}{\text{Market Price of Common Stock per Share}}$$

$$\text{Book Value of Equity per Common Share} = \frac{\text{Book Value of Equity for Common Stock}}{\text{Number of Common Shares}}$$

Dividend Payout Ratio: The percentage of earnings paid to shareholders in dividends. The payout ratio provides an idea of how well earnings support the dividend payments. More mature companies will typically have a higher payout ratio.

This is also known as the dividend cover.

$$\text{Dividend Payout Ratio} = \frac{\text{Cash Dividends}}{\text{Net Income}}$$

The payout ratio can also be calculated as follows.

$$\text{Dividend Cover/ Payout ratio} = \frac{\text{Annual Dividends}}{\text{Earnings per share}}$$

Example 9.3:

The following balance sheet and trading, Profit and Loss Account were drawn for Horst's Plc. Use these statements to calculate:

- Debt-Equity Ratio
- Interest Coverage ratio
- Price Earning Ratio
- Dividend Yield
- Dividend Payout ratio

Horst Plc Trading Profit and Loss Account for the period ended 30/09/2xx3

	£	£
Sales		451,600
Cost of Sales		-213,900
Gross Profit		237,700
Operating Expenses		-109,000
Net Profit before interest and tax		128,700
interest		-12,200
Net profit after interest before tax		116,500
Tax		-19,000
Net profit after interest and tax		97,500
Dividends payable		-34,500
Retained Profits		63,000

Horst Plc Balance Sheet as at 30/09/2xx3

	£
Fixed Assets	
Vehicles	89,300
Plant and Machinery	100,650
Current Assets	
Debtors	36,600
Stock	31,200
Bank	21,800
Current Liabilities	
Creditors	-43,050
Accrued Dividends	-34,500
Accrued Taxes	-19,000
Net Assets less Liabilities	183000

Financed by:	
100,000 Shares @£1 per share issued	100,000
Long-term Loan	20,000
Retained Profits	63,000
	183,000

Note: The share of Horst Plc is trading currently at London Stock Exchange at 600p
(Shares in the LSE are quoted in pence 100p = £1)

$$\text{Debt to Equity Ratio} = \frac{\text{Total Long-term Liabilities}}{\text{Total Stockholders' Equity}}$$

$$= \frac{20,000}{100,000 + 63,000} = 0.123$$

CHAPTER 9: RATIOS FOR FINANCIAL STATEMENT ANALYSIS

The debt equity ratio is used to evaluate the long-term stability of a business. In Horst's Plc above the debt represents 12% of the total business equity. Again, this ratio has to be used in conjunction with other ratios and industrial averages.

$$\text{Interest Coverage Ratio} = \frac{\text{Income before Interest and Income Tax Expenses}}{\text{Gross Interest Expense}}$$

$$\frac{128{,}700}{12{,}200} = 10.55 \text{ times}$$

This ratio simply measures whether the business can meet the gross interest charges that arise from loan and debenture liabilities. In this case, the gross interest can be covered 10.55 times over by the income before tax and interest.

$$\text{Price Earnings (PE) Ratio} = \frac{\text{Market Price of Common Stock per Share}}{\text{Earnings per Share}}$$

$$\text{Earning per share} = \frac{\text{Net Income}}{\text{Ordinary Shares Outstanding issued}}$$

Net Income = Net Profits - Interest - Taxes

$$\text{EPS} = \frac{97{,}500}{100{,}000} = 0.975$$

$$\text{PE Ratio} = \frac{6}{0.975} = 6.15$$

The EPS is a better measure of profitability as the net income refers to the Net Profit after interest and taxes. It also relates profitability to the outstanding shares of the business. Therefore, at Horst Plc each share has earned £0.975. The performance must be compared to the industrial average to determine whether the Horst Plc is performing better or worse than other businesses.

The Price Earning ratio is an important ratio to buyers and sellers of publicly traded shares these are also known as speculators as they buy shares hoping that their prices will rise so that they can sell them at a profit. In this case, the PE is 6.15, which means that the speculators in the market value the share at 6 times more than the actual earning per share. This could mean that the share is overvalued in the stock market or speculators believe that the EPS is undervaluing the business. It could also be that the speculators expect that the

AN INTRODUCTION TO ACCOUNTING

value of the business will rise six-fold in the near future justifying the market valuation of the share. Lastly, the speculators could simply be misinformed about the business and therefore overvaluing it.

$$\text{Dividend Yield} = \frac{\text{Annual Dividends per Common Share}}{\text{Market Price of Common Stock per Share}}$$

$$DY = \frac{0.345}{6} = 0.057$$

$$\text{Dividend Payout Ratio} = \frac{\text{Cash Dividends}}{\text{Net Income}}$$

$$DPR = \frac{34{,}500}{97{,}500} = 0.354$$

The dividend yield is used to determine how much shareholder gets out of the dividends as a proportion of the whole share value. Either shareholders buy shares as a source of income through regular dividends or for the capital gain, they expect if the market price of the share rises. The dividends yield ratio can therefore be used to determine whether a share has reasonable dividends yields.

Dividend payout, as the name suggests is the ratio of the dividends paid out and the income available to shareholders. Again, this is a measure of how much a share pays out as dividends.

9.7: Liquidity ratios

These are ratios used to evaluate the ability of a business to pay for arising liabilities. It measures the cash flow risks the business may face in the future. There are two useful ratios used to measure liquidity, these are the current ratio and quick ratio.

$$\text{Current Ratio} = \frac{\text{Current Assets}}{\text{Current Liabilities}}$$

Generally, the acceptable ratio is usually two and above, this means that the liabilities are half the available assets. This ratio must however be evaluated with other factors such as the repayment periods allowed for the debtors as compared to the creditors. If the creditors give the business a longer period, to pay for their debts but the business gives the debtors less time then a lower ratio may be acceptable. A current ratio of less than one means that there are lower current assets then there are liabilities and the business may therefore be insolvent or fixed assets have to be converted to cash to meet the maturing debt obligations.

The quick ratio is a more precise measure of liquidity as the stock is excluded from the ratio as they may take long to be realised as cash and may therefore not be handy to pay maturing debts.

$$\text{Quick Ratio} = \frac{\text{Current Assets - Stock}}{\text{Current Liabilities}}$$

Therefore, the quick ratio is a better indicator of the business' short-term liquidity than the current ratio as it only considers the current assets that can quickly be converted into cash and used to pay for maturing obligations.

9.8: Limitations of ratios:

Though ratios are useful tools in the evaluation of the performance of a business, a closer look at their components reveal a number of weaknesses. Profitability ratios match profits to gross and net income and further to capital employed and assets of the business. Sales figures may reflect increased absolute sales either due to reduced prices or due to the scarcity of the sale item, which has increased the sales total. The two reasons for increased sales may produce the same gross and net profit margins but for very different reasons. This could easily mislead the users of the accounts.

Secondly, the activity efficiency ratios depend on the valuation of the assets. Assets in different businesses may be valued differently making it difficult to do cross-sectional analyses. For example, where one business values its stock using the FIFO method and another business values the stock using the Averaging approach, it may therefore be misleading to compare the two businesses activity efficiency.

It is important therefore that ratios be used in conjunction with other tools to analyse the performance of the business. Users of ratios should be aware that the data used to calculate ratios is derived from historical data; information about preceding periods that may not necessarily reflect what might happen in the future.

Qualitative analysis is very important when evaluating a business' performance. Information about the future prospects of a business may not be quantifiable but may significantly affect the perception of shareholders about the business. A wholesome

AN INTRODUCTION TO ACCOUNTING

approach to business analyses must therefore be adopted to provide a better picture of its performance.

Revision Questions:

1. Discuss the limitations and problems that face the use of ratios to analyse the performance of businesses.
2. What is the implication of a high stock turnover ratio, what are the advantages and disadvantages of high stock turnover?
3. Profitability ratios are used to measure the efficiency of a business. Explain the difference between the ROCE, ROA and the Profit margin ratios.
4. Why is it not advisable to use ratios as the only tools for evaluating the performance of a business?
5. Define EPS and explain why it is important in calculating PE ratios. What would a high PE indicate about the underlying value of the share and market price of the share?
6. The following profit and Loss account and balance sheet were prepared for Banks Plc.

Banks Plc Trading, Profit and Loss Account for the period ended 31/12/2xx1

		£	£
Sales			898,500
	Opening Stock	104,100	
	Purchases	210,000	
	Closing Stock	-111,000	-203,100
Gross Profit			695,400
Operating Expenses			
	Salaries and Wages	150,600	
	Rent and Rates	48,000	
	Depreciation costs	90,000	
	Auditor's Fees	18,400	
	Administration Costs	130,000	
	Distribution Costs	65,000	-502,000
Net Proft before interest and tax			193,400
	Interest Payable		-16,000
Net Profits before tax after interest			177,400
	Tax payable		-28,000
Net Profit after interest and tax			149,400
Proposed dividends			-80,000
Retained Profits			69,400

CHAPTER 9: RATIOS FOR FINANCIAL STATEMENT ANALYSIS

Using the information in the profit and loss account calculate the profitability margins of the Bank Plc and comment on the performance of the business.

7. The following balance sheets relate to Banks Plc for the year 31/12/2xx1 and for the previous year 31/12/2xx0.

Using these balance sheets calculate the Return on Capital Employed and the Return on Assets and the implication of the ratios to the performance of the business.

Bank's Plc Balance Sheets for the years ended 31/12/2xx1 and 31/12/2xx0

	31/12/2xx1 £	31/12/2xx0 £
Fixed Assets		
Vehicles	300,000	360,000
Plant and Machinery	500,000	600,000
Furniture and Fittings	150,000	30,000
Current Assets		
Stock	151,300	104,100
Trade Debtors	138,500	83,400
Bank	106,500	60,500
Total Assets	1,346,300	1,238,000
Current Liabilities		
Trade Creditors	-114,300	-121,900
Accrued Auditor's Fees	-18,400	0
Tax Payable	-28,000	-19,900
Proposed Dividends	-80,000	-60,000
Total Assets less current liabilities	1,105,600	1,036,200
Financed by		
Issued Share Capital 700,000@£1 per share	700,000	700,000
Share premium account	80,600	80,600
Long term liabilities		
Loans	150,000	150,000
Retained Profits	175,000	105,600
	1,105,600	1,036,200

8. Using the information in the balance sheets above calculate the Current Ratio and Quick Ratio for Bank's Plc. Comment on your results and what they mean to the business and contrast Quick ratio to the Current Ratio
9. Using the Balance sheet in question 7 and the Profit and Loss Account in Question 6 calculate the EPS and the PE ratios and comment on their implication to the business and the stock market
10. Using the Balance Sheets and Trading, Profit and Loss accounts in questions 6 and 7, calculate at least three capital structure ratios and comment on the performance of the business in the light of these ratios.

Chapter 10: Budgetary Planning

Learning outcomes:
At the end of this chapter, the learner should be able to describe and discuss:
1. The basic concepts of the planning process
2. The nature of budgets
3. The purpose of budgets
4. Budgetary control

10.1: Introduction

Businesses are formed for a variety of reasons. The three basic reasons why businesses are set up include:
- To generate a profit from available resources through the application of an efficient management process
- To provide public goods and services at cost: Such organisations are not interested in making profits, but rather in the efficient and effective provision of services
- For philanthropic purposes, these organisations are more interested in meeting the needs of the needy than making a profit.

Generally, private enterprises are formed for the sole purpose of generating a profit. Those who start private enterprises are known as entrepreneurs, they risk their resources on ideas with an aim of generating wealth. Profit is gained from using available resources to produce wealth. Profit is the difference between costs of the resources applied and the income generated from the business activity.

Private enterprises include sole traders, which are business entities set up and owned by one person all the decisions about such entities are made by this one individual. He/she enjoys all the profits that he or she makes from his/her enterprise. However, he/she also bears all the losses that he/she might incur in the course of his business operations.

Another type of enterprise is the partnership a partnership is formed where two or more people form a business. They have to agree on how they will share the profits, losses and responsibilities that arise during the course of their business. Partnerships are advantageous in that the partners can share ideas and the work. Having a partnership also means that the losses can be distributed between the partners lightening the burden. A disadvantage is that the profits have to be shared between the partners thus reducing the total profits available to each partner.

A private company on the other hand is governed by the strict government regulations; this is because the owners have a limited liability to companies. Limited companies both public and private have various characteristics that distinguish them from the sole trader and the partnership. These include the fact that companies are regarded as legal persons and have rights as any other person to sue and be sued as such entities, they can own property and bear their obligations as such individuals. This means that the owners of a company have a limited liability to creditors and other entities that the company might be indebted to. The shareholders can only lose what they invested in terms of the shares they hold.

10.2: The basic concepts of the planning process

A business must have aims and objectives governed by its mission statement that has been derived from the vision. The company must plan its activities beforehand to ensure that they employ their resources efficiently.

A vision is a picture in the present about the future of the business, it gives the wider view of what the business intends to achieve in the future. A mission statement on the other hand is an explanation of the vision. It expounds on what has been set out in the vision. For example, the company may set out a vision to be the most effective and efficient firm in meeting their customers' needs. The mission statement may go on to state what the vision means in exact terms so it may read:

Vision: *That by the year 2xx5, our company will be the largest provider of consultancy services in Europe*

Mission statement: *To ensure expansion throughout the major cities of Europe beginning with London by increasing our customer base. This expansion will be led by an efficient and effective service for our customers.*

Ensuring that our customer's needs are met on time (efficient) and that the intended results are achieved (effective), will guarantee an expansion of our customer base.

Aims: To achieve the mission statement the company must come up with specific aims. Aims are directions towards an intended outcome. In this case, to achieve the mission statement there needs to be specific aims that show how the mission statement will be achieved. Business aims include:

1. The main aim of most businesses is to make a profit. This is especially true for private companies. Public sector businesses may make a profit if there is a possibility of doing so, but they are mainly formed to provide services at a reasonable costs while meeting strict regulations set by those who are responsible for the funding of those public activities
2. Another aim is to provide goods or services to people in their locality, either nationally or internationally. Voluntary organisations and public entities might be more driven to provide such goods or services than they are in making a profit.
3. Another common aim is growth and expansion. There are two ways of looking at this aim, expansion could mean that a business wants to operate in another market where they can enjoy increased sales and hence profits or they want to increase the

number of people who can access their goods or services. The former relates mainly to the private sector whereas the latter relates to the public sector, which would like to reach more of the community with its goods and services.
4. Other businesses choose to improve the quality of their goods and services to either help those who use them to derive more utility from then (especially in the public sector) or to increase the sales, for the private sector businesses.
5. Other aims include being environmentally friendly and corporate social responsibility where the businesses seek to give back to the communities in which they operate. This aim serves to give the business prominence in its area of operation apart from the purely philanthropic objectives, corporate social responsibility, gives the company prominence in the community and serves as a method of advertising

For the business named above, the following could be a few of their aims
- *Increase profitability by reducing costs*
- *Serve our customers efficiently and effectively*
- *Expand our customer base*
- *Be involved in various community based efforts in our cities of operation*
- *Be innovative in meeting our customers' needs*

Objectives: The aims are further broken down into objectives. Objectives are the specific ways in which the aims of the business will be met. Objectives have certain characteristics. These include:

1. **Specificity:** all objectives must be in reference to a specific outcome. The outcome of an objective should be expressly stated.

2. **Measurable:** all objectives must have a measurable outcome. Measurable outcomes are used to determine whether the desired result has been achieved, or the progress that has been made thus far in achieving those results is in line with those objectives.

3. **Achievable:** More often than not objectives can be unattainable either because of constraints of time, resources or the lack of clarity of the intended outcomes. For objectives to be robust then it is important the implementers evaluate whether or they can achieve the intended outcomes.

4. **Realistic:** given the resources available and the time allowed each objective should be evaluated based on whether it is realistic. This is an outward looking basis of evaluation it requires that the plans look at their environment and decide whether the assumptions they have made about in making their plans are realistic.

5. **Time related:** Time constraints are an important factor; some of the objectives are time related. For example increasing the sale of winter clothes in summer is not realistic due to the demand for summer clothes and the relative lack of interest in winter clothing in a hot season. Time conscious planning also means that the planners include time lines showing the time by which they expect certain tasks to be completed.

These five characteristics create the acronym **SMART**. Objectives are said to be smart using the example above; the objectives that could possibly be related to the aim of increasing profitability would be:

1. *To reduce the overall operating costs by 14% by the end of the financial year 2xx4/2xx5*
2. *To increase our market share from 3% to 6% by the end of the financial year 2xx4/2xx5*

The two objectives stated above clearly show the specific targets that are to be achieved by the end of the financial year 2xx4/2xx5. The targets are also measurable using the percentages. They are time related as they are to be achieved from the time they are put down to the end of the financial year. Whether on not they are realistic would have to be determined by including external factors to the business. For example, how easy would it be for the businesses that control 97% of the market to lose 3% to us?

Targets or goals are the strategies that are used to achieve the objectives. For example to reduce operating costs by 14% would mean that the business would have to look into their operations and decide which costs they are going to reduce. Many strategies of reducing costs these are measured using targets. A target describes an outcome of a task. For example, the business can set a target of reducing costs by centralising all the administration and secretarial services for the business. This would mean that a target has been set to cut down the number of people who carry out the administration tasks. The target could thus be reducing the number of employees in the administration department from 10 to 7. The tasks to achieve this would be a process of evaluation to decide which employees should be laid off. This would then be followed by a process of terminating the contracts of those who are to be laid off and ensuring that they are well catered for and their redundancy payments made fairly and on time.

Thus, the planning process in a business is geared toward achieving a preset vision. In the case above the vision for expansion, is met by the aim of increasing profitability, which in turn is met by the objective of reducing costs. The reduction of costs on the other hand is met by reducing the number of employees in the administration department.

Planning and hence setting the objectives of a business starts with a clear vision and all the activities of the business are geared towards achieving that goal.

10.3: The nature of budgets

A budget is an itemised summary of estimated or intended expenditures for a given period along with proposals for financing them. A budget hence has two parts: Firstly, a list of intended expenditures for a specific period and secondly a source of incomes with which to finance the expenditure. A budget is also a plan expressed in quantitative, usually monetary terms, covering a specific period, usually one year. In other words, a budget is a systematic plan for the utilisation of the workforce and material resources.

There are two types of budgets: Capital budgets, which are directed towards proposed expenditures for new projects and often require special financing and operating budgets, which, are directed towards achieving short-term operational goals of the organization, for instance, production or profit goals in a business firm. Operating budgets may be sub-divided into various departmental of functional budgets.

Budgeting is an integral part of long-term planning. The vision and mission statement discussed earlier in this section form the backbone of budgeting. Budgets serve six distinct functions:

1. Planning: once overall long-term plans have been made then their implementation will require resources. Budgets help the business planners to refine their plans, by addressing the allocation of resources to various business needs. It forces the planners to look at the financial implications of plans.
2. Coordination: A budget helps managers establish interrelations between various aspects and expenses to be incurred in next period. It therefore helps the managers coordinate activities and the expenses.
3. Communication: financial planning and budgeting helps clarify the targets to employees and managers. The monetarisation of targets also enables communication in less confusing terms as compared to long policy papers.
4. Motivation: clear attainable targets that are created by the refining effect of a budget also increase motivation as employees and managers know what is expected of them.
5. Evaluation is connected to planning, by matching the performance of the business to the plan. You can tell whether the business is performing as per the expectations.
6. Control is also achieved as the adherence to budget plans can be ascertained at various points during the year.

The main characteristics of a budget are:

1. It is prepared in advance and is derived from the long-term strategy of the organization.
2. It relates to future periods for which objectives or goals have already been laid down.

It is expressed in quantitative form, physical or monetary units, or both.

Different types of budgets are prepared for different purposed e.g. Sales Budget, Production Budget, Administrative Expense Budget, and Raw-material Budget etc. All these sectional budgets are afterwards integrated into a master budget, which represents an overall plan of the organization.

Budgeting is very important to business as it helps the management to:

1. Manage the financial resources effectively by allocating them appropriately to different needs and projects.
2. It is also an important tool for monitoring performance in a business
3. It improves decision-making and the planning process by matching available resources to the needs of the business. Using a budget during planning ensures that all the possible needs are taken into account and prioritisation for allocation of financial resources is done correctly.
4. Budgets like cash flow statements can be used to identify possible cash flow problems and hence make provisions for such eventualities.
5. It can also be used as a benchmark of performance for the employees hence increasing their motivation by staying within the budgets. Budgets are powerful tools in increasing motivation as they refocus the workers to the common goals.
6. Budgets also clearly identify areas of responsibility for the management through budget centres. It can be used for performance evaluation of the management.

Budgets are essentially a list of expenses matched against a list of income that has already been realised or is to be realised in the future.

10.4: Budgetary Control:

Budgetary control is the continuous comparison between the actual financial results and the budgeted financial results. This comparison is used to identify deviations from the planned performance and responsibility is allocated to individuals within the business to ensure that the budgetary plan is adhered to. The individuals will also be charged with the responsibility of dealing with any deviations; if negative, such deviations are corrected while the positive deviations are enhanced.

Individuals charged with budgetary control are allocated a budgetary centre. Budgetary responsibility centres are functional areas headed by a manager and are allocated financial resources for their use according to a budget.

There are four distinct types of centres:

- Revenue centres are centres, which through their outputs generate revenues. The inputs to these centres are however not related to the outputs in monetary terms, for example the retail store of a business.
- Expense centres are centres where the input is measured in monetary terms but is not related to its output in monetary terms. It is the opposite of the revenue centre, for example, the manufacturing department of a business.
- Profit centres are where the input and output are related in monetary terms and the difference is the measure of the outcome from such a centre
- Investment centres where the output is measured in monetary terms and compared to the assets invested in that centre.

CHAPTER 10: BUDGETARY PLANNING

Characteristics of a good budget

To create a successful budget a business needs to imbue the following characteristics in it:

1. Ensure the participation of the employees and all the individuals who will be expected to participate in its implementation.
2. Ensure that the budget is comprehensive and covers every aspect of the business.
3. A good budget should set out the expected standards of performance for the business. It should serve as a benchmark to evaluate whether or not the intended outcomes of the business are being achieved.
4. A budget should also have a built in flexibility this allows for changing circumstances. An inflexible budget is unable to adjust and hence it becomes wholly unachievable.
5. A budget should also set up conduits for feedback this ensures that performance can be monitored continuously.
6. A budget should also have a basis of analysis of costs and revenues; this could be through cost centres such as product lines to name just a few.

10.5: Advantages of Budgets

A budget helps businesses in the following ways:

1. It brings about efficiency and improvement in the working of the organization.
2. It is a way of communicating the plans to various units of the organization. By establishing the divisional, departmental, sectional budgets, exact responsibilities are assigned. It thus minimizes the possibilities of buck passing if the budget figures are not met.
3. It is a way or motivating managers to achieve the goals set for the units.
4. It serves as a benchmark for controlling on-going operations.
5. It helps in developing a team spirit where participation in budgeting is encouraged.
6. It helps in reducing wastage and losses by revealing them in time for corrective action.
7. It serves as a basis for evaluating the performance of managers.
8. It serves as a means of educating the managers.

10.6: Budgetary Control

No system of planning can be successful without having an effective and efficient system of control. Budgeting is closely connected with control. The exercise of control in the organisation with the help of budgets is known as budgetary control. The process of budgetary control includes:

1. Preparation of various budgets
2. Continuous comparison of actual performance with budgetary performance

3. Revision of budgets in the light of changed circumstances.

A system of budgetary control should not become rigid. There should be enough scope of flexibility to provide for individual initiative and drive. Budgetary control is an important device for making the organization more efficient on all fronts. It is an important tool for controlling costs and achieving the overall objectives.

Installing a Budgetary Control System

Budgetary control is achieved by consciously installing it in a given business planning process. The setting up of a definite plan of organization is the first step towards installing budgetary control system in an organization a budget manual should be prepared giving details of the powers, duties, responsibilities and areas of operation of each executive in the organization.

A budget manual must be prepared, this shows the timeline of the budgeting process, responsibilities of the persons engaged in preparing and implementing the budget.

The budget must then be sufficiently approved by those in authority to ensure that it has the requisite support in the implementation stages. The standards to be observed in the preparation of the budget should be clearly stated in the budget manual. Clear reports, statements, forms and other records should also be maintained.

The accounts classification to be employed should be consistent as it allows for future comparison between the budgeted activities and the actual outcomes. It is necessary that the framework within which the costs, revenues and other financial amount are classified must be identical both in accounts and in the budget department.

The responsibility for preparation and implementation of the budgets may be fixed as under:

Budget Controller

Although the chief executive is finally responsible for the budget programme, it is better if a large part of the supervisory responsibility is delegated to an official designated as the Budget Controller or Budget Director. Such a person should have knowledge of the technical details of the business and should report directly to the president or the Chief Executive of the organization.

Fixing the budget period

Budget period means the period for which a budget is prepared and employed. The budget period depends upon the nature of the business and the control techniques. For example, a seasonal industry will budget for each season while an industry requiring long periods to complete work will budget for four, five or even larger number of years. However, it is necessary for control purposes to prepare budgets both for long as well as short periods.

Budget Procedures

Having established the budget organization and fixed the budget period, the actual work or budgetary control can be taken upon the following pattern:

10.7: Steps in Budgetary Control

The budget manual is a written document or booklet that specifies the objectives of budgeting organization and procedures. Following are some of the important matters covered in a budget manual:

- A statement regarding the objectives of the organization and how they can be achieved through budgetary control
- A statement regarding the functions and responsibilities of each Executive by designation regarding both preparation and execution of budgets
- Procedures to be followed for obtaining the necessary approval of budgets
- The authority of granting approval should be stated in explicit terms.
- Whether one, two or more signatures are to be required on each document should also be clearly stated
- Timetable for all stages of budgeting
- Reports, statements, forms and other records to be maintained
- The accounts classification to be employed; It is necessary that the framework within which the costs, revenues and other financial amount are classified must be identical both in accounts and the budget departments.

There are many advantages attached to the use of a budget manual. It is a formal record defining the functions and responsibilities of each executive. The methods and procedures of budgetary control are standardized. There is synchronisation of the efforts of all which result in maximisation of the profits of the organisation.

Making a forecast

A forecast is an estimated of the future financial conditions or Operating results. Any estimation is based on consideration of probabilities. An estimate differs from a budget in that the latter embodies an operating plan of an organisation.

A budget envisages a commitment to certain objectives or targets, which the management seeks to attain based on the forecasts prepared. A forecast on the other hand is an estimate based on probabilities of an event. A forecast may be prepared in financial or physical terms for sales, production cost, or other resources required for business. Instead of just one

AN INTRODUCTION TO ACCOUNTING

forecast, a number of alternative forecasts may be considered with a view to obtaining the most realistic overall plan.

Alternative combination of forecasts should be used in budgeting to ensure that all the important information is captured. Alternative combinations of forecasts are considered with a view to contain the most efficient overall plan to maximize profits. When the optimum -profit combination of forecasts is selected, the forecasts should be regarded as being finalised.

Sales budget

In making a well-rounded sales budget, the following factors should be considered.

1. **Past sales figures and trend:** The record of previous experience forms the most reliable guide as to future sales as the past performance is related to actual business conditions. However, the other factors such as seasonal fluctuations, growth of market, trade cycles etc., should not be lost sight of including sales representatives' estimates. Sales representatives are in a position to estimate the potential demand of the customers more accurately because they come in direct contact with the customers. However, proper discount should be made for over-optimistic or too conservative estimates of the sales representatives depending upon their temperament.
2. **Plant Capacity** It should be the endeavour of the business to ensure proper utilisation of plant facilities and that the sales budget provides an economic and balanced production on the factory.
3. **General trade prospects** The general trade prospects considerable affect the sales. Valuable information can be gathered in this connection from trade papers and magazines.
4. **Orders on hand:** In case of industries where production is quite a lengthy process, orders on hand also have a considerable influence on the sales level.
5. **Proposed expansion** or discontinuance of products; It affects sales and therefore, it should be considered.
6. **Seasonal fluctuations** Experience will be the best guide in this respect. However, efforts should be made to minimise the effects of seasonal fluctuations by giving special concessions or off-season discounts thus increasing the volume of sales.
7. **Potential market:** Market research should be carried out for ascertaining the potential market, for the company's products. Such an estimate is based on expected population growth, purchasing power of consumers and buying habits of the people.
8. **Availability of material and supply:** Adequate supply of raw materials and other supplies must be ensured before drafting the sales programme.
9. **Financial aspect:** Expansion of sales usually requires an increase in capital outlay, therefore the sales budget must be kept within the bounds of financial capacity.

Other factors:

      i. The nature and degree of competition within the industry;
     ii. Cost of distributing goods;
    iii. Governments controls, rules and regulations related to the industry;
    iv. Political situation - national and international as it may have an influence upon the market.

The sales manager, after taking into consideration all these factors, will prepare the sales budget in terms if quantities and money, distinguishing between products, periods and areas of sale.

Production budget

Factors to consider include:

1. **Inventory policies** Inventory standards should be predetermined so that there is neither a shortage nor over-stocking of goods.
2. **Sales requirement** The quantity of goods to be sold would decide largely how much is to be produced. Therefore, this budget depends upon the sales budget.
3. **Production stability** For reduction of costs, stability in employment and better utilization of plant facilities, the production should be evenly distributed throughout the year. In case of seasonal industries, since it is not possible to have stable levels of production or inventory, an effort should be made to have the optimum balance between the two.
4. **Plant capacity** How much can be produced depends upon the available plant capacity. There must be sufficient capacity to produce the annual requirements and to meet seasonal high demands.
5. **Availability of material and labour** Adequate and timely supply of raw material and labour should have an important effect on the planning of production and the time taken in the production process.

Capital Expenditure Budget

The budget provides guidance as to the amount of capital that may be needed for procurement of capital assets during the budget period. The budget is prepared after taking into account the available productive capacities probable reallocation of existing assets and possible improvement in production techniques. If necessary separate budgets may be prepared for each item of assets, such as the building budget, a plant and equipment budget etc.

Cash budget

The cash budget can be prepared by any of the following methods;

1. Receipts and payments method
2. The adjusted profit and loss method
3. The balance sheet method

Receipts and payments method: In this method, the cash receipts from various sources and the cash payments to various agencies are estimated. In the opening balance of cash, estimated cash receipts are added and from the total, the total of estimated cash payments is deducted to find out the closing balance.

The adjusted profit and loss method: In case of this method, the cash budget is prepared based on opening cash and bank balances, projected profit and loss account and the balances of the various assets and liabilities.

The balance sheet methods: With the help of budget balances at the end except cash and bank balances, a budgeted balance sheet can be prepared and the balancing figure would be the estimated closing cash/ bank balance.

Thus under this method, closing balances other than cash/bank will have to be found out first to be put in the budgeted balance sheet.

Research and Development Budget

Research and development costs are to be incurred so that the products or the methods of the concern do not become out of date. The research and development budget is a forecast of all such expenses.

10.8: Classification of Budgets

Budgets can be classified into different categories based on time, function or flexibility. The different budgets covered under each category are shown

1. Time: budgets can be classified according to whether they are long-term, short term or current
2. Function: budgets can further be classified into the functional areas they relate to for example sales, marketing, production and so on
3. Flexibility: whether they are fixed, flexible or rolling

Some of the budgets covered in the above classification.

CHAPTER 10: BUDGETARY PLANNING

Rolling Budget

Some organizations follow the practice of preparing a rolling or progressive budget. In such organizations, a budget for a year in advance will always be there. Immediately after a month, or a quarter, passes, as the case may be, a new budget is prepared for twelve months. The figures for the month/quarter, which has rolled down, are dropped and the figures for the next month/quarter are added. For example, if a budget has been prepared for the year 2xx5 after the expiry of the first quarter ending 31st march 2xx5, a new budget for the full year ending 31st march, 2xx5 will be prepared by dropping the figures for the quarter, which has rolled past, and adding the figures for the new quarter ending 31st march 20x5. The figures for the remaining three quarters ending 31st December 2xx5 may also be revised, if necessary.

Preparing budgets

After the forecasts have been finalised the preparation of budgets follows. The budget activity starts with the preparation of the sales budget. Then the production budget is prepared based on sales budget and the production capacity available. Financial budget (i.e., cash or working capital budget) will be prepared based on sales forecasts and the production budget. All these budgets are combined and coordinated into a master budget. The budget may be revised in the course of the financial period if it becomes necessary to do so in view of the unexpected developments, which have already taken place or are likely to take place.

Choice between fixed and flexible budgets

A budget may be fixed or flexible. A fixed budget is based on a fixed volume of activity. It may lose its effectiveness in planning and controlling if the actual capacity utilisation is different from what was planned for any particular unit of time e.g., a month or a quarter. The flexible budget is more useful for changing levels of activity as it considers fixed and variable costs separately, fixed costs remain unchanged over a certain range of output. Such costs change when there is a change in capacity level.

The variable costs change in direct proportion to output. If flexible budgeting approach is adopted, the budget controller can analyses the variance between actual costs and budgeted costs depending upon the actual level of activity attained during a period of time. This will be explained in detail a little later.

Revision Questions

1. Discuss the connection between long term planning and budgeting.
2. Describe the six different functions of budgeting.
3. Discuss the stages of budgeting and their importance to the budgeting process.

4. There are at least three methods of classifying budgets, discuss them giving examples of each.
5. Discuss the characteristics of a good budget.
6. What are the factors to consider when preparing the sales budget?
7. Discuss the relationship between vision, mission statement and business objectives. Why is it important that a business prepare its plans along these lines?
8. How can budgets be used to motivate employees in a business?
9. How would a business go about setting up a budgetary control system?
10. Discuss the statement 'Objectives must be SMART' why is it important that objectives are SMART?

Glossary of Accounting terms:

Accounting concepts:
These can be defined as all the basic ideas in accounting that are used to govern the application of accounting practices and conventions.

Accounting controls:
These procedures are employed in a business to ensure that the recording of accounting information is done correctly and that it reflects the actual state and performance of a business. It is therefore a system of practices and procedures that is usually overseen by the management and its provisions enforced by the management.

Accounting Equation:
One of the basic accounting concepts is the accounting equation, which shows that however big the business becomes, the balance between the sum of the assets and liabilities and the capital invested is always the same. This idea is expressed as an equation as: Assets= Liabilities + Owner's equity

Accounting information:
Once data has been collected in from the operation of a business, it is processed through various skills and systems to give information, which is then used to make important decisions in the business. Accounting information can therefore be defined as the processed data from the operations of a business that is presented to its users in a form that can be used to make financial decisions regarding the business for example a Balance sheet.

Accounts Receivable Turnover Ratio
This is the ratio of total sales owed as debt by the business' customers. The more a business makes sales on credit the more dependent that business will be on its customers' ability to pay and the higher the risk that they may fail to honour their debt incurring more expenses for the business in terms of bad debts.

Accruals:
The term 'accruals' is used in two different ways in accounting; the accruals convention is the practice in accounting that states that incomes and expenditures should be recorded in the period they occur. On the other hand, accrued expenses (that some authors may put down in the balance sheet as 'accruals') refers to the accounts payable by the business for goods or services supplied and therefore expenses 'accrued' and not paid for.

Administrative Costs
Costs incurred in the general running of the business are known as administrative costs. Such costs cannot be allocated to a particular cost centre and are regarded as expenses incurred in the general administrative work involved in the management of resources to ensure efficient production occurs.

Adverse Opinion:
An auditor may render an adverse opinion if he is dissatisfied that the account he or she has been asked to audit does not represent the true and fair position of a business and therefore relying on such accounts to make financial decisions on the business may have adverse outcomes to the user.

Assets:
Assets are items held by a business that are used to produce further wealth within that business. Assets can be either tangible or intangible.

Audit Plan:
Auditing requires meticulous planning to ensure that all aspects of a business that accounts intend to communicate are covered. An audit plan describes the conduct and scope of an audit. This is usually discussed and agreed upon by the management of the business and the auditor.

Average Cost (AVCO)
At the end of each accounting period, a business must value the stock it holds. This helps in determining how much has been sold and the value the stock shall take at the beginning of the next period. AVCO is one of the methods that is used to determine this value and is calculated as the average cost of all the stock held by the business by simply dividing the total value of all the stock by the total number of units held in stock. This has the effect of eliminating different values for the same type of units simply because they bought at different prices and at different times. Further different prices for the same units does not give a true picture of the stock as the consumer does not distinguish these differences and all the stock will be resold at the same price. Other methods include LIFO (Last in Fast Out) and FIFO (First in First Out.

Bad Debts:
A bad debt is an irrecoverable debt. It is recorded as an expense to the business as it reduces the net profit.

Balance Sheet:
This final statement of accounts is used to record the final balances of the items of the accounting equation. The name balance sheet is derived from the fact that the statement is used to record the status of the balance between the capital and related assets and liabilities.

Books of Prime Entry:
To capture financial information, a set of accounting books is opened that is used to record each and every transaction at the time and place where it occurs, these are known as books of prime or original entry. It is from these books that we develop financial information. An example of a book of prime entry is the cashbook.

Budget:
A budget is a statement of future incomes and the related expenses. A budget is drawn up to show how resources available now, or that are anticipated will be allocated to expenses in the future. It is an important tool in business planning as it helps anticipate resource needs and problems that may arise in the future.

Budget Controller:
This is the person charged with the responsibility of ensuring that, as much as possible, the allocation of resources in the budget is adhered to when the budget is implemented. Such a person may also be charged with overseeing that allocated resources are used for the purposes intended.

Budgetary Control:
This is the authority and responsibility exercised by the budget controller in ensuring that the budget is adhered to.

Called Up Capital:
A company that issues shares must have an authorised share capital. This is the maximum number of shares that it can issue to its shareholders. Once shares are issued, the shareholders may be required to pay for the share at once or in bits. Called-up share capital is the capital that relates to that bit of the total value of shares that the shareholders have been requested to pay for.

GLOSSARY OF ACCOUNTING TERMS

Capital Expenditure:
This is a once-off payment for assets that will be used in a business for example payment for a business van. Capital expenditure can be contrasted to revenue expenditure, which is a recurrent payment for a recurrent purchase of a good or service, for example, telephone bills.

Capital Leverage:
This is the ratio between debt incurred in the growth of the business and the amount contributed by the owners to the growth of the said business.

Cash Accounting:
This form of accounting does not take into account any transactions that have not occurred on a cash basis, in reality it is difficult to imagine a business that neither takes nor gives credit.

Cash Budget:
A cash budget concentrates on the business' cash balances, it is also known as a forecast cash flow statement.

Check of Accuracy:
The double entry system means that a debit entry always has an equal credit entry, albeit the credit entry is in different accounts. This means that the sum of credits should equal the sum of debits. If these sums are not equal then we can preliminarily conclude that there is an error. This is known as a check of accuracy in accounting. Note that whereas a failure of the sum of debits to equal credits is an indication of an error, the equality of these sums does not mean that the accounts are error free.

Compensating Errors:
A compensating error is an error that affects both the debit and credit sides of a trial balance. This is where an error on the credit side is compensated for by an error on the debit side, and vice versa. A compensating error invalidates a check of accuracy test.

Compilation Engagement:
A compilation engagement involves the professional accountant in collecting, classifying and summarising financial information. No audit procedures are undertaken and no assurance is expressed in the report.

Cooperatives:
Cooperatives are organisations formed by people who come together to pursue a common goal. For example, a Farmers' Cooperative that is interested in the sale of its members' farm produces.

Cost of Sales:
The cost of goods actually sold in a business is known as cost of sales, it excludes general expenses that cannot be allocated to a specific cost centre. The cost of goods sold is made up of the opening stock at the beginning of the period in question, added to the purchases less the closing stock.

Current Assets:
Assets on a balance sheet are classified according to whether or not they can be liquidated in one accounting period. Current assets are assets that are can be converted into cash within an accounting period.

Current Liabilities:
Current liabilities are obligations that can be fulfilled within one accounting period. They are different from loans and other long-term liabilities in that they do not extend over different accounting periods and often are paid off at once.

Debentures:
Debentures refer to loans that are secured generally on the well-being (credit rating) of a business rather than a specific asset of the business.

Debt to Equity Ratio
This is the ratio between the debt that the business has acquired to purchase assets and run the business and the amount that has been contributed by the shareholders, a balance should be struck between the debt the business has taken on and the its needs. A high debt to equity ratio may indicate a rapid expansion; this may not be sustainable.

Deferred Revenues:
Deferred revenues are payments received by a business before it supplies the goods or services.

Disclaimer of Opinion:
Sometimes the auditors may be unable to express their opinions on such a large part of the accounts that they decline to express any opinion, as any opinion cannot be supported by the available information.

Dividend Payout Ratio:
It is important that a business knows how much of its net profits are given out as dividends. Therefore, we compare the two figures directly using the dividend ratio, which is the total dividends issued, divided by the net earnings, also known as the income after interest and tax.

Enron:
Enron was a U.S. energy-trading and utilities company that housed one of the biggest accounting frauds in history. Enron's executives employed accounting practices that falsely inflated the company's revenues, which, at the height of the scandal, made the firm become the seventh largest corporation in the United States. Once the fraud became known, the company quickly unravelled and filed for Chapter 11 bankruptcy on Dec 2, 2001.

Enron shares traded as high as $85 before the fraud was discovered, but plummeted to $0.30 in the sell-off after the fraud was revealed. Shareholders received company payouts as compensation for their losses, but former company executives also settled to pay shareholders out of their own pockets. Enron was the first big-name account scandal, but it was soon followed by the uncovering of frauds at other companies such as WorldCom and Tyco International, and has become a symbol of modern corporate crime.

Except For Limitation of Scope:
In some auditing cases, the auditors state that they can only give an opinion for a limited scope of reports and not the others, as they do not have sufficient evidence regarding the material out of this defined scope.

Executive Directors:
A person who is responsible for the actual running of an organisation is said to be in the executive. An executive director is a director who is active in the day-to-day running of a business.

First in First Out (FIFO) Approach:
First In First Out is a method of valuing the cost of goods sold that uses the cost of the oldest items in the inventory first in arriving at the value of the stock included in the cost of sales.

Fixed Assets:
Fixed assets are items of value held by a business not expected to be sold in the next fiscal period and whose use extends over a number of financial years.

GLOSSARY OF ACCOUNTING TERMS

Historical Cost Convention:
This is the convention in accounting that dictates that assets be valued at the cost of purchase regardless of their present day market values.

Inventories:
Inventory usually refers to goods that are being held for resale or are being converted into goods that can be resold.

Ledgers:
A book in which the monetary transactions of a business are posted in the form of debits and credits. These are generally known as the books of original or prime entry.

Liabilities:
In accounting, a liability refers to financial obligations or debts that arise because of a credit agreement between two parties that are transacting business.

Marketable Securities:
Marketable securities are investments that are very easy to convert into cash as they have a lifetime that is less than a year for example a government's treasury bonds.

Matching:
Where possible revenues should be matched to the expenses that have been employed in generating it, this may however not be possible at all times due to general expenses incurred in the overall administration of the business.

Memorandums of Association:
A memorandum of association is a legal document that sets out the objectives, names, addresses, and a list of the members of company.

Overdrafts:
An overdraft is a short-term loan facility extended to holders of bank accounts by the banks based on their credit rating to help smooth the differences in cash inflow and outflow.

Owner's Equity:
This is the portion of the total investment into a business made by the owners of the business. Where the business is a company, then the equity would then be the amounts paid by the shareholders.

Par Value:
The par value is also known as the face value, often the face value of shares is the price attached to the share at its initial issue. While the market value of the share changes, the par value does not as the market value includes the value that the market attaches to the business regardless of its par value, which is the initial true value.

Partnership:
In business, a partnership is an agreement between individuals to conduct business together. The relationship arising from this agreement is codified in a Partnership agreement.

Prepayments:
Prepayments are expenses paid for before they occur.

Private Companies:
The shareholders of this type of company cannot sell their shares to the public and therefore cannot raise funds from the public. Shareholders wishing to join a private company must be approved by other shareholders already in the company. A private company is also not under an obligation to make its accounts public.

Public Companies:

The shares of a public company are sold to the public in a secondary market known as the stock market. There are stringent requirements imposed on public companies to make their accounts public. Anyone can buy shares in a public company and can sell the said shares to anyone else in the public.

Qualified Opinion:

An auditor may give a qualified opinion if he or she is not satisfied by the manner in which accounts that he or she is auditing are kept. A qualified opinion is issued where the auditor cannot comment on a certain section of the accounts because the accounts needed are not available thereby limiting the scope of audit report or where there is a departure from the accounting guidelines.

Quick Ratio:

The Quick ratio measures how liquid a company is and therefore how ready it is to meet its short-term obligations. The measure is the ratio between its short-term liabilities and its short-term high liquidity assets.

Realisation:

Realisation is an accounting convention where a business recognises a sale or a purchase at the time when the legal ownership changes hands rather than when cash payment is made for the transaction.

Replacement Value Approach:

To value the cost of the goods in a sale we may have to value to the stock that remains at the end of the trading period. Replacement value approach is a valuation method where goods held in stock are valued at the cost that would be incurred if the stock were to be replaced at the time of valuation.

Residual Value:

Residual value is the value of assets after a full depreciation has been carried out on them over a period of being used in a business.

Rolling Budget:

A rolling budget is a budget that is periodically adjusted to reflect a more realistic picture of the performance of the business. An annual budget may be revised quarterly using discarded predications that are not true for that quarter and predicting for a fifth quarter to create a new annual budget. If this process is repeated for each quarter then we say we have a rolling budget.

Segmental Analysis:

In preparing final accounts, very large businesses may be required to produce analysis for various segments of their business. Each segment, for this purpose, may be treated as a separate entity with its own final statements such as cash flow statements, balance sheets and trading profit and loss accounts. These statements may appear side by side on the complete annual report of that business.

Separate Entity:

A business is treated as a separate entity from its owners when we prepare accounts Treating the financial affairs of a business as those of a separate entity helps accountants understand the performance and the state of the business without it being confused with the financial matters of the owners of the business.

Share Capital:

Shareholders contribute to the equity of the business capital in portions of equal value known as shares. The total value of shares contributed by the shareholders, who are the owners of the business, is known as share capital.

GLOSSARY OF ACCOUNTING TERMS

Single Entry:
In small businesses, all financial transactions may be recorded individually in a single account with an accompanying explanation of the transaction. Single entry is the opposite of double entry that is a more elaborate method of recording financial information in larger organisations with more transactions

Stakeholders:
People who have an interest in a business are known as stakeholders. Stakeholders could be people who have invested money in the business, people who benefit from the existence of the business such as customers or employees. Therefore, stakeholders are people who could be affected by the activities of the business.

Stock:
See inventories

Substance over Form:
This is an accounting convention that states that when recording financial transactions it is more important to capture the real substance or economic effect of the transaction than merely adhering to the form of recording that is prescribed by the accounting conventions.

T-Account:
A T-account is a simple ledger account with a debit and a credit side. This ledger accounts are called T-accounts because they look like the letter 'T'.

Trial Balance:
A trial balance is a list of the debit and credit balances of ledger or T-accounts. A trial balance, in keeping with the accounting equation, should have the same total figure for the sums of the debit and credit balances.

Uncalled Capital:
After a share issue, a company may decide to request for payment of only part of the total share value. The amount that has not been requested of the total value of the shares is known as the uncalled share capital.

Valuing At Cost:
In keeping with the historical cost convention, assets should be valued at their cost price. The cost price is the price at which they were purchased regardless of their market price.

Veil of Incorporation:
The shareholders of a company are said to enjoy limited liability. The 'limited liability' limits their losses to the amounts they have contributed to the business. This means that if the obligations incurred in the operations of the business cannot be paid from the assets of the business then the owners cannot be asked to pay for such obligations. The shareholders can also not be sued for the actions of the company. This protection afforded to the shareholders and the stewards of the company is known as the 'veil of incorporation'

Subject Index

A

Accounting concepts · 217
Accounting controls · 217
Accounting conventions · 17, 109, 112
Accounting equation · 13, 17, 88
Accounting Equation · 11, 217
Accounting information · 109, 217
Accounting Standards Board · 109
Accounting Standards Committee · 109
Accounting systems · 64
Accounts Receivable Turnover Ratio · 189, 217
Accrual accounting · 110
Accruals · 165, 217
Administrative Costs · 156, 217
Adverse opinion · 136
Adverse Opinion · 217
Agreed-upon procedures · 137
Amortisation · 158
Articles of Association · 143
ASB · 110, 120, 121, 122
ASC · 109
Assets · 3, 10, 11, 12, 13, 14, 15, 16, 17, 19, 20, 25, 26, 27, 29, 49, 60, 73, 80, 89, 90, 91, 116, 165, 166, 169, 185, 186, 189, 190, 192, 199, 201, 217, 218, 219, 220
Assets Turnover Ratio · 189
Audit Plan · 134, 218
Auditing Practices Board · 109
Auditing regulatory bodies · 131
Average Cost (AVCO) · 77, 218

B

Bad Debts · 96, 218
Balance sheet · 165, 201
Balance Sheet · 13, 71, 88, 89, 101, 105, 151, 164, 165, 179, 181, 186, 201, 218
Barter and other non-cash transactions · 173
Books of Prime Entry · 218
Budget · 100, 156, 207, 210, 211, 213, 214, 215, 218, 219, 222
Budget Controller · 210, 218
Budgetary Control · 208, 209, 210, 211, 218
Budgetary Planning · 3, 203

C

Called-up share capital · 165, 166
Capital and revenue expenditure · 115
Capital Expenditure Budget · 213
Capital Leverage · 219
Cash Accounting · 219
Cash Budget · 219
Cash flow statements · 101, 151, 171, 174
Check of Accuracy: · 10, 41, 219
Cheques ledger · 10
Comparability · 118
Comparative information · 159
Compensating Errors · 219
Compilation · 219
Conceptual framework · 127
Confidentiality · 133
Consistency · 66, 114, 118
Continuing operations · 154
Cooperatives · 142, 219
Cost of Sales · 35, 72, 73, 155, 156, 219
Creditors · 15, 16, 19, 44, 45, 50, 56, 60, 67, 68, 87, 92, 165
Current Assets · 15, 19, 80, 90, 166, 219
Current Liabilities · 90, 167, 219

D

Debentures · 149, 158, 220
Deferred Revenues · 168, 220
Depreciation · 33, 73, 80, 81, 83, 95, 115, 156, 174, 175, 176
Directors fees and emoluments · 157
Disagreement · 136
Disclosure · 135, 146
Discontinued operations · 154
Distribution Costs · 155
Dividend Payout Ratio · 194, 220
Dividend Yield · 194, 195
Dividends · 95, 147, 158, 175
Double entry · 47
Due care · 133

E

Earnings per share · 159
Enron · 146, 220
Equity · 11, 12, 13, 14, 17, 20, 168, 169, 192, 195
Exceptional items · 154, 158
Except for limitation of scope · 136, 220
Executive Directors · 220
External auditing · 130
Extraordinary items · 152, 154, 170, 173, 178

AN INTRODUCTION TO ACCOUNTING

F

Financial recording and reporting · 8
Financial Reporting Standards (FRS) · 109, 131, 152
Financing Cash flows · 171
First In First Out (FIFO) Approach: · 74
Fixed Assets · 15, 19, 80, 90, 220
Foreign currency cash flows · 172
FRS 3 · 152, 155

G

Going concern · 113
Goodwill · 117
Gross Profits · 48, 73, 155, 186

H

Historical Cost Convention · 116, 221

I

Intangible assets · 90, 166
Integrity · 132
Interest Cover · 193, 195
Interest Coverage Ratio · 193
Internal audit · 130
International Accounting Standards · 9, 109, 118, 119, 132
International Accounting Standards Board (IASB) · 119
International Accounting Standards Committee (IASC) · 119
Inventories · 166, 167, 174, 221
Inventory Turnover Ratio · 190
Investment · 126, 208
Issued share capital · 148

L

Last In First Out (LIFO) · 77
Ledgers · 221
Liabilities · 3, 10, 11, 13, 14, 16, 17, 20, 25, 26, 29, 49, 89, 90, 91, 167, 168, 217, 219, 221
Lifting the veil · 150
Limited liability · 120, 143
Liquidity · 198
Liquidity ratio · 198
London Stock Exchange · 145
Long-Term Liabilities · 168

M

Market-to-book ratio · 193
Marketable Securities · 167, 221
Matching · 115, 221
Materiality · 113
Minority interests · 155, 158
Monetary terms · 117

N

Net Assets · 16, 19, 60, 90
Net Worth · 90
Normal income/profit · 125

O

Objectivity · 118, 133
Operating cash flows · 171
Ordinary shares · 148
Owner's equity · 11, 13, 168, 221
Overdrafts · 221

P

Par Value · 221
Partnership · 141, 221
Preference shares · 149
Prepaid expenses · 167
Prepayments · 165, 221
Price Earning Ratio · 195
Price Earnings (PE) Ratio · 193
Private companies · 120, 144
Production Budget · 207
Professional behaviour · 133
Professional competence · 133
Profit · 6
Profit Margin · 185, 186
Profitability ratios · 184, 185, 199, 200
Project reports · 100
Prospective investors · 9
Prudence · 114
Public Companies · 141, 151, 222
Purchases · 34, 35, 39, 40, 48, 49, 50, 51, 54, 67, 72, 75, 85, 87, 91, 95, 102, 104

Q

Qualified Opinion · 222
Quick Ratio · 201, 222

SUBJECT INDEX

R

Ratios · 183, 184, 189, 192, 193
Realisation · 112, 113, 222
Registrar of Companies · 144
Relevance · 118, 122
Replacement Value Approach · 79, 222
Research and development costs · 156, 157, 214
Residual Value · 83, 222
Return on Assets · 185, 186, 201
Return on Equity · 185, 186
Returns inwards · 39, 50, 67, 92
Returns Outwards · 35, 51
Review · 109, 120
Rolling Budget · 215, 222

S

Sale, · 34
Sales Budget · 207
Sales Daybook' · 64
Sales Ledger · 10
Segmental Analysis · 174, 222
Separate Entity · 117, 222
Share Capital · 148, 222
Share premium · 165
Shareholders · 89, 141, 142, 143, 159, 193
Single Entry · 9, 223
Sole trader · 71, 141, 203
Stakeholders · 14, 17, 223
Stewardship · 119, 120, 130, 145

Stock · 3, 14, 15, 25, 34, 35, 36, 44, 45, 47, 48, 67, 68, 72, 74, 79, 85, 86, 87, 89, 90, 91, 120, 127, 144, 145, 151, 165, 175, 223
Statement of Principles for Financial reporting · 120, 121
Subnormal profits · 126
Substance over form · 118, 127, 223
Supernormal profits/income · 125

T

T-Account · 10, 24, 42, 47, 223
Tangible and intangible assets · 80, 90
Technical standards · 133
Toyota · 6
Trial Balance · 47, 55, 101, 223
True and fair · 131
Turnover · 155, 189, 190

U

Uncalled Capital · 148, 223

V

Valuing At Cost · 223
Veil of incorporation · 146, 223
Vicarious liability · 150

www.ingramcontent.com/pod-product-compliance
Ingram Content Group UK Ltd.
Pitfield, Milton Keynes, MK11 3LW, UK
UKHW051117200426
11947UKWH00038B/1799